Seeking After the HEART of GOD

— FOR 52 WEEKS —

MAX LUCADO

Seeking After the Heart of God for 52 Weeks

Published by HarperChristian Resources, 3950 Sparks Drive SE, Suite 101, Grand Rapids, MI 49546, USA. HarperChristian Resources is a registered trademark of HarperCollins Christian Publishing, Inc.

Requests for information should be addressed to customercare@harpercollins.com.

ISBN 978-0-310-17942-9 (softcover)
ISBN 978-0-310-17943-6 (ebook)

HarperChristian Resources titles may be purchased in bulk for church, business, fundraising, or ministry use. For information, please e-mail ResourceSpecialist@ChurchSource.com.

HarperCollins Publishers, Macken House, 39/40 Mayor Street Upper, Dublin 1, D01 C9W8, Ireland (https://www.harpercollins.com).

Art direction: Ron Huizinga
Cover Design: © 2025 HarperCollins Christian Publishing
Interior Design: Inside Out Design

First Printing April 2026 / Printed in the United States of America

CONTENTS

UNIT 5: SEEKING A WORSHIPFUL HEART

UNIT 6: SEEKING AN HONEST HEART

UNIT 7: SEEKING A REPENTANT HEART

UNIT 8: SEEKING AN OBEDIENT HEART

INTRODUCTION

Ever wonder why the Bible mentions the heart so frequently? The term appears roughly one thousand times, from Genesis to Revelation, and is used in a variety of contexts.[1] Scripture admonishes you to "love the LORD your God with all your heart" (Deuteronomy 6:5) and to "guard your heart" above all else (Proverbs 4:23). Jesus said it is "out of a person's heart" that evil thoughts arise (Mark 7:21–22). Paul stated that it is "with your heart that you believe and are justified" (Romans 10:10). God told the Jewish exiles living in Babylon, "You will seek me and find me when you seek me with all your heart" (Jeremiah 29:13).

Clearly, what is meant by *heart* in these passages is more than the beating of a physical organ. Biblically, the heart refers to our *entire being*. It is the seat of emotions, instincts, and passions, but it is also the source of each individual's intellectual and spiritual life.[2] God "knows the secrets of the heart" (Psalm 44:21); he knows *everything* about us. As he told the prophet Jeremiah, "I the LORD search the heart and examine the mind, to reward each person according to their conduct" (Jeremiah 17:10).

Given this meaning of *heart*, it is surprising to find that God described David as "a man after his own heart" (1 Samuel 13:14). He is the only person in the Bible given this exact designation. This raises some interesting and important questions for us to consider. What made David a man after *God's* own heart? How exactly did he stand out from others? What was so unique about David that God was compelled to describe him in this way?

A look at David's story provides us with clues. When we first see him in action, facing down the Philistine giant Goliath, it is evident that he has a *courageous* heart. His time spent in the wilderness as a fugitive shows us David's heart that *trusted* in the Lord. The psalms written throughout his life reveal that he had a *prayerful* and *worshipful* heart. When we consider how David honored his promise to Jonathan, even after this close friend's death, we recognize that he had an *honest* heart.

Based on these qualities, we could surmise that being a man after God's own heart meant that he always chose the path of righteousness. But the biblical story shows this is not the case. David's many flaws included coveting, pride, anger, neglect of duties (as both a king and father), abuse of power, impulsivity (acting first without consulting God), adultery, and even murder . . . to name just a few. David made many, many, many mistakes in his life.

However, the full story of David's life tells us of another meaningful trait: a *repentant* heart. Sometimes his repentance came soon after the act; sometimes it came much later, but ultimately David admitted his sin and sought restoration from the Lord. Above all, David's life demonstrates an *obedient* heart devoted to God. David was a man who continually and steadfastly sought to do "everything" that God wanted him to do (Acts 13:22). What made David stand out from the rest was that his heart was always pointed toward God.

Seeking After the Heart of God for 52 Weeks will guide you through each of these qualities that David possessed and shed light on how we, too, can have a heart that continuously seeks after God's will, despite the challenges of life and our own failures and missteps. Each week begins with a short reading that explores the trait, encourages daily practice, and invites you to bask in God's presence. This is followed by a brief summary of the reading in "The Heart of the Matter," a space for writing out the memory verse, a concluding section titled "After God's Own Heart," and then two passages of Scripture to read and seven daily Bible study questions to work through during the week.

David wrote, "One thing I ask from the LORD, this only do I seek: that I may dwell in the house of the LORD all the days of my life" (Psalm 27:4). There is great joy to be found in spending time in God's presence! So lean into this study and commit to engaging with him each day of the coming year. Experience God's deep love for you, and become, like David, a person after God's own heart.

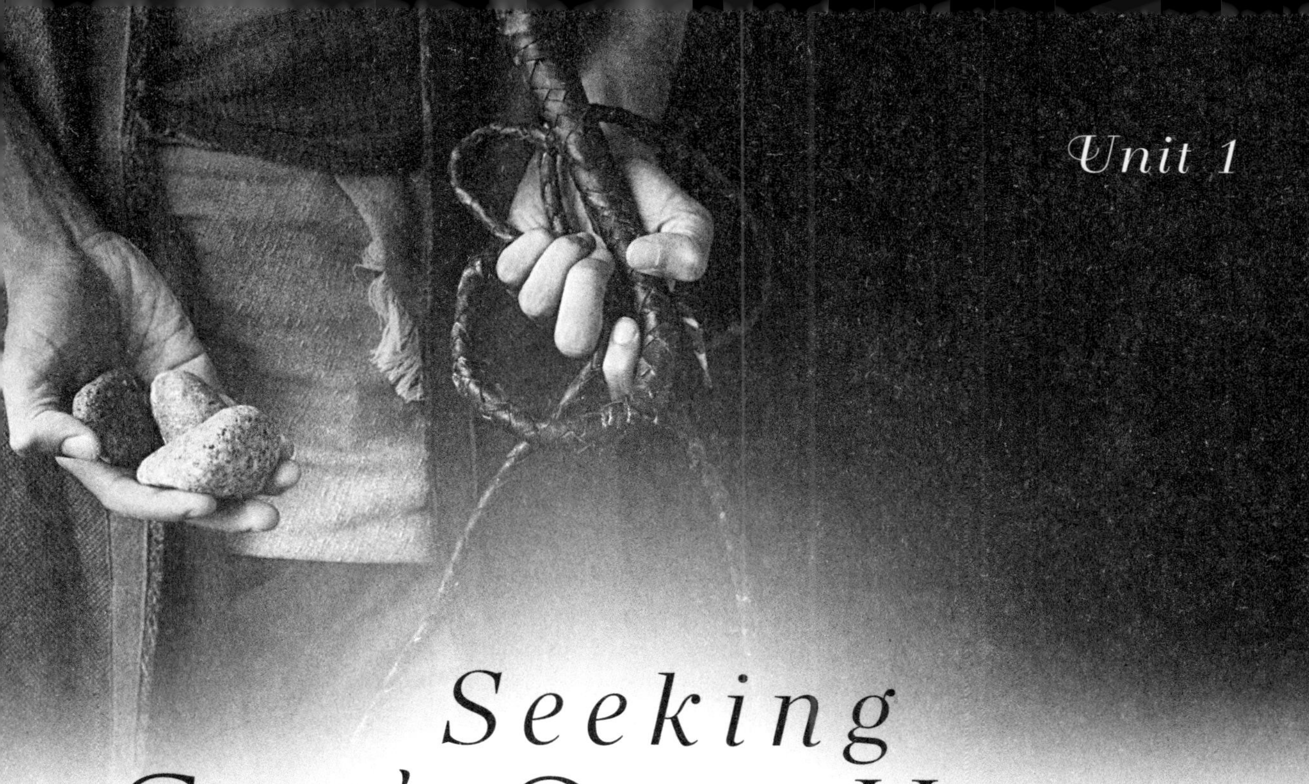

Unit 1

Seeking God's Own Heart

WEEK 1: A MATTER OF THE HEART
WEEK 2: UGLY RELIGION
WEEK 3: THE CALLOUSED HEART
WEEK 4: A HEART LIKE HIS

The story of David begins, not on the battlefield, but on the ancient hillsides of Israel as a silver-bearded priest ambles down a narrow trail. A heifer lumbers behind him. Bethlehem lies before him. Anxiety brews within the old priest. Farmers in their fields notice his presence. Those who know his face whisper his name. Those who hear the name turn to stare at his face. "Samuel?"

God's chosen priest. Mothered by Hannah. Mentored by Eli. Called by God. When the sons of Eli turned sour, young Samuel stepped forward. When Israel needed spiritual focus, Samuel provided it. When Israel wanted a king, Samuel anointed one . . . Saul.

The very name causes Samuel to groan. *Saul. Tall Saul. Strong Saul. The Israelites wanted a king, so we have a king. They wanted a leader, so we have . . . a louse.* Samuel glances from side to side, fearful that he may have spoken aloud what he intended only to think.

No one hears him. He's safe . . . as safe as you can be during the reign of a king gone manic. Saul's heart is growing harder, his eyes even wilder. He isn't the king he used to be. In God's eyes, he isn't even king anymore.

Saul's decline had begun when he disobeyed the Lord's command to wait for Samuel before making a sacrifice. The impatient king decided seven days was long enough for the prophet to arrive. At that point, Saul took it on himself to offer the burnt offering to the Lord, even though he was not a priest or Levite—a clear violation of God's laws.

Samuel could still remember the words he had spoken to Saul that day: "You have done a foolish thing. . . . You have not kept the command the LORD your God gave you; if you had, he would have established your kingdom over Israel for all time. But now your kingdom will not endure; the LORD has sought out a man after his own heart and appointed him ruler of his people, because you have not kept the LORD's command" (1 Samuel 13:13–14).

Samuel didn't know the identity of this "man after God's own heart" at the time. He still didn't know the exact person God had in mind as he approached Bethlehem. All he knew is what God had revealed to him: "How long will you continue to feel sorry for Saul? I have rejected him as king of Israel. Fill your container with olive oil and go. I am sending you to Jesse who lives in Bethlehem, because I have chosen one of his sons to be king" (1 Samuel 16:1 NCV).

So Samuel set out to find this man who would be king over Israel.

— PRAYER —

Father, you are forgiving and good, abounding in mercy. Your heart is pure. Give me a heart like yours. Fill me with forgiveness. Flood me with mercy. When my heart is divided and distracted, remind me of what matters. May I seek your heart over wealth, prestige, and looks. May I care what you think of me more than what the world thinks. In your name, amen.

— MEMORY VERSE —

"Blessed are the pure in heart, for they will see God."

MATTHEW 5:8

Week 1: A MATTER OF THE HEART

Samuel walks the trail toward Bethlehem. His stomach churns and his thoughts race. It's hazardous to anoint a king when Israel already has one. Yet it's more hazardous to live with no leader in such explosive times.

One thousand BC was a bad era for the ramshackle collection of tribes called Israel. Joshua and Moses were history-class heroes. Three centuries of spiritual winter had frozen people's faith. One writer described the days between Joshua and Samuel with this sentence: "In those days Israel did not have a king. All the people did whatever seemed right in their own eyes" (Judges 21:25 NCV).

Corruption fueled disruption. The people had demanded a king—but rather than save the ship, Saul had nearly sunk it. Israel's first monarch turned out to be a psychotic blunderer.

Then there were the Philistines: a warring, bloodthirsty, giant-breeding people who monopolized iron and blacksmithing. They were grizzlies; Hebrews were salmon. Philistines built cities; Hebrews huddled in tents. Philistines forged iron weapons; Hebrews fought with crude slings and arrows. Philistines thundered in flashing chariots; Israelites retaliated with farm tools and knives.

Corruption from within. Danger from without. Saul was weak. The nation, weaker. So what did God do? He did what no one had imagined. He issued a surprise invitation to a nobody from Nowheresville. In this case, "Nowheresville" was Bethlehem—a sleepy village that time had forgotten nestled in the foothills some six miles south of Jerusalem.

Bethlehem sat two thousand feet above the Mediterranean, looking down on gentle, green hills that flattened into gaunt, rugged pastureland. Jesus would one day issue his first cry beneath Bethlehem's sky. But a thousand years before the babe in the manger, Samuel enters the village, pulling a heifer. His arrival turns the heads of the citizens. Prophets don't visit Bethlehem. Has he come to chastise someone or hide somewhere? Neither, the stoop-shouldered priest assures. He has come to sacrifice the animal to God and invites the elders and Jesse and his sons to join him.

The scene has a dog and pony show feel to it. Samuel examines Jesse's boys one at a time like canines on leashes, more than once ready to give the blue ribbon. But each time God stops him.

Eliab, the oldest, seems the logical choice. Envision him as the village Casanova: wavy-haired, strong-jawed. He wears tight jeans and has a piano-keyboard smile. *This is the guy*, Samuel thinks. "Wrong," God says.

Abinadab enters as brother and contestant number two. You'd think a GQ model had just walked in. Italian suit. Alligator-skin shoes. Jet-black, oiled-back hair. Want a classy king? Abinadab has the bling-bling. But God's not into classy.

Samuel asks for brother number three, Shammah. He's bookish, studious. Could use a charisma transplant but busting with brains. Jesse whispers to Samuel, "Valedictorian of Bethlehem High." Samuel is impressed, but God isn't. He reminds the priest, "God does not see the same way people see. People look at the outside of a person, but the LORD looks at the heart" (1 Samuel 16:7 NCV).

Seven sons pass. Seven sons fail. The procession comes to a halt.

Samuel counts the siblings: one, two, three, four, five, six, seven. "Jesse, don't you have eight sons?" A similar question caused Cinderella's stepmother to squirm. Jesse likely did the same. "I still have the youngest son. He is out taking care of the sheep" (verse 11 NCV).

The Hebrew word for "youngest son" is *haqqaton*. It implies more than age; it suggests rank. The *haqqaton* was more than the youngest brother; he was the little brother—the runt.

Sheep watching fits the family *haqqaton*. Leave him with woolly heads and open skies. And that's where we find David, in the pasture with the flock.

The Bible dedicates sixty-six chapters to his story, more than anyone else outside of Jesus. The New Testament mentions his name fifty-nine times. He will establish and inhabit the world's most famous city, Jerusalem. The Son of God will be called the Son of David. The greatest psalms will flow from his pen. We'll call him king, warrior, minstrel, and giant-killer. But today he's not even included in the family meeting; he's just a forgotten, uncredentialed kid, performing a menial task in a map-dot town.

As you read David's story, you might wonder what God saw in him. The fellow fell as often as he stood. He stared down Goliath, yet ogled at Bathsheba; defied God-mockers in the valley, yet joined them in the wilderness. An Eagle Scout one day. Chumming with the Mafia the next. He could lead armies but couldn't manage a family.

Still, David was the one whom God called "a man after my own heart" (Acts 13:22). God gave the appellation to no one else. Not Abraham or Moses or Joseph. He called Paul an apostle, John his beloved, but neither was tagged a man after God's own heart. That God saw David as such gives hope to us all. For we ride the same roller coaster. We alternate between swan dives and belly flops, soufflés and burnt toast.

So, what caused God to pick him? We want to know. After all, we've walked David's pasture, the pasture of exclusion. We are weary of society's surface-level system, of being graded according to the inches of our waist, the square footage of our house, the color of our skin, the make of our car, the size of our office, the presence of diplomas.

Hard work ignored. Devotion unrewarded. The boss chooses clout over character. The teacher picks pet students instead of prepared ones. Parents show off their favorite sons and leave their runts out in the field. Oh, the Goliath of exclusion.

Are you sick of him? Then it's time to quit staring at him. Who cares what he, or they, think? What matters is what your Maker thinks. "People look at the outward appearance, but the LORD looks at the heart" (1 Samuel 16:7). Those words were written for the *haqqatons* of society, for misfits and outcasts. God uses them all.

God saw what no one else saw: a God-seeking heart. David, for all his foibles, sought God like a lark seeks sunrise. He took after God's heart because he stayed after God's heart. In the end, that's all God wanted or needed . . . wants or needs. Others measure your waist size or wallet. Not God. He examines hearts. When he finds one set on him, he calls it and claims it.

Why did God choose David? The same reason he chooses you. It's a matter of the heart.

THE HEART OF THE MATTER

- God's ways will not always make sense to you—but obey him anyway.
- God looks not to the outer appearance of a person but to the inner character.
- God seeks out those who have a heart to follow after him.
- You need David's story because his story is your own.

MEMORY VERSE

Your memory verse for this unit is Matthew 5:8. Take a few moments to review this verse, and then write it out from memory in the space below.

After God's Own Heart

You know what it feels like. You're discerning, kind, and forgiving, but you've always felt that people have judged you for your looks.

You're inquisitive, understanding, and optimistic, but you've never had much money, and so you feel that others have looked down on you.

You're passionate, wise, and courageous, but you've never "climbed the ladder" at work, so it seems to you that no one is impressed by you.

For all the *haqqatons* who've never felt seen by society, know that God sees you. He sees straight into you—to your heart. It is your heart that he cares about when the world cares about everything else. It is the trusting, repentant, prayerful, and worshipful heart he wants. Not the wealth . . . or looks . . . or prestige. To God, it is the pure in heart who are the true heroes, the preferred leaders, the elevated saints.

So continue seeking God's heart. As you do, yours will become more and more like his.

WEEKLY BIBLE STUDY

READ: 1 SAMUEL 16:1–14 AND ACTS 13:13–41

1. According to 1 Samuel 16:1–2, why did God send Samuel to Jesse? What kind of king do you think Saul was—and what effect had he had on the nation and his people?

2. What did God instruct Samuel to look for in the next king (see verse 7)? How does this differ from the way kings were typically selected then and the way we select our leaders today?

3. How do you think David felt when Samuel anointed him in the presence of his brothers? What happened to David and Saul after David was anointed (see verses 13–14)?

4. Paul went on several missionary journeys in a region known as Antioch. Why do you think he included David and Saul's story in the sermon he gave (see Acts 13:20–22)?

5. What kind of man was David—and what was significant about his lineage (see verse 23)? What would Paul's audience have already known about David?

6. David was a man after God's own heart, but he was not God himself. What does Paul say was different about David and Jesus (see verses 34–37)?

7. Have you ever been judged for your outward appearance rather than your heart? Why do you think people tend to judge others based on superficial qualities?

Week 2: UGLY RELIGION

God chose David to be the next king of Israel because he was a man who sought "after his own heart" (1 Samuel 13:14). But what qualities did David possess that revealed this was true of him? *What does it mean to have a heart that seeks after God?*

For this, let's look to a story in the Gospels about the one called the "Son of David." Jesus was on the road to Jerusalem one day when the crowd decided not to allow two blind men to come to him. "As Jesus and his disciples were leaving Jericho, a large crowd followed him. Two blind men were sitting by the roadside, and when they heard that Jesus was going by, they shouted, 'Lord, Son of David, have mercy on us!'" (Matthew 20:29–30).

"The people warned the blind men to be quiet, but they shouted even more, 'Lord, Son of David, have mercy on us!' Jesus stopped and said to the blind men, 'What do you want me to do for you?' They answered, 'Lord, we want to see.' Jesus . . . touched their eyes, and at once they could see. Then they followed Jesus" (Matthew 20:31–34 NCV).

Matthew doesn't tell us why the people refused to let the blind men get close to Jesus—but it's easy to figure it out. They wanted to protect Jesus. He was on a mission, a critical mission. The future of Israel was at stake. He was an important man with a crucial task. He hadn't time for "indigents" on the side of the road.

Besides, don't they have any sense of propriety? Don't they have any dignity? These things must be handled in the proper procedure. First talk to Nathanael, who talks to John, who talks to Peter, who then decides if the matter is worth troubling the Master or not.

The crowd was sincere in this, but the crowd was wrong.

And so, by the way, are we when we think God is too busy for little people or too formal for poor protocol. When people are refused access to Christ by those closest to him, the result is empty, hollow religion.

Ugly religion.

In the Old Testament, Hezekiah, king of Israel, stirrer of religious revival in the land, called upon the people to abandon false gods and return to the true God. He told the people to come to Jerusalem to celebrate the Passover. But there were two problems.

One, it had been so long since the people partook of the Passover that no one was ceremonially clean. No one was prepared to partake. Even the priests had been worshiping idols and had failed to observe the necessary rituals for purity.

Two, God had commanded that the Passover be celebrated on the fourteenth day of the first month. By the time Hezekiah could assemble the people, it was the second month.

So the Passover was kept a month late by impure participants.

Hezekiah prayed for them: "LORD, you are good. . . . Please forgive all those who try to obey you even if they did not make themselves clean as the rules of the Temple command" (2 Chronicles 30:18–19 NCV). Do you see the dilemma?

What does God do when the motive is pure but the method is poor? "The LORD listened to Hezekiah's prayer, and he healed the people" (verse 20 NCV). The right heart with the wrong ritual is better than the wrong heart with the right ritual.

One time when I was in Atlanta, Georgia, at a conference, I called home and talked to Denalyn and the girls. Jenna was little at the time and said she had a special treat for me. She took the phone over to the piano and began to play an original composition.

From a musical standpoint, everything was wrong with the song. She pounded more than she played. There was more random than rhythm in the piece. The lyrics didn't rhyme. The syntax was sinful. Technically the song was a failure. But to me, the song was a masterpiece. Why? Because she wrote it for me.

You are a great daddy.
I miss you very much.
When you're away I'm very sad and I cry.
Please come home very soon.

What dad wouldn't like that? What father wouldn't bask in the praise of even an off-key adulation? Some of you are scowling. "Wait a minute, Max. Are you saying that the method we use to approach God is immaterial? Are you saying that the only thing that matters is why we go to God and that how we approach him is relative?"

No, that's not what I'm saying (but I do appreciate the question). Ideally, we approach God with the right motive and the right method. And sometimes we do. Sometimes the words of our prayer are as beautiful as the motive behind the prayer. Sometimes the way we sing is as strong as the reason we sing. Sometimes our worship is as attractive as it is sincere.

But many times it isn't. Many times our words falter. Many times our music suffers. Many times our worship is less than what we want it to be. God didn't tell Hezekiah to shut down the celebration. Jesus didn't tell the blind men to go away. I didn't tell Jenna to practice a bit more and call me again after she had improved.

The blind men, Hezekiah, and Jenna all did the best they could with what they had—and that was enough. "You will search for me," God declared. "And when you search for me with all your heart, you will find me! I will let you find me" (Jeremiah 29:13–14 NCV).

What a promise!

THE HEART OF THE MATTER

- Focusing on protocol and formality will keep others from Christ.
- Blocking access to Jesus results in empty, hollow, and *ugly* religion.
- God cares more about the right heart over the right ritual.
- When you seek God with all your heart . . . you will find him!

MEMORY VERSE

Your memory verse for this unit is Matthew 5:8. Take a few moments to review this verse, and then write it out from memory in the space below.

After God's Own Heart

You've passed the church countless times. It's on your route to work. A large stone structure with stained glass and a manicured lawn. You've watched churchgoers walk in and out of its doors every Sunday. But you've never been inside.

Why? You're not a "church" person. But you have recently become a *Jesus* person and you're craving Christian community. The beauty of the church, the pristine outfits of the attendees—you fear you won't fit in. Not with your history. Not with your wardrobe.

Still, you know that Jesus has called you. You need community. The building is right here. And so, one Sunday morning, dressed in your ratty jeans and old sneakers, you follow the other congregants inside, hoping to disappear in the crowd.

Instead, you're greeted warmly at the front door, and then again when you sit down inside. A child in front of you turns and smiles. *Maybe I belong here*, you think.

Yes, you do.

WEEKLY BIBLE STUDY

READ: 2 CHRONICLES 30:1–27 AND MATTHEW 20:29–34

1. Hezekiah called for Israel and Judah to celebrate Passover in Jerusalem. How had the people failed to properly observe Passover according to the law (see 2 Chronicles 30:3, 5, 18)?

2. How did Hezekiah intercede on behalf of the people and their failings (see verses 18–19)? What does God's response tell you about his opinion on rituals and the heart?

3. How did Israel celebrate as a result of God's forgiveness and healing (see verses 21, 23, 26)? When have you experienced this kind of joyful worship in your life?

4. The crowd rebuked the blind men for calling out to Jesus (see Matthew 20:31). What does this response tell you about the state of their hearts versus the state of the blind men's hearts?

5. What kind of heart did Jesus have toward the two blind men? What do you think the crowd might have thought of Jesus' compassion?

6. Old Testament prophecy indicated the Messiah would come from David's line. Why is this significant when you consider what the blind men called Jesus (see verse 31)?

7. When have you chosen religion before God—a time you let appearances, power, or another superficial quality get between you and Jesus? What did this teach you about your heart?

Week 3: THE CALLOUSED HEART

Peculiar, this childhood memory of mine.

For many, early church recollections are made of zippered Bibles, patent leather Easter shoes, Christmas pageants, or Sunday schools. Mine is not so religious. Mine is comprised of calluses, straight pins, and dull sermons.

There I sit, all six years of me, flat-topped and freckled. My father's hand in my lap. It is there to keep me from squirming. A robust preacher is behind the pulpit, one of God's kindest but most monotonous servants. Bored, I turn my attention to my father's hand.

If you didn't know he was a mechanic, one look at his hands would tell you as much. Thick, strong, scrubbed clean, but still bearing traces of last week's grease.

I'm intrigued as I run my fingers over the calluses. They rise on the palm like a ridge of hills. Layer upon layer of nerveless skin. The hand's defense against hours of squeezing wrenches and twisting screwdrivers.

On the back of the pew in front of me is a collection of attendance cards. At the top of each card is a red ribbon for the visitors to wear. The ribbon is attached to the card by a straight pin. I have an idea. *I wonder how thick those calluses are?*

I take the pin, and with the skill of a surgeon, I begin the insertion. I look up at Dad. He doesn't move. I go deeper. No response. Another eighth of an inch. No flinch. While the rest of the church is intent on the words of a preacher, I'm fascinated by the depth of a callus.

I decide to give it a final shove.

"Umph," he grunts, yanking his hand away, closing his fist, which only pushes the pin further. He glares at me, my mother turns, and my brother giggles. Something tells me that the same hand will be used later that Sunday to make another point.

Peculiar, this childhood memory. But even more peculiar is that decades later, I find myself doing the same thing that I did at age six: in church, trying to penetrate calluses with a point. Only now I'm in the pulpit, not the pew. And my tool is truth, not a pin. And the calluses are not on the hand but on the heart. Thick, dead skin wrapped around the nerves of the soul. The result of hours of rubbing against the truth without receiving it. Toughened, crusty, lifeless tissue that defies feeling and ignores touch. The calloused heart.

When our oldest daughter, Jenna, was two, I lost her in a department store. One minute she was at my side and the next she was gone. I panicked. All of a sudden only one thing mattered—I had to find my daughter. Shopping was forgotten. The list of things I'd come to get was unimportant. I yelled her name. What people thought didn't matter.

For a few minutes, every ounce of energy had one goal—to find my lost child. (I did, by the way. She was hiding behind some jackets!)

No price is too high for a parent to pay to redeem his child. No effort too demanding. A parent will go to any length to find his own.

So will God.

Mark it down. God's greatest creation is not the flung stars or the gorged canyons; it's his eternal plan to reach his children. Behind his pursuit of us is the same brilliance behind the rotating seasons and the orbiting planets. Heaven and earth know no greater passion than God's personal passion for you and your return. He has made his faithfulness clear.

Noah saw it as the clouds opened and the rainbow appeared. Abraham felt it as he placed his hand on aging Sarah's belly. Jacob found it through failure. Joseph experienced it in prison. God is tireless, relentless. He refuses to quit.

Listen as he articulates his passion: "My heart beats for you, and my love for you stirs up my pity. I won't punish you in my anger, and I won't destroy Israel again. I am God and not a human; I am the Holy One, and I am among you" (Hosea 11:8–9 NCV).

Before you read any further, reflect on those last four words: "I am among you." Do you believe that? Do you believe God is near? He wants you to. He wants you to know he is in the midst of your world. Wherever you are as you read these words, he is present. In your car. On the plane. In your office, your bedroom, your den. He's near.

And he is more than near. He is active. Noah's God is your God. The promise given to Abraham is given to you. God is in the thick of things in your world. He has not taken up residence in a distant galaxy. He has not removed himself from history. He has not chosen to seclude himself on a throne in an incandescent castle.

He has drawn near. He has involved himself in the carpools, heartbreaks, and funeral homes of our day. He is as near to us on Monday as on Sunday. In the schoolroom as in the sanctuary. At the coffee break as much as the communion table.

Why? Why did God do it? What was his reason?

"The Spirit himself joins with our spirits to say we are God's children" (Romans 8:16 NCV). God loves you for whose you are. You are his child. It was this love that pursued the Israelites. It was this love that sent the prophets. It was this love that wrapped itself in human flesh and descended the birth canal of Mary. It was this love that walked the hard trails of Galilee and spoke to the hard hearts of the religious.

"This is extraordinary, Lord GOD," David exclaimed as he considered God's love (2 Samuel 7:19 NCV). You are right, David. God's love is not normal love. He is patient with our mistakes. He is long-suffering with our stumbles. He doesn't get angry with our questions. He doesn't turn away when we struggle. And in response, what do we do?

Like David, we consider God's love, soften our hearts, and seek after him.

THE HEART OF THE MATTER

- God is in pursuit of the toughened, crusty, lifeless, calloused heart.
- No price was too high for God to pay to redeem his children.
- God is near, not distant. He is in the thick of things in your world.
- Your response to God's love is to soften your heart and seek after him.

MEMORY VERSE

Your memory verse for this unit is Matthew 5:8. Take a few moments to review this verse, and then write it out from memory in the space below.

After God's Own Heart

As humans, we are most familiar with conditional love. I love you *if* you do this for me. I love you *if* you're this type of person. I love you *if* you make me feel a certain way. I love you *if*. . . But God does not love us *if*. God loves us *because*. Because we are his. This is not a normal kind of love. This love is pure, long-suffering, and persistent.

Life has a way of hardening our hearts. Sin, disappointment, and rejection create a thick wall around the most vulnerable parts of us. We go from trusting others to protecting ourselves from them. The calluses grow thicker and thicker. But just as our calluses grow, so does God's love. He knows we've been hurt, so he is patient with us. He knows we're distrusting, so he is kind to us. Eventually, God's long-suffering softens even the hardest of hearts and frees us to experience, perhaps for the first time, unconditional love.

WEEKLY BIBLE STUDY

READ: LUKE 15:1–8 AND MATTHEW 13:1–23

1. What was the Pharisees' and scribes' complaint about Jesus (see Luke 15:1–2)? What does this say about the state of their hearts?

2. What does the Shepherd do in the parable of the lost sheep (see verses 3–4)? What does this tell you about the Shepherd's pursuit of the lost?

3. What does the Shepherd do when he finds his lost sheep (see verses 6–8)? What do you think happens in heaven when someone with a calloused heart softens their heart toward Jesus?

4. What happened to the seeds that fell along a path, rocky ground, thorns, and good soil in the parable of the sower (see Matthew 13:4–8)? What does each type of soil represent?

5. When Jesus explains the parable to his disciples, what does he say each type of soil represents (see verses 18–23)?

6. Based on this parable, what is the result of a calloused heart? What is the result of a soft heart?

7. What is the state of your heart today—calloused, heavy, or soft toward God? How could these stories inspire you to surrender your heart to Jesus so he can make it more like his?

Week 4: A HEART LIKE HIS

What if, for one day, Jesus were to become you?

What if, for twenty-four hours, Jesus wakes up in your bed, walks in your shoes, lives in your house, assumes your schedule? Your boss becomes his boss, your mother becomes his mother, your pains become his pains. With one exception, nothing about your life changes. Your health doesn't change. Your circumstances don't change. Your schedule isn't altered. Your problems aren't solved. Only one change occurs.

What if, for one day and one night, Jesus lives your life with his heart? Your heart gets the day off, and your life is led by the heart of Christ. His priorities govern your actions. His passions drive your decisions. His love directs your behavior.

What would you be like? Would people notice a change? Your family—would they see something new? Your coworkers—would they sense a difference? What about the less fortunate? Would you treat them the same? And your friends? Would they detect more joy? How about your enemies? Would they receive more mercy from Christ's heart than from yours?

And you? How would you feel? What alterations would this transplant have on your stress level? Your mood swings? Your temper? Would you sleep better? Would you see sunsets differently? Death differently? Taxes differently? Any chance you'd need fewer aspirin or sedatives? How about your reaction to traffic delays? (Ouch, that touched a nerve.) Would you still dread what you are dreading? Better yet, would you still do what you are doing?

Would you still do what you had planned to do for the next twenty-four hours? Pause and think about your schedule. Obligations. Engagements. Outings. Appointments. With Jesus taking over your heart, would anything change?

Keep working on this for a moment. Adjust the lens of your imagination until you have a clear picture of Jesus leading your life, then snap the shutter and frame the image. What you see is what God wants. He wants you to "think and act like Christ Jesus" (Philippians 2:5 NCV).

God's plan for you is nothing short of a new heart. If you were a car, God would want control of your engine. If you were a computer, God would claim the software and the hard drive. If you were an airplane, he'd take his seat in the cockpit. But you are a person, so God wants to change your heart.

"You were taught to be made new in your hearts, to become a new person. That new person is made to be like God—made to be truly good and holy" (Ephesians 4:23–24 NCV).

God wants you to be just like Jesus. He wants you to have a heart like his.

I'm going to risk something here. It's dangerous to sum up grand truths in one statement, but I'm going to try. If a sentence or two could capture God's desire for you, it might read like this: *God loves you just the way you are, but he refuses to leave you that way. He wants you to be just like Jesus.*

God loves you just the way you are. If you think his love for you would be stronger if your faith were, you are wrong. If you think his love would be deeper if your thoughts were, wrong again. Don't confuse God's love with the love of people. The love of people often increases with performance and decreases with mistakes. Not so with God's love. He loves you right where you are. To quote my wife's favorite author (me!):

> God's love never ceases. Never. Though we spurn him. Ignore him. Reject him. Despise him. Disobey him. He will not change. Our evil cannot diminish his love. Our goodness cannot increase it. Our faith does not earn it any more than our stupidity jeopardizes it. God doesn't love us less if we fail or more if we succeed. God's love never ceases.[3]

God loves you just the way you are, but he refuses to leave you that way.

When my daughter Jenna was a toddler, I used to take her to a park not far from our apartment. One day as she was playing in a sandbox, an ice cream vendor approached us. I purchased her a treat, and when I turned to give it to her, I saw her mouth was full of sand. Where I intended to put a delicacy, she had put dirt.

Did I love her with dirt in her mouth? Absolutely. Was she any less my daughter with dirt in her mouth? Of course not. Was I going to allow her to keep the dirt in her mouth? No way. I loved her right where she was, but I refused to leave her there. I carried her over to the water fountain and washed out her mouth. Why? Because I love her.

God does the same for us. He holds us over the fountain. "Spit out the dirt, honey," our Father urges. "I've got something better for you." And so he cleanses us of sins: dishonesty, prejudice, bitterness, greed, immorality.

We don't enjoy the cleansing; sometimes we even opt for the dirt over the ice cream. "I can eat dirt if I want to!" we pout and proclaim. Which is true—we can. But if we do, the loss is ours. God has a better offer. He wants us to be just like Jesus.

Isn't that good news? You aren't stuck with today's personality. You aren't condemned to "grumpydom." You are tweakable. Even if you've worried each day of your life, you needn't worry the rest of your life. So what if you were born a bigot? You don't have to die one.

Where did we get the idea we can't change? From whence come statements such as, "It's just my nature to worry," or, "I would rather avoid conflict than tell the truth," or, "I have a bad temper. I can't help the way I react"? Who says? Would we make similar statements about our bodies? "It's just my nature to have a broken leg. I can't do anything about it." Of course not. If our bodies malfunction, we seek help. Shouldn't we do the same with our hearts? Shouldn't we seek aid for our dishonest ways? Can't we request treatment for our selfish tirades? Of course we can. Jesus can change our hearts. He wants us to have a heart like his.

Can you imagine a better offer?

THE HEART OF THE MATTER

- God's plan for you is nothing short of a new heart.
- God loves you just the way you are, but he refuses to leave you that way.
- You aren't stuck with today's personality. You are tweakable.
- You can request a better heart—and Jesus will give it to you!

MEMORY VERSE

Your memory verse for this unit is Matthew 5:8. Take a few moments to review this verse, and then write it out from memory in the space below.

After God's Own Heart

Stuck. Stuck in our ways. Stuck in our sin. Stuck in a family with a reputation. As humans with limited perspective, we often feel stuck. We think we were just born the way we were and will never change. But God is in the business of change. And Jesus is the change-maker.

He can make dirty hearts clean, restless hearts peaceful, and skeptical hearts trusting. He can make the fearful courageous, the downtrodden full of worship, and the shamed set free. Whatever the state your heart is in today does not have to be where it is tomorrow. Your looks, your height, your skills, your mannerisms, your status—all of these might not change. But the one thing that matters most can indeed change: *your heart.*

WEEKLY BIBLE STUDY

READ: PSALM 86:1–17 AND EPHESIANS 4:17–32

1. Based on Psalm 86, what was the state of David's heart? How was he feeling about his struggles—and where did he find hope?

2. Based on this psalm, how would you describe the heart of God? What descriptions of God stand out that you need to be reminded of today?

3. David asked for an "undivided heart" (verse 11). When has your heart felt divided? What other things besides God tend to vie for your heart's attention?

4. Paul compares those who don't know Christ to those who do in Ephesians 4:17–32. What does he say the hearts, minds, and lives are like of those who don't know Christ?

5. When you encounter Jesus, what happens to your old self—to your heart (see verses 22–24)? How does that affect who you are and who you are like?

6. How should this change in your heart affect your actions (see verses 25–29)? How are you to treat others, speak to others, and deal with your own sin and anger?

7. How have you experienced a heart change—whether that was from knowing Jesus or experiencing his love through someone else? How did this change affect how you treated others?

Unit 2

Seeking A Courageous Heart

WEEK 5: AN ANCIENT FOE
WEEK 6: DO NOT BE AFRAID
WEEK 7: LOOK FOR THE GOOD
WEEK 8: FREE TO FLY
WEEK 9: QUIET COURAGE
WEEK 10: TOSSED BY THE WAVES

The slender, beardless boy kneels by the brook. Mud moistens his knees. Bubbling water cools his hand. Were he to notice, he could study his handsome features in the water. Tanned, sanguine skin and eyes that steal the breath of Hebrew maidens.

He searches not for his reflection, however, but for rocks. Smooth stones. The kind that stack neatly in a shepherd's pouch, rest flush against a shepherd's leather sling. Flat rocks that balance heavy on the palm and missile with comet-crashing force into the head of a lion, a bear, or, in this case, a giant.

Goliath stares down from the hillside. Only disbelief keeps him from laughing. He and his Philistine herd—a bloodthirsty gang of hoodlums—have rendered their half of the valley into a forest of spears. Goliath towers above them all: nine feet, nine inches tall in his stocking feet, wearing 125 pounds of armor, and snarling like the main contender at a wrestling match. He wears a size-20 collar, a 101/2 hat, and a 56-inch belt. His biceps burst, and his boasts belch through the canyon. "This day I defy the armies of Israel! Give me a man and let us fight each other" (1 Samuel 17:10).

Who will go one-on-one with me? Give me your best shot.

Goliath has been doing this every morning and every evening for the past *forty* days. Ever since the Philistines first "gathered their forces for war and assembled at Sokoh in Judah" (verse 1). Saul, flush with the success of recent victories over the Ammonites and Amalekites, had readily mustered the Israelite forces to meet the Philistine threat.

But things had changed since those victories. For one, God had rejected Saul as king over Israel . . . and he knew it. And Saul also hadn't counted on there being a *giant* in the Philistine ranks. When he directed the Israelites to pitch their tents in the Valley of Elah, he wasn't expecting to face so fearsome a foe. It didn't help matters that Goliath's formidable size and strength was accompanied by his formidable taunts.

"Why do you come out and line up for battle? Am I not a Philistine, and are you not the servants of Saul? Choose a man and have him come down to me. If he is able to fight and kill me, we will become your subjects; but if I overcome him and kill him, you will become our subjects and serve us. . . . This day I defy the armies of Israel! Give me a man and let us fight each other" (verses 8–10).

What was needed in this moment was courage. But alas, there was none to be found among the Israelites. Not even in Saul himself. "On hearing the Philistine's words, Saul and all the Israelites were dismayed and terrified" (verse 11).

No one volunteered . . . until the day David showed up on the scene.

— PRAYER —

God, my Goliaths are no match for you. Yet still, I worry. I focus on my giants instead of you. As I study your Word, lift my eyes so all I see is you. As I seek you and your heart, may my giants disappear. Replace my heart of fear with your heart of courage. In Jesus' name. Amen.

— MEMORY VERSE —

"Be strong and courageous. Do not be afraid or terrified because of them, for the LORD your God goes with you; he will never leave you nor forsake you."

DEUTERONOMY 31:6

Week 5: AN ANCIENT FOE

David had just clocked out of sheep watching that morning to deliver bread and cheese to his brothers on the battlefront. That's when he heard Goliath defying God. That's when he saw the Israelites fleeing from him in fear. That's when he made his decision.

"Who is this uncircumcised Philistine that he should defy the armies of the living God?" he says to the men around him (1 Samuel 17:26). Then, taking his staff in hand, he walks to the brook that runs through the valley, bends down, and picks up five smooth stones. These he puts in his shepherd's bag—a pouch that he is carrying with him—and takes his sling in his hand. "Then he went to meet the Philistine" (verse 40 NCV).

Goliath scoffs at the kid when he sees him. Nicknames him Twiggy. "Am I a dog, that you come to me with sticks?" (verse 43 NASB). Skinny, scrawny David. Bulky, brutish Goliath. The toothpick versus the tornado. The toy poodle taking on the Rottweiler.

What odds do you give David against his giant?

Better odds, perhaps, than you give yourself against yours. Your Goliath doesn't carry a sword or shield. He brandishes blades of unemployment, abandonment, sexual abuse, or depression. Your giant doesn't parade up and down the hills of Elah; he prances through your office, your bedroom, your classroom. He brings bills you can't pay, grades you can't make, people you can't please, whiskey you can't resist, pornography you can't refuse, a past you can't shake, and a future you can't face.

You know well the roar of Goliath.

The one David determined to face foghorned his challenges morning and night: "For forty days, every morning and evening, the Philistine champion strutted in front of the Israelite army" (verse 16 NLT). Yours does the same. First thought of the morning, last worry of the night—your Goliath dominates your day and infiltrates your joy.

How long has he stalked you? Goliath's family was an ancient foe of the Israelites. Joshua drove them out of the Promised Land three hundred years earlier. He destroyed them all except for the residents of three cities: Gaza, Gath, and Ashdod (see Joshua 11:21–22). Gath bred giants like Yosemite grows sequoias. Guess where Goliath was raised. See the *G* on his letter jacket? Gath High School.

Saul's soldiers saw Goliath and mumbled, "Not again. My dad fought his dad. My granddad fought his granddad."

You've groaned similar words. "I'm becoming a workaholic, just like my father." "Divorce streaks through our family tree like oaks wilt." "My mom couldn't keep a friend either. Is this ever going to stop?"

Goliath: the long-standing bully of the valley. Tougher than a two-dollar steak. More snarls than twin Dobermans. He awaits you in the morning, torments you at night. He stalked your ancestors and now looms over you. He blocks the sun and leaves you standing in the shadow of a doubt. "When Saul and his troops heard the Philistine's challenge, they were terrified and lost all hope" (verse 11 MSG).

But what am I telling you? You know Goliath. You recognize his walk and wince at his talk. You've seen your Godzilla. The question is, is he all you see? You know his voice—but is it all you hear? David saw and heard more. Look at the first words he spoke, not just in the battle, but in the Bible: "What will a man get for killing this Philistine and ending his defiance of Israel? Who is this pagan Philistine anyway, that he is allowed to defy the armies of the living God?" (verse 26 NLT).

David shows up discussing God. The soldiers mentioned nothing about him. His brothers never spoke his name. But David takes one step onto the stage and raises the subject of the living God. He does the same with King Saul: no chitchat about the battle or questions about the odds. Just a God-birthed announcement: "The LORD, who delivered me from the paw of the lion and from the paw of the bear, He will deliver me from the hand of this Philistine" (verse 37 NKJV).

He continues the theme with Goliath. When the giant mocks David, the shepherd boy replies:

> "You come against me with sword and spear and javelin, but I come against you in the name of the LORD Almighty, the God of the armies of Israel, whom you have defied. This day the LORD will deliver you into my hands, and I'll strike you down and cut off your head. This very day I will give the carcasses of the Philistine army to the birds and the wild animals, and the whole world will know that there is a God in Israel. All those gathered here will know that it is not by sword or spear that the LORD saves; for the battle is the LORD's, and he will give all of you into our hands" (verses 45–47).

No one else discusses God. David discusses no one else but God. A subplot appears in the story. More than "David versus Goliath," this is "God-focus versus giant-focus."

David sees what others don't and refuses to see what others do. All eyes, except David's, fall on the brutal, hate-breathing hulk. All compasses, sans David's, are set on the polestar of the Philistine. The people know his taunts, demands, size, and strut. They have majored in Goliath.

David majors in God. He sees the giant, mind you; he just sees God more. God is where his courage comes from. Look carefully at David's battle cry: "You come against me with sword and spear and javelin, but I come against you in the name of the LORD Almighty, the God of the armies of Israel, whom you have defied" (verse 45).

> *Focus on giants—you stumble.*
> *Focus on God—your giants tumble.*

Lift your eyes, giant-slayer. The God who made a miracle out of David stands ready to make one out of you.

THE HEART OF THE MATTER

- Your giant may seem overwhelming, but God's power is greater.
- Shift your focus from fear of your struggles to faith in God's strength and promises.
- Confront your challenges with confidence, knowing the battle belongs to the Lord.
- Giants fall when you trust God's power instead of relying on your own strength.

MEMORY VERSE

Your memory verse for this unit is Deuteronomy 31:6. Take a few moments to review this verse, and then write it out from memory in the space below.

After God's Own Heart

The shadow of the giant looms large. Everywhere you look, it is there. In your dreams. In your thoughts. In your journal. What—or who—is your Goliath? How long have you let him terrorize you? Forty days, like the Israelites? More?

David exhibited great courage when he went to face Goliath. But it wasn't courage in *himself* he was depending on but courage in the *living God*. This was courage that had been instilled in him when he faced a lion and a bear during his days as a shepherd boy. It was courage rooted in the memory of a God who had saved him once and whom he knew could save him again. This type of courage is not easily shaken nor easily overshadowed by the giant of fear. This courage is rooted in something deeper and more powerful than yourself.

So take courage, friend. Your giant has already been slayed.

WEEKLY BIBLE STUDY

READ: 1 SAMUEL 17:1–49 AND EPHESIANS 6:10–20

1. What made Goliath such a formidable foe for Saul and the Israelites (see 1 Samuel 17:4–7)? What effect did his presence have on the Israelite army (see verses 11, 24)?

2. What kind of man was David compared to Goliath, outwardly and inwardly? What gave David the courage the other Israelite soldiers lacked (see verses 26, 45–47)?

3. What was David's weapon of choice to defeat Goliath (see verses 40, 48–49)? What does this say about how we choose our "weapons" against our Goliaths?

4. What or whom does Paul say our battles are against (see Ephesians 6:12)? How have you experienced this—a battle against a source of evil that felt beyond your physical world?

5. Review the pieces of God's armor in verses 10–17 and then think about a spiritual battle you are facing. What piece of armor do you need to fight that battle? Why that piece?

6. Paul advised to "pray in the Spirit" with "all kinds of prayers and requests" (verse 18). How has prayer helped you fight your spiritual battles and given you courage to face your giants?

7. How long have you felt taunted by the fear of the Goliath in your life? In what ways do these passages give you the courage to go out and confront your giant?

Week 6: DO NOT BE AFRAID

Could you use some courage like David had? Are you backing down more than you are standing up? If so, let the Master lead you out into the valley. Let him remind you why you should "fear not" when it comes to your foe. Listen to the time Jesus scattered the butterflies out of the stomachs of his nervous disciples in Matthew 10:5–31 and see if his words help you.

Remember, the disciples were common men given a compelling task. Before they were the stained-glassed saints we see in the windows of cathedrals, they were somebody's next-door neighbors trying to make a living and raise a family. They weren't cut from theological cloth or raised on supernatural milk. But they were an ounce more devoted than they were afraid and, as a result, they did some extraordinary things.

They would have done nothing, however, had they not learned to face their fears. Jesus knew that. So he spoke words of courage to them.

Jesus was about to send the disciples out on their own. For a limited time, they were to go into the cities and do what he had done—but without him. Jesus assembled them to give some final instructions. Perhaps the disciples looked nervous. They had reason to be nervous. What Jesus was about to tell them would raise the pulse rate of the stoutest heart.

First, Jesus tells them not to take any extra money or extra clothing on their journey.

"No money?"

Then he assures them that they are being sent out like sheep among wolves.

"Uh, what do you mean, Jesus?"

His answer is not reassuring. He tells them they will be taken before the authorities (uh-oh), flogged (ouch), and arrested (groan).

And it gets worse before it gets better.

Jesus goes on to describe the impact their mission will have on people: "Brother will betray brother to death, and a father his child; children will rebel against their parents and have them put to death. You will be hated by everyone because of me, but the one who stands firm in the end will be saved" (verses 21–22).

Some eyes duck. Some eyes widen. Someone swallows. Feet shift. A brow is wiped. And though no one says it, you know someone is thinking, *Is it too late to get out of this?*

That's the setting for Jesus' words of courage to his disciples. Three times in five verses he says, "Do not be afraid" (verses 26, 28, 31). Read the words and see his call and cause for courage. See the reason you should sleep well tonight: "So do not be afraid of them, for there is nothing concealed that will not be disclosed, or hidden that will not be made known" (verse 26).

On the surface, those words would seem like a reason for panic rather than a source of peace. Who of us would like to have our secret thoughts made public? Who would get excited over the idea that every wrong deed we've ever done will be announced to everyone?

You're right, no one would. But we're told over and over that such a thing *will* happen: "Everything is uncovered and laid bare before the eyes of him to whom we must give account" (Hebrews 4:13). "He reveals deep and hidden things; he knows what lies in darkness, and light dwells with him" (Daniel 2:22). "He will bring to light what is hidden in darkness and will expose the motives of the heart" (1 Corinthians 4:5).

To think of the disclosure of my hidden heart conjures up emotions of shame, humiliation, and embarrassment in me. There are things I've done that I want no one to know. There are thoughts I've thought that I would never want to be revealed. So why does Jesus point to the day of revelation as a reason for *courage*?

The answer is found in Romans 2:16. Let out a sigh of relief as you underline the last three words of this verse: "This will take place on the day when God judges people's secrets through Jesus Christ."

Did you see it? Jesus is the screen through which God looks when he judges our sins. Now read another chorus of verses and focus on their promise: "Therefore, there is now no condemnation for those who are in Christ Jesus" (Romans 8:1). "Through him everyone who believes is set free from every sin" (Acts 13:39). "For I will forgive their wickedness and will remember their sins no more" (Hebrews 8:12).

If you are in Christ, these promises are not only a source of joy. They are also the foundations of true courage. You are guaranteed that your sins will be filtered through and hidden in the sacrifice of Jesus. When God looks at you, he sees the One who surrounds you. That means that failure is not a concern for you. Your victory is secure.

Picture it this way. Imagine you are an ice skater in competition. You are in first place with one more round to go. If you perform well, the trophy is yours. You are nervous, anxious, and frightened. Then, only minutes before your performance, your trainer rushes to you with the thrilling news: "You've already won! The judges tabulated the scores, and the person in second place can't catch you. You are too far ahead."

Upon hearing that news, how will you feel? Exhilarated!

And how will you skate? Timidly? Cautiously? Of course not.

How about courageously and confidently? You bet you will. You will do your best because the prize is yours. You will skate like a champion because that is what you are! You will hear the applause of victory.

Hence, these words from Hebrews: "Therefore, brothers and sisters, since we have *confidence* to enter the Most Holy Place by the blood of Jesus . . . let us draw near to God with a sincere heart and with the *full assurance* that faith brings" (10:19, 22, emphasis added).

The truth will triumph. The Father of truth will win, and the followers of truth will be saved. Earthly fears are no fears at all when you are focused on your heavenly Father.

THE HEART OF THE MATTER

- Following Jesus at times can feel scary, intimidating, and unsettling.
- All truth will be revealed. What was in the dark will be brought into the light.
- We will be judged *through Jesus Christ*, so we have no reason to be afraid.
- "Do not be afraid." These words Jesus spoke to his disciples he speaks to us today.

MEMORY VERSE

Your memory verse for this unit is Deuteronomy 31:6. Take a few moments to review this verse, and then write it out from memory in the space below.

After God's Own Heart

In our world, there is no shortage of reasons to fear. Job insecurity, health scares, children going down a path you didn't expect. And if there aren't enough fears in your own life, just hop on the internet. There you will be flooded with hundreds more reasons to feel afraid of the world you live in and where it is headed.

You need the comforting words Jesus spoke to his disciples: "Do not be afraid." Do not be afraid, for he is with you. Do not be afraid, for he hears you. Do not be afraid, for he sees you. Do not be afraid, for he forgives you.

In the same way you would assure a child who is afraid of monsters under the bed, God assures you when it comes to your fears. What you are afraid of is no match for his strength, power, and wisdom. You are in Christ, and because you are in Christ, you are safe.

WEEKLY BIBLE STUDY

READ: MATTHEW 10:16–31 AND HEBREWS 10:19–25

1. What does Jesus say would happen when his disciples were arrested (see Matthew 10:19–20)? What does this reveal about how you will be supported in the mission he gives you?

2. Jesus said nothing that is hidden will remain hidden (see verse 26). When you consider the hidden parts of your life being brought to light, how do you feel? Why do you feel that way?

3. How does God feel about you (verses 29–31)? How does this truth affect the way you feel about the things you've kept hidden that will one day be revealed?

4. Why can you have confidence when you enter God's presence (see Hebrews 10:19–22)? Do you have that sense of confidence when you approach the Father? Why or why not?

5. What happens to your guilt when you are in Christ (see verse 22)? How could this truth give you more confidence to approach God's throne when you pray and worship?

6. This confidence shouldn't only affect your personal relationship with God. How does this confidence affect the body of believers? What should it inspire us to do (see verses 24–25)?

7. How has guilt or shame held you back from approaching God's throne? How do this week's passages encourage you to approach it with confidence?

Week 7: LOOK FOR THE GOOD

Dirt carpeted the floor. Rats scurried beneath the grated vent. Roaches roamed the walls and crawled over sleeping prisoners. The only source of light peeked through three holes near the fifteen-foot ceiling. The cell offered no bunk, no chair, no table, and no way out for American General Robbie Risner. For seven and a half years, North Vietnamese soldiers had held him and dozens of other soldiers in the Zoo, a POW camp in Hanoi.

Misery came standard issue. Solitary confinement, starvation, torture, and beatings were routine. Screams echoed throughout the camp, chilling the blood of other prisoners.

Listen to Risner's description: "Everything was sad and dismal. It was almost the essence of despair. If you could have squeezed the feeling out of the word *despair*, it would have come out gray, dull, and lead-colored, dingy and dirty."[4]

How do you survive seven and a half years in such a hole? Cut off from family. No news from the United States. What do you do? Here is what Risner did. He stared at a blade of grass. Several days into his incarceration, he wrestled the grate off a floor vent, stretched out on his belly, lowered his head into the opening, and peered through a pencil-sized hole in the brick and mortar at a singular blade of grass. Aside from this stem, his world had no color. So he began his days with head in vent, heart in prayer, staring at the green blade of grass. He called it a "blood transfusion for the soul."[5]

You don't have to go to Hanoi to face a "gray, dull, and lead-colored, dingy and dirty" existence. Do you know the tint of a colorless world? If so, do what Risner did. Go on a search. Fix your eyes on a color outside your cell.

What you see defines who you are. "Your eyes are windows into your body. If you open your eyes wide in wonder and belief, your body fills up with light. If you live squinty-eyed in greed and distrust, your body is a musty cellar. If you pull the blinds on your windows, what a dark life you will have!" (Matthew 6:22–23 MSG).

Jesus is discussing not the eyes of your head but the eyes of your heart—your attitude, your outlook, your vision, not of things but of life. You, like General Risner, make daily decisions. Do you set your eyes on the gray harshness or search for the blade of a different color?

Jerry Rushford directed the Pepperdine Bible Lectures for nearly thirty years in Malibu, California. He masterfully coordinated a week of classes and speakers—hundreds of teachers and thousands of attendees. You would have been hard-pressed to find anything wrong with the event, but inevitably someone did. For that reason, Jerry always closed the final session with this tongue-in-cheek phrase: "If you look hard enough, long enough, you'll find, I'm sure, something to complain about. But we hope you'll look at the good."

If you look hard enough and long enough, you'll find something to complain about.

Adam and Eve did. Doesn't the bite into the forbidden fruit reflect a feeling of discontent? Surrounded by all they needed, they set their eyes on the one thing they couldn't have. They found something to complain about.

The followers of Moses did. They could have focused on the miracles: the Red Sea becoming the Yellow Brick Road, fire escorting them by night and a cloud accompanying them by day, manna reflecting the morning sunrise and quail scampering into the camp at night. Instead they focused on their problems. They sketched pictures of Egypt, daydreamed of pyramids, and complained that life in the desert wasn't for them. They found something to complain about.

What about you? What are you looking at? The one fruit you can't eat? Or the million you can? The manna or the misery? His plan or your problems?

Paul wrote, "Finally, brethren, whatever things are true, whatever things are noble, whatever things are just, whatever things are pure, whatever things are lovely, whatever things are of good report, if there is any virtue and if there is anything praiseworthy—meditate on these things" (Philippians 4:8 NKJV).

This is more than a silver-lining attitude. More than seeing the cup as half full rather than half empty. This is an admission that unseen favorable forces populate and direct the affairs of humanity. But when we see as God wants us to see, we see heaven's hand in the midst of sickness, Jesus working on a troubled youth, the Holy Spirit comforting a broken heart. We see not what is seen but what is unseen. We see with faith and not flesh, and since faith begets hope, we are hope-filled. For we know there is more to life than what meets the eye.

We see the "Christ; who will sustain you to the end" (1 Corinthians 1:7–8 RSV). We believe that Jesus "who began a good work in you will carry it on to completion until the day of Christ Jesus" (Philippians 1:6). We believe that our Savior was serious when he said, "My Father is working still" (John 5:17 RSV).

And since God is working, we look at people differently. We don't dismiss the kid with the learning disorder, the husband with the drinking problem, the preacher with the pride issue. We don't give up on people because we know that beneath the grate, beyond the rats, stands a stalk of grass, and we focus on it.

Does your world feel like General Risner's POW cell? Look long enough, hard enough, and it will. Even the garden of Eden looks gray to some. But it needn't look gray to you. Learn a lesson from the prisoner. Give every day a chance. Peer through the bricks, past the rats, to find the blade of grass. And once you find it, don't look anywhere else.

THE HEART OF THE MATTER

- Even in the most miserable of circumstances, there is always a bit of hope.
- The eyes of your heart will determine your outlook on life.
- Sometimes even followers of Christ forget their blessings.
- Setting your mind on what is good, pure, and holy requires great courage.

MEMORY VERSE

Your memory verse for this unit is Deuteronomy 31:6. Take a few moments to review this verse, and then write it out from memory in the space below.

After God's Own Heart

Sometimes courage looks like standing up for the oppressed. Sometimes it looks like going after a promotion. Sometimes it looks like fighting a spiritual battle. And sometimes your greatest act of courage will be to simply wake up and face the day. In these moments, courage is difficult because hope is distant. And hope requires courage.

It's easier to assume the worst. It's easier for the prisoner to assume death, for the orphan to assume loneliness, for the divorcee to assume a life of heartache. Why get your hopes up when your history tells you hope always lets you down?

It's when you hear this voice of defeat that you need a blade of grass. Any small joy, any glimpse of beauty, any ounce of kindness—cling to it! The more you look for joy, the more you will find it and the more aware of joy you will be. Your outlook depends on *where* you look.

WEEKLY BIBLE STUDY

READ: MATTHEW 6:19–24 AND PHILIPPIANS 4:4–9

1. Jesus warned his listeners not to get caught up in amassing worldly possessions (see Matthew 6:9). How does our reliance on earthly things affect our hearts?

2. What connection does Jesus make between our treasures and our hearts (see verse 21)?

3. How does our outlook—what we see—affect our spirit (see verses 22–23)? When has a lack of contentment caused you to feel anxious about a circumstance you were facing?

4. What does Paul say you should do when you're feeling anxious (see Philippians 4:6–7)? How has showing gratitude helped you feel more courageous in the face of anxiety?

5. What does Paul say our mindset should be (see verse 8)? How does this list compare to the types of thoughts you tend to have when you're feeling anxious or afraid?

6. What makes it especially difficult to put these instructions from Paul "into practice" (verse 9) when you feel anxious or afraid?

7. Where in your life do you feel discontent? How could you focus on whatever is true, noble, or lovely—and how such thoughts affect your courage?

Week 8: FREE TO FLY

Hans Babblinger of Ulm, Germany, wanted to fly. He wanted to soar like a bird. The problem was, he lived in the sixteenth century. There were no planes, no helicopters, no flying machines. He was a dreamer born too soon. What he wanted was impossible.

Hans, however, made a career out of helping people overcome the impossible. He made artificial limbs. In his day, amputation was a common cure for disease and injury, so he kept busy. His task was to help the handicapped overcome circumstances.

Babblinger longed to do the same for himself. With time, he used his skills to construct a set of wings. The day soon came to try them out, and he tested his wings in the foothills of the Bavarian Alps. Good choice. Upcurrents are common in the region. On a memorable day with friends watching and sun shining, he jumped off an embankment and soared safely down.

His heart raced. His friends applauded. And God rejoiced. How do I know God rejoiced? Because God always rejoices when we dare to dream. In fact, we are much like God when we dream. The Master exults in newness. He wrote the book on making the impossible possible. God has made an eternity out of making the earthbound airborne. And he gets angry when people's wings are clipped.

Such is the message of the fig tree drama, a peculiar scene involving a fruitless fig tree. Jesus and his disciples are walking to Jerusalem on Monday morning after spending the night in Bethany. He is hungry and sees a fig tree on the side of the road. However, as he approaches the tree, he notices that though it has leaves, it has no fruit.

So Jesus denounces the tree: "May no one ever eat fruit from you again" (Mark 11:14). The tree immediately dries up (see verse 20). The next day, Tuesday, the disciples see what happened to the tree. They are amazed. Just twenty-four hours before, the tree had been green and healthy; now it is barren and dry.

"Rabbi, look!" Peter exclaims. "The fig tree you cursed has withered!" (Mark 11:21).

Jesus responds, "Have faith in God. I tell you the truth, you can say to this mountain, 'Go, fall into the sea.' And if you have no doubts in your mind and believe that what you say will happen, God will do it for you. So I tell you to believe that you have received the things you ask for in prayer, and God will give them to you" (verses 22–24 NCV).

You won't find the words *dream* or *fly* or *wing* in the story. But look closely and you'll see a story of a God who issues a call for the Babblingers of the world to mount the cliff and test their wings. Jesus does to the tree on Monday morning what he will do to the temple on Monday afternoon: He curses it. Note, he's not angry at the tree. He's angry at what the tree represents. He is disgusted by lukewarm, placid, vain believers who have pomp but no purpose.

God can't stomach lukewarm faith. He is angered by a religion that puts on a show but ignores the service. This is precisely the religion that Jesus was facing during his last week. And the religion he had faced his entire ministry.

When he served, the religious leaders complained. They complained his disciples ate on the wrong day. They complained he healed on the wrong day. They complained he hung out with the wrong crowd. Even worse, every time he tried to set people free, they attempted to tie them down. Those closest to the temple were quickest with the shackles. When a courageous soul tried to fly, they were there to say it couldn't be done.

By the way, they told Hans the same thing. Seems the king was coming to Ulm and the bishop and the citizens wanted to impress him. Word had gotten out about Hans's flying feat, so they asked him to do a loop for the king.

They wanted one change, however. Since the crowd would be large and the hills were difficult to climb, could Hans choose a place in the lowlands in which he could fly?

Hans chose the bluffs near the Danube. They were broad and flat and the river was a good distance below. He would jump off the edge and float down to the water.

Poor choice. The updraft in the hills was nonexistent near the river. So in front of the king, his court, and half the village, Hans jumped and fell like a rock straight into the river. The king was disappointed and the bishop mortified. Guess what the bishop preached the next Sunday? "Man was not meant to fly." Hans believed him. Imprisoned by a pulpit, he put his wings away and never again tried to fly. He died soon after, buried with his dreams.

The cathedral of Ulm isn't the first church to cage a flyer. Through the years pulpits have grown proficient in telling people what they can't do. They did in the day of Christ, they did in the day of Hans Babblinger, and they do today—and you can be sure it is just as nauseating to God today as it was then.

But as we are looking at religion, we would do well to look in the mirror. It's convenient to point fingers at organized religion and say, "Amen, tell 'em like it is!" It's comfortable to do that, but inadequate. While we are talking about setting people free to fly, think about yourself. How are you at giving wings? How have you been at setting people free?

The message of the fig tree is not for all of us to have the *same* fruit. The message is for us to have *some* fruit. Not easy. Jesus knows that. "If you have faith and do not doubt, you will be able to do what I did to this tree and even more" (Matthew 21:21 NCV).

Faith in whom? Religion? Hardly. The faith is in God.

God wants you to fly. He wants you to fly free of yesterday's guilt. He wants you to fly free of today's fears. He wants you to fly free of tomorrow's grave. Sin, fear, and death—these are the mountains he has moved. These are the prayers he will answer. That is the fruit he will grant. This is what he longs to do: He longs to set you free so you can fly . . . fly home.

THE HEART OF THE MATTER

- God loves it when you dare to dream because he can make the impossible possible.
- Faith in God empowers you to overcome obstacles and achieve the impossible.
- Jesus calls you to bear fruit, not settle for a life of unfulfilled potential.
- Release guilt, fear, and doubt—trust God to set you free to pursue your dreams.

MEMORY VERSE

Your memory verse for this unit is Deuteronomy 31:6. Take a few moments to review this verse, and then write it out from memory in the space below.

After God's Own Heart

As children, we dream big. We're not afraid of our dreams. We tell adults what we'll be when grow up. A doctor! An astronaut! A princess! And we believe it with all our hearts. Until . . . life gets a hold of us. Little by little, we learn our dreams aren't to be trusted. Our dreams rarely come true. Our dreams are often crushed, sometimes inside the church's walls.

We lose our courage to dream.

What would you dream today if you had no fear? What would you believe if you had no doubt? What would you do if you fully believed Jesus was with you and could make it happen? This is the type of faith Jesus wants you to have. What the world has chipped away, he will restore. When you dream with him, anything is possible.

WEEKLY BIBLE STUDY

READ: EXODUS 3:1–12 AND MARK 11:12–25

1. God revealed himself to Moses in a burning bush (see Exodus 3:1–4). What instructions did he give to Moses? What calling did the Lord make on his life (see verses 5–10)?

2. How did Moses respond to this calling (see verse 11)? What does that reveal about how Moses felt about the mission that God was giving to him?

3. What reassurance did God give to Moses to embolden him (see verse 12)? What does this tell you about God's presence when you respond to his call on your life?

4. Why does Jesus curse the fig tree (see Mark 11:12–13)? What is the importance of the detail Mark adds that "his disciples heard him say it" (verse 14)?

5. How is the barren fig tree a metaphor for empty religion? Why do you think Jesus had such a strong reaction to the tree and those trading in the temple (see verses 15–17)?

6. What instruction does Jesus give the disciples when they see the withered fig tree (see verses 22–25)? How does your faith and prayer life compare to what Jesus describes here?

7. Have you lost your courage to pursue a particular dream? How do the passages you've read this week encourage you to start believing in yourself again?

Week 9: QUIET COURAGE

Step with me into a dank dungeon in Judea. Peer through the door's tiny window. Consider the plight of the man on the floor. He has just inaugurated history's greatest movement. His words have triggered a revolution that will span two millennia. Future historians will describe him as courageous, noble, and visionary.

At this moment he appears anything but. Cheeks hollow. Beard matted. Bewilderment etched on his face. He leans back against the cold wall, closes his eyes, and sighs. John had never known doubt. Hunger, yes. Loneliness, often. But doubt? Never. Only raw conviction, ruthless pronouncements, and rugged truth. Such was John the Baptist.

Until now.

Now the sun is blocked. Now his courage wanes. Now the clouds come. And now, as he faces death, he doesn't raise a fist of victory; he raises only a question. His final act is not a proclamation of courage but a confession of confusion: "Find out if Jesus is the Son of God or not" (see Matthew 11:2–3).

He doesn't sound too courageous. We'd rather John die in peace. We'd rather the trailblazer catch a glimpse of the mountain. After all, didn't Moses get a view of the valley? Isn't John the cousin of Jesus? If anybody deserves to see the end of the trail, doesn't he?

Apparently not. The miracles he prophesied, he never saw. The kingdom he announced, he never knew. And the Messiah he proclaimed, he now doubts. He doesn't look like a hero.

Heroes seldom do.

Can I take you to another prison for a second example? This time the jail is in Rome. The man is named Paul. What John did to present Christ, Paul did to explain him. John cleared the path; Paul erected signposts. Like John, Paul shaped history. And like John, Paul would die in the jail of a despot. No headlines announced his execution. When the ax struck Paul's neck, society's eyes didn't blink. To them Paul was a peculiar purveyor of an odd faith.

Peer into the prison and see him for yourself: bent and frail, shackled to the arm of a Roman guard. Behold the apostle of God. Who knows when his back last felt a bed or his mouth knew a good meal? Three decades of travel and trouble, and what's he got to show for it?

There's squabbling in Philippi, competition in Corinth, the legalists are swarming in Galatia. Even some of Paul's own friends have turned against him. Dead broke. No family. No property. Nearsighted and worn out. He never received a salary. Had to pay his own travel expenses. Kept a part-time job on the side to make ends meet.

Doesn't look like a hero.

Doesn't sound like one either. He introduced himself as the worst sinner in history. He was a Christian-killer before he was a Christian leader. At times his heart was so heavy, his pen dragged itself across the page. "What a miserable man I am! Who will save me from this body that brings me death?" (Romans 7:24 NCV).

Only heaven knows how long he stared at the question before he found the courage to defy logic and write, "I thank God for saving me through Jesus Christ our Lord!" (verse 25). One minute he's in charge; the next he's in doubt. One day he's preaching; the next he's in prison.

And that's where I'd like you to look at him. Look at him in the prison. Pretend you don't know him. You're a guard or a cook or a friend of the hatchet man, and you've come to get one last look at the guy while they sharpen the blade. What you see shuffling around in his cell isn't too much. But what I lean over and tell you is, "That man will shape the course of history."

You chuckle, but I continue. "Nero's fame will fade in this man's light." You turn and stare. I continue. "His churches will die. But his thoughts? Within two hundred years his thoughts will influence the teaching of every school on this continent." You shake your head.

"See those letters? Those letters scribbled on parchment? They'll be read in thousands of languages and will impact every major creed and constitution of the future. Every major figure will read them. Every single one." You say, "No way. He's an old man with an odd faith. He'll be killed and forgotten before his head hits the floor."

What rational thinker would disagree? Paul's name would blow like the dust his bones would become. Just like John's. No levelheaded observer would think otherwise. Both were courageous, but small. Radical, yet unnoticed. No one—I repeat, no one—bade farewell to these men thinking their names would be remembered longer than a generation.

Their peers simply had no way of knowing—and neither do we. For that reason, a hero could be next door and you wouldn't know it. I know, I know, the folks in your neighborhood don't fit your image of a courageous hero. They look too, too . . . well, normal. Give us four stars, titles, and headlines. But something tells me that for every hero in the spotlight, there are dozens in the shadows. They don't draw crowds. They don't even write books!

But behind every avalanche is a snowflake. Behind a rockslide is a pebble. An atomic explosion begins with one atom. And a revival can begin with one sermon.

Do heroes know when they are heroic? Rarely. Are historic moments acknowledged when they happen? You know the answer to that one. (If not, a visit to the manger will remind you.) We seldom see history in the making, and we seldom recognize heroes. Which is just as well, for if we knew either, we might mess up both.

But we'd do well to keep our eyes open. Tomorrow's hero may be in our midst.

THE HEART OF THE MATTER

- Don't underestimate the impact of small, faithful acts in your life.
- Even the greatest heroes wrestled with uncertainty and found strength in God.
- Your unseen efforts today could shape history tomorrow.
- There could be a hero in your midst. You just need eyes to see that person.

MEMORY VERSE

Your memory verse for this unit is Deuteronomy 31:6. Take a few moments to review this verse, and then write it out from memory in the space below.

After God's Own Heart

They often aren't kings or queens. Nor are they presidents, CEOs, military leaders, or officials. They are in the background, sweeping the floor while everyone else is asleep. Packing the lunches early in the morning. Grading papers late at night. Building the stage others will stand on. Tending the flock in the field while the older brothers speak with the priest at the house.

God's heroes sometimes surprise us. They often are not our heroes, or the ones we would choose. But God notices the faithful servants, quiet and consistent. The teachers, kind and patient. The parents, loving and forgiving. Occasionally they are recognized but most days they're not. This doesn't stop them from doing the Lord's work. They know where their award awaits them. They don't need the trophy, check, or promotion. They elevate others and wait their turn. Their courage is quiet. Their lives, heroic.

WEEKLY BIBLE STUDY

READ: LUKE 1:26–38 AND 2 CORINTHIANS 11:16–31

1. What do you learn about Mary based on the description in Luke 1:26–27?

2. How does Mary respond to Gabriel and his message for her (see verses 28–33)? What does this tell you about Mary, her status in society, and how she viewed herself before God?

3. What did Gabriel say would happen to enable her to give birth to the Messiah (see verses 35–37)? How do you think these words emboldened Mary's heart?

4. Paul talks about "boasting in the way the world does" (2 Corinthians 11:18) and then gives his own "boast." What is the difference between Paul's boasting and the world's boasting?

5. Review the list of afflictions Paul faced in spreading the gospel (see verses 23–28.) How do you think Paul's contemporaries viewed him based on the type of life he was living?

6. Paul said he would boast of the things that show his weakness (see verse 30). In the Christian life, how is weakness a sign of strength? How does that determine your definition of courage?

7. When it comes to facing your Goliath today, do you feel weak like Paul or trusting like Mary? What is Jesus saying to you through their stories?

Week 10: TOSSED BY THE WAVES

Peter learned a critical lesson in courage one night on the Sea of Galilee. The story begins in Matthew 14:24: "But the boat was now in the middle of the sea, tossed by the waves, for the wind was contrary" (NKJV).

As famous lakes go, Galilee is a small, moody one. Its size and location make it more vulnerable to the winds out of the Golan Heights that cause life-threatening storms.[6] Peter and his fellow storm riders knew they were in trouble. What should have been a sixty-minute cruise became a nightlong battle. Winds whipped the sails, leaving the disciples "in the middle of the sea, tossed by the waves."

Apt description, perhaps, for your stage in life? In the middle of a divorce, tossed about by guilt. In the middle of debt, tossed about by creditors. In the middle of a recession, tossed about by stimulus packages and bailouts.

The disciples fought the storm for nine cold, wet hours. At about 4:00 a.m. they spotted someone coming on the water. "'A ghost!' they said, crying out in terror" (verse 26 MSG). Jesus replied to the disciples' fear with an invitation worthy of inscription on every church: "Don't be afraid. . . . Take courage. I am here!" (verse 27 NLT).

Power inhabits those words. To awaken in an ICU and hear your husband say, "I am here." To lose your retirement yet hear your family say, "We are here." When a Little Leaguer spots Mom and Dad in the bleachers watching the game, "I am here" changes everything.

Perhaps that's why God repeats it so often. "I am with you always, to the very end of the age" (Matthew 28:20). "I give them eternal life, and they shall never perish; no one will snatch them out of my hand" (John 10:28). "Nothing can ever separate us from God's love" (Romans 8:38 NLT).

We cannot go where God is not. Look into the storm; Christ is coming toward you.

Peter took Jesus at his word. "Lord, if it is You, command me to come to You on the water" (Matthew 14:28 NKJV). "So He said, 'Come.' And when Peter had come down out of the boat, he walked on the water to go to Jesus" (verse 29 NKJV).

Peter never would have made this request on a calm sea. Had Christ been strolling across a glass-like surface, Peter would have applauded, but I doubt he would have stepped out of the boat. Storms prompt us to take unprecedented journeys. For a few historic steps, Peter did the impossible: "he walked on the water."

My editors would have flooded the margin with red ink: "Elaborate! How quickly did Peter exit the boat? What was the expression on his face? Did he step on any fish?" But Matthew moves quickly to the main message of the event: where to stare in a storm. "But when [Peter] saw that the wind was boisterous, he was afraid; and beginning to sink he cried out, saying, 'Lord, save me!'" (verse 30 NKJV).

A flash of lighting, a gust of wind, and Peter shifted his attention away from Jesus and toward the squall. When he did, he sank. Give the storm waters more attention than the Storm Walker, and get ready to do the same.

Whether or not storms come, we cannot choose. But where we stare during a storm, that we can. I experienced this firsthand while sitting in my cardiologist's office. My heart rate was misbehaving, beating at the pace of a NASCAR race, to the rhythm of Morse Code. So I went to a specialist. After reviewing my tests, the doctor nodded knowingly and told me to wait in his office. I quickly noticed his abundant harvest of diplomas. They were everywhere, from everywhere. One degree from university. Another degree from residency.

The more I looked at his accomplishments, the better I felt. *I'm in good hands*, I thought. Then the nurse entered and handed me a sheet of paper that described my condition. I lowered my gaze from the diplomas to the summary of the disorder. As I read, contrary winds began to blow. Unwelcome words like atrial fibrillation, arrhythmia, embolic stroke, and blood clot caused me to sink into my own Sea of Galilee.

My courage from a moment ago was gone. So I changed strategies. I counteracted the diagnosis with the diplomas. In between paragraphs of bad news, I looked at the wall for reminders of good news. That's what God wants us to do: Counterbalance fear with long looks at God's accomplishments. "We must *pay much closer attention* to what we have heard, so that we do not drift away from it" (Hebrews 2:1 NASB, emphasis added).

Do whatever it takes to keep your gaze on Jesus. When a friend of mine spent several days in the hospital at the bedside of her husband, she relied on hymns to keep her courage. Every few minutes she stepped into the restroom and sang a few verses of "Great Is Thy Faithfulness." Do likewise! Make the deliberate decision to set your hope on Jesus.

Courage is always a possibility.

After a few moments of flailing in the water, Peter turned back to Christ and cried, "Lord, save me!" (Matthew 14:30). "Immediately Jesus stretched out his hand and caught him. 'O you of little faith, why did you doubt?' And when they got into the boat, the wind ceased" (verses 31–32 NKJV).

Jesus could have stilled this storm hours earlier. But he didn't. He wanted to teach the followers a lesson. Jesus could have calmed your storm long ago too. But he hasn't. Maybe he wants to teach you the same lesson: "Storms are not an option, but fear is."

THE HEART OF THE MATTER

- Storms are inevitable, but where you focus determines whether you sink or stand.
- Storms will prompt you to take unprecedented journeys.
- Fix your eyes on Jesus, not the chaos around you, to find courage and peace.
- Storms are not an option, but fear is, so keep your eyes on Jesus.

MEMORY VERSE

Your memory verse for this unit is Deuteronomy 31:6. Take a few moments to review this verse, and then write it out from memory in the space below.

After God's Own Heart

We remember Jesus when the storm hits. We remember him during those first few shaky steps, calling out to him, praying, relying on our Savior. But what about in the middle of the storm? When you've endured the downpour for weeks? When the rain hasn't let up, the pain hasn't subsided? Turning your eyes to Jesus is one thing. Keeping them on him is another.

Storms chip away at our courage. Our strength wanes, and the overwhelm causes us to shift our gaze—to other saviors, to ourselves, to self-help books, to empty promises, to anything but Jesus. But even though we look away, Jesus doesn't go anywhere. He is still there. All we have to do is look up. The storm may not end, but the hand reaching out will steady us. Soon we find our courage again and the peace we experience guards us against the winds and rain.

WEEKLY BIBLE STUDY

READ: PSALM 31:9–24 AND MATTHEW 14:22–33

1. Based on Psalm 31:9–13, what kind of storms was David facing? How did these trials affect him physically, emotionally, and spiritually?

2. What did David say to himself to keep his eyes fixed on God in the midst of these storms (see verses 14–15)? Has doing the same helped you? If so, how?

3. What was David's final plea in this psalm (see verse 24)? When have you waited on the Lord to help you weather a storm—and how does that require courage and strength?

4. Where was Jesus when the disciples encountered the storm on the Sea of Galilee (see Matthew 14:23–24)? Why do you think he allowed the disciples to initially experience the storm alone?

5. How do Jesus' words in verse 27 echo David's words in Psalm 31:24? How does Jesus' presence bring you courage and still your heart when storms are raging around you?

6. When Peter began sinking and cried out for help, how quickly did Jesus respond (see Matthew 14:31)? What does this tell you about Jesus' willingness to respond when you cry out to him?

7. What storm have you faced this week that tempted you to take your eyes off Jesus? Were you able to refocus on the Savior to regain the courage to be strong in the storm? How?

Unit 3

Seeking A TRUSTING HEART

Poor David. The Valley of Elah proved to be boot camp for the king's court. When Goliath lost his head, the Hebrews made David their hero. People threw him a ticker-tape parade and sang, "Saul has slain his thousands, and David his ten thousands" (1 Samuel 18:7 NKJV). Saul explodes like the volcano he is. He eyes David "from that day forward" (verse 9 NKJV). The king is already a troubled soul, prone to angry eruptions, mad enough to eat bees. David's popularity splashes gasoline on Saul's temper. "I will pin David to the wall!" (verse 11 NKJV).

Saul tries to kill Bethlehem's golden boy six different times. First, he invites David to marry his daughter Michal. Seems like a kind gesture, until you read the crude dowry Saul required. One hundred Philistine foreskins. *Surely one of the Philistines will kill David*, Saul hopes. They don't. David doubles the demand and returns with the proof.

Saul doesn't give up. He orders his servants and Jonathan to kill David, but they refuse. He tries with the spear another time but misses. Saul sends messengers to David's house to kill him, but his wife, Michal, lowers him through a window.

David the roadrunner stays a step ahead of Saul the coyote.

Saul's anger puzzles David. What has he done but good? He has brought musical healing to Saul's tortured spirit, hope to the enfeebled nation. He is the Abraham Lincoln of the Hebrew calamity, saving the republic and doing so modestly and honestly. He behaves "wisely in all his ways" (18:14 NKJV). "All Israel and Judah loved David" (verse 16 NKJV). David behaves "more wisely than all the servants of Saul, so that his name became highly esteemed" (verse 30 NKJV).

Yet Mount Saul keeps erupting, rewarding David's deeds with flying spears and murder plots. We understand David's question to Jonathan: "What have I done? What is my iniquity, and what is my sin before your father, that he seeks my life?" (20:1 NKJV).

Oh, to have a friend like Jonathan. A soul mate who protects you, who seeks nothing but your interests, wants nothing but your happiness. An ally who lets you be you. You feel safe with that person. No need to weigh thoughts or measure words. You know their faithful hand will sift the chaff from the grain, keep what matters, and with a breath of kindness, blow the rest away.[7] God gave David such a trusted friend. He gave you one as well.

David found a companion in a prince of Israel; you have a friend in the King of Israel, Jesus Christ. Just as Jonathan protected David, Jesus vows to protect you. "I give them eternal life, and they will never perish. No one can snatch them away from me" (John 10:28 NLT).

— PRAYER —

Lord God, when I can't trust anyone else, I can trust you. Just as David trusted you while he ran from Saul, help me trust you as I face my enemies. Help me lean into your strength and not my own. The world has taught me to be weary of others. But may I never be weary of you. Teach my heart to trust again. In your name I pray, amen.

— MEMORY VERSE —

Trust in the LORD with all your heart and lean not on your own understanding; in all your ways submit to him, and he will make your paths straight.

PROVERBS 3:5–6

Week 11: SEASONS OF DRYNESS

The Dead Sea is dying. Drop by drop, at a rate of three feet a year. Galilee sends her fresh fluid through the Jordanian Canal, water worthy of a Messiah's baptism. But the Dead Sea impoverishes it: darkening, acidizing, creating a saline cemetery.

You find little life in her waters or her surroundings. Ominous cliffs rise to the west, flattening out at two thousand feet. Erosion has scarred the land into a tyranny of caves and ruts: a home for hyenas, lizards, buzzards . . . and David. Not by choice, mind you. He didn't want to swap the palace for the badlands. No one chooses the wilderness.

But sometimes we have no vote. Calamity hits and the roof rips. The tornado lifts and drops us in the desert. Not the desert in southeastern Israel, but the desert of the soul.

A season of dryness.

Isolation marks such seasons. Saul has effectively and systematically isolated David from every source of stability. His half-dozen assassination attempts ended David's military career. His pursuit drove a wedge in David's marriage. After David's wife, Michal, helped him escape, Saul demanded an explanation from her. "I had to," she lied. "He threatened to kill me if I didn't help him" (1 Samuel 19:17 TLB).

David races from Saul's court to Samuel's house. But no sooner does he arrive than someone tells Saul, "Take note, David is at Naioth in Ramah!" (verse 19 NKJV). David flees to Jonathan, his soul mate. Jonathan wants to help, but what can he do? Leave the court in the hands of a madman? No, Jonathan has to stay with Saul.

No place in the court. No position in the army. No wife, no priest, no friend. Nothing to do but run. He escapes to Gath, the hometown of Goliath. He tries to forge a friendship based on a mutual adversary. If your enemy is Saul and my enemy is Saul, we become friends, right?

In this case, wrong.

The Gittites aren't hospitable. "Isn't this David, the king of the land?" they ask. "Isn't he the one the people honor with dances, singing, 'Saul has killed his thousands, and David his ten thousands'?" (21:11 NLT). David panics. We'd like to hear a prayer to his Shepherd. We'd appreciate a pronouncement of God's strength. But David doesn't see God. He sees trouble. So he takes matters into his own hands.

He pretends to be insane, scratching on doors and drooling down his beard. Finally the king of Gath says to his men, "'Must you bring me a madman? We already have enough of them around here! Why should I let someone like this be my guest?'" (verses 14–15 NLT).

He can't go to the court of Saul or the house of Michal, the city of Samuel or the safety of Nob. So he goes to the only place he can—the place where no one goes, because nothing survives. The wilderness. To the honeycombed canyons that overlook the Dead Sea. He finds a cave, the cave called Adullam. In it he finds shade, silence, and safety. He stretches on the cool dirt and closes his eyes and begins his decade in the wilderness.

Can you relate to David's story? Has your Saul cut you off from the position you had and the people you love? Are you seeking refuge in Gath?

Under normal circumstances you would never go there. But these aren't normal circumstances, so you loiter in the breeding ground of giants. The hometown of trouble. Her arms or that bar. You walk shady streets and frequent questionable places. And, while there, you go crazy. So the crowd will accept you, so the stress won't kill you, you go wild. You wake up in a Dead Sea cave, in the grottoes of Adullam, at the lowest point of your life and ask, "What do I do now?"

Let David be your teacher. Sure, he goes wacko for a few verses. But in the cave of Adullam, he gathers himself. The faithful shepherd boy surfaces again. The giant-killer rediscovers courage. Yes, he has a price on his head. Yes, he has no place to lay his head, but somehow he keeps his head. He returns his focus to trusting God and finds refuge.

Refuge surfaces as a favorite word of David's with forty-plus appearances in the Psalms. But never did David use the word more poignantly than in Psalm 57. The introduction to the passage explains its background: "A song of David when he fled from Saul into the cave."

Envision Jesse's son in the dimness: on his knees, perhaps on his face, lost in shadows and thought. He has nowhere to turn. Go home, he endangers his family; go to the tabernacle, he imperils the priests. Saul will kill him; Gath won't take him. Here he sits. All alone.

But then he remembers: He's not. He's not alone. And from the recesses of the cave a sweet voice floats: "Be merciful to me, O God, be merciful to me! For my soul trusts in you; and in the shadow of your wings I will make my refuge" (verse 1 NKJV).

Make God your refuge. Trust him. Not your job, your spouse, your reputation, or your retirement account. Let him, not Saul, encircle you. Let him be the ceiling that breaks the sunshine, the walls that stop the wind, the foundation on which you stand.

A cave dweller addressed our church recently. He bore the smell of Adullam. He'd just buried his wife, and his daughter was growing sicker by the day. Yet, in the dry land he found God. I wrote his discovery on the flyleaf of my Bible: "You'll never know that Jesus is all you need until Jesus is all you have."

Wilderness survivors find refuge in God's presence. They trust him in all seasons—even the driest ones.

THE HEART OF THE MATTER

- Isolation and hardship often lead to moments of reflection and personal growth.
- Challenges can strip away your security, compelling you to rely on Christ.
- God is with you even during the driest and most desperate seasons in life.
- Make God your refuge. Let him—not your "Saul"—encircle you.

MEMORY VERSE

Your memory verse for this unit is Proverbs 3:5–6. Take a few moments to review this verse, and then write it out from memory in the space below.

After God's Own Heart

Where is your Gath? The place you fled to when the loved one was buried, the dream never came to fruition, the bank account was drained. What did you hope Gath would do for you? Restore your faith, your health, your wealth? What did it do instead?

And where is your Adullam? The place you ended up after every other place and every other person had failed you. The cave where you sought refuge. The place where you met God. You entered into the darkness for a season, but when you emerged, it was light.

Trusting God during the good, fruitful, and joyful seasons can be easy. Trusting him during the wilderness may be hard. Too embarrassed to face God? Too scared, uncertain, confused? This is why David fled. Sometimes we do the same. But, like Israel's king, may we remember where to find refuge. May we trust in the Lord our God.

WEEKLY BIBLE STUDY

READ: 1 SAMUEL 19:1–17, 20:12–17, AND PSALM 57:1–11

1. How did Jonathan respond to his father's instruction to kill David? What was the initial result of Jonathan's intervention (see 1 Samuel 19:1–7)?

2. What ultimately led David to separate again from Saul? What caused David to flee even from his home—initiating his "dry season" (see verses 9–12)?

3. What covenant did Jonathan make with the house of David (see 20:12–17)? How did Jonathan, throughout this entire ordeal with Saul, prove to be a loyal friend to David?

4. David is believed to have written Psalm 57 when he fled King Saul. What is David's cry in this psalm? What is his expectation of God's intervention (see verses 1–3)?

5. How does David describe the men who were pursuing him (verses 4, 6)? What does this say to you about his state of mind in this moment?

6. What confidence in the Lord does David express in verses 7–11? How do these proclamations display David's trust in God even as he feared his enemies?

7. What specific fear, anxiety, or trouble are you running from today? How do you think God might be calling you to be still and wait on him even as fear pursues you?

Week 12: GOD'S BIG ARMS

I stand six steps from the bed's edge. My arms extended. Hands open. On the bed, Sara—all four years of her—crouches, poised like a playful kitten. She's going to jump. But she's not ready. I'm too close.

"Back more, Daddy," she stands and dares.

I dramatically comply, confessing admiration for her courage. After two giant steps, I stop. "More?" I ask.

"Yes!" Sara squeals, hopping on the bed.

With each step she laughs and claps and motions for more. When I'm on the other side of the canyon, when I'm beyond the reach of mortal man, when I am but a tiny figure on the horizon, she stops me. "There, stop there."

"Are you sure?"

"I'm sure!" she shouts. I extend my arms. Once again she crouches, then springs. Superman without a cape. Skydiver without a chute. Only her heart flies higher than her body. In that airborne instant, her only hope is her father. If he proves weak, she'll fall. If he proves cruel, she'll crash. If he proves forgetful, she'll tumble to the hard floor.

But such fear she does not know, for her father she does. She trusts him. He is not superhuman, but he is strong. He is not holy, but he is good. He's not brilliant, but he doesn't have to be to remember to catch his child when she jumps. And so she flies.

And so he catches her, and the two rejoice at the wedding of her trust and his faithfulness.

I stand a few feet from another bed. This time no one laughs. The room is solemn. A machine pumps air into a tired body. A monitor metronomes the beats of a weary heart. The woman on the bed is no child. She was, once. Decades back. She was. But not now.

Like Sara, she must trust. Only days out of the operating room, she's just been told she'll have to return. Her frail hand squeezes mine. Her eyes mist with fear. Unlike Sara, she sees no father. But the Father sees her. "Trust him," I say to us both. Trust the voice that whispers your name. Trust the hands to catch.

I sit across the table from a good man. Good and afraid. His fear is honest. Stocks are down. Inflation is up. He has payroll to meet and bills to pay. He hasn't squandered or gambled or played. He has worked hard and prayed often, but now he's afraid. Beneath the flannel suit lies a timid heart.

He stirs his coffee and stares at me with eyes that know he's about to fall and fall fast. He's Peter on the water, seeing the storm and not the face. He's Peter in the waves, hearing the wind and not the voice.

"Trust," I urge. But the word thuds. He's unaccustomed to such strangeness. He's a man of reason. Even when the kite flies beyond the clouds, he still holds the string. But now the string has slipped. And the sky is silent.

I stand a few feet from a mirror and see the face of a man who failed . . . who failed his Maker. Again. I promised I wouldn't, but I did. I was quiet when I should have been bold. I took a seat when

I should have taken a stand. If this were the first time, it would be different. But it isn't. How many times can one fall and expect to be caught?

Trust. Why is it easy to tell others and so hard to remind yourself? Can God deal with death? I told the woman so. Can God deal with debt? I ventured as much with the man. Can God hear yet one more confession from these lips? The face in the mirror asks.

I sit a few feet from a man on death row. Jewish by birth. Tentmaker by trade. Apostle by calling. His days are marked. I'm curious about what bolsters this man as he nears his execution. So I ask some questions.

"Do you have family, Paul?" *I have none.*

"What about your health?" *My body is beaten and tired.*

"What do you own?" *I have my parchments. My pen. A cloak.*

"And your reputation?" *Well, it's not much. I'm a heretic to some, a maverick to others.*

"Do you have friends?" *I do, but even some of them have turned back.*

"Then what do you have, Paul? No belongings. No family. Criticized by some. Mocked by others. What do you have, Paul? What do you have that matters?"

I sit back quietly and watch. Paul rolls his hand into a fist. He looks at it. I look at it. What is he holding? What does he have? He extends his hand so I can see. As I lean forward, he opens his fingers. I peer at his palm. It's empty.

I have my faith. It's all I have. But it's all I need. I have kept the faith.

Paul leans back against the wall of his cell and smiles. For that's what faith is. Faith is trusting what the eye can't see.

Your eyes look in the mirror and see a sinner, a failure, a promise-breaker. But by faith you look in the mirror and see a robed prodigal bearing the ring of grace on your finger and the kiss of your Father on your face. "But wait a minute," someone asks. "How do I know this is true? How do I know these aren't just fanciful hopes?"

Part of the answer can be found in Sara's little leaps of faith. Her sister, Andrea, was in the room watching, and I asked Sara if she would jump to Andrea. Sara refused. I tried to convince her. She wouldn't budge. "Why not?" I asked.

"I only jump to big arms."

If we think the arms are weak, we won't jump. For that reason, the Father flexed his muscles. "God's power is very great for those who believe," Paul taught. "That power is the same as the great strength God used to raise Christ from the dead" (Ephesians 1:19–20 NCV).

Next time you wonder if God can catch you, read that verse. The very arms that defeated death are the arms awaiting you. And the next time you wonder if you will survive the jump, think of Sara and me. If a flesh-and-boneheaded dad like me can catch his child, don't you think your eternal Father can catch you?

THE HEART OF THE MATTER

- You can trust the arms of your loving heavenly Father will always catch you.
- Faith grows when you rely on God even in uncertain or overwhelming situations.
- Faith means trusting what the eye cannot see.
- When you trust God's arms are big enough to catch you, the leap is easy.

MEMORY VERSE

Your memory verse for this unit is Proverbs 3:5–6. Take a few moments to review this verse, and then write it out from memory in the space below.

After God's Own Heart

Maybe you've been trying to muster courage with self-talk and power poses but have found it's not working. The missing link could be trust. Trust comes before courage—not trust in yourself or your work ethic but trust in God. If your courage is weak, perhaps your trust is, too.

Or maybe your view of God is too small. The God in whom you place your trust cannot be small or weak. He must be strong. He must be fighting for you. He must not shrink in the face of strength, because your courage depends on him.

Big courage begins with big trust. And that starts with believing in a big God—"the Creator of the heavens, who stretches them out, who spreads out the earth with all that springs from it, who gives breath to its people, and life to those who walk in it" (Isaiah 42:5). A courageous heart is one that trusts in a God who is big enough to catch you in his big arms.

WEEKLY BIBLE STUDY

READ: JOB 38:1–41 AND EPHESIANS 1:18–23

1. God speaks to Job from a whirlwind after his friends tried to explain the reason for his suffering. What does God say about their arguments when he first appears (see Job 38:2)?

2. What point was God making by asking Job and his friends the rhetorical questions that follow (see verses 4–41)? What was he revealing about his sovereignty?

3. Do you think about God in the way he describes himself in these chapters? How does this passage make you think differently about his power and control over the universe?

4. Faith means trusting what the eye cannot see. How might God's questions to Job have bolstered his faith? How does understanding God's authority help you in seasons of suffering?

5. What is Paul's prayer for the believers in Ephesians 1:18–19? What does he want them to understand about the God whom they serve?

6. It's easier to trust in God when you believe his arms are big enough to catch you. What does Paul add in verses 19–21 about the power that God possesses?

7. In what areas of your life are you lacking trust that your heavenly Father will catch you? How do the passages you've read this week give you confidence that his power is sufficient?

Week 13: NEVER ALONE

Joy Veron was all alone in her hospital room. Alone with her fears, her pain, and her memory of the SUV rolling over her body. Vacation became tragedy when her car slipped out of gear and began rolling toward a steep Colorado mountain ravine, carrying her three children.

Joy and her parents had been looking at a cabin her parents were considering buying. When they saw the vehicle moving, they dashed to stop it. Joy arrived first. Fearful she didn't have time to open the driver's side door, she placed herself in front of the SUV. Her interference slowed it down enough for her father to climb into the passenger side and bring the car to a stop. Joy's back was broken, and the internal damage was severe.

Joy was airlifted to a hospital. Her condition was so fragile the doctors waited twelve days before doing surgery. She emerged from the operation with a dangerously high fever. For seven days her temperature raged. So did her fears. Joy pleaded with her mom for help. Her mother, who had maintained a bedside vigil, stepped out to call friends for prayer.

"I'll be back soon," she told her daughter.

Joy was all alone. But not for long. A man opened the door and walked into the room. Joy did not recognize him. If the man was a doctor or nurse, he wasn't one of hers. He had a striking appearance, tall and dressed in white. He had high cheekbones and silver-white hair that was parted in the middle and ran down his back in a ponytail.

The visitor stepped toward her bed and lifted her chart. After a few moments he spoke to her with a soothing voice. "Joy, you are going to be all right. You will get through this." He looked at her, and then as quickly as he had entered, he left.

Joy instantly believed him. "Had the doctor, a nurse, or a family member said those words, I would have doubted them. But when this stranger spoke, there was a knowing in my inner person. He knew me. And I believed him. I knew I was going to be okay."

When her mother reentered, Joy told her about the man. "Mom, he said I am going to be fine!" Joy's mom ran out to find the visitor but saw no one matching his description. The staff knew nothing of such a man. They searched the hospital but could not find him.

Joy knows why. She believes the visitor was heaven-sent just for her. She treasures the words he spoke: "You are going to be all right. You will get through this." And she has.[8]

Who was this visitor? Did God send an emissary to bring her hope? Joshua would like to weigh in on this discussion. He has a story that parallels Joy's, a divine encounter during a dark, difficult time. He was alone with a challenge. "Joshua was near Jericho" (Joshua 5:13).

David had his Goliath. Elijah had his Jezebel. John had the Roman Empire. And Joshua had the people of this fortified city. It towered like a titan on the barren plains north of the Dead Sea. Successive walls encircled the stone houses.[9]

The outer wall was seven feet wide and sixteen feet high. On top of this wall a second wall was built, this one eight feet tall. A thick forest of palm trees, eight miles long and three miles wide, stood as a barrier east of the city. Steep hills protected the western wall.[10] High walls. Protected sides. Joshua and his soldiers had never faced such a challenge.

They had fought battles in the wilderness but always on their terms on an open plain. Never, ever had they fought a fortified city. They had never passed this way before.

Perhaps you haven't either. Perhaps you are facing a challenge unlike any you have ever faced before. It looms on the horizon like an angry Jericho. Imposing. Strong. It consumes your thoughts and saps your strength. It wakes you up and keeps you awake. It is the biggest challenge of your life. It sits between you and a Promised Land life.

Like Joshua, you can see it. Like Joshua, you must face it. And, like Joshua, you don't have to face your Jericho alone.

> When Joshua was near Jericho, he looked up and saw a man standing in front of him with a drawn sword in his hand. Joshua went up to him and asked, "Are you for us or our enemies?"
>
> "Neither," he replied, "but as commander of the army of the LORD I have now come." Then Joshua fell facedown to the ground in reverence, and asked him, "What message does my Lord have for his servant?"
>
> The commander of the LORD's army replied, "Take off your sandals, for the place where you are standing is holy." And Joshua did so (verses 13–15).

When it comes to heaven-to-earth communiqués, God seems to follow one rule: There is no rule. In the case of Abram, three strangers came for dinner. (Angel food cake for dessert, perhaps?) In the story of Moses, a blazing bush left him wide-eyed and barefoot. A talking donkey got the attention of Balaam. A blazing angel guarded the empty tomb of Jesus.

The Bible is famous for surprise encounters.

The message to Joshua is unmistakable. *Jericho may have its walls, but, Joshua, you have more. You have God. He is with you. Trust in the Lord.*

Isn't that the word Joshua needed? A reminder of God's mighty presence? Isn't that all any of us need? We can trust that God is near! We are never alone. In our darkest hour, in our deepest questions, the Lord of hosts never leaves us.

When my daughters were small, they would occasionally cry out in the middle of the night. The wind would brush a branch against a window. They would hear a noise on the street. They would shout, "Daddy!" I would do what all daddies do. I would walk down the hall and step into their room. When I did, the atmosphere changed. Strange noises? Odd sounds? Didn't matter. Daddy was here.

You need to trust this: Your Father is here. Here with his heavenly hosts. You will never face a Jericho alone.

THE HEART OF THE MATTER

- God is present in your most overwhelming and impossible challenges.
- His reassurance brings peace when fear and uncertainty threaten to consume you.
- The Lord is willing and able to help you face your "Jerichos."
- You can trust that your heavenly Father is here with his heavenly hosts!

MEMORY VERSE

Your memory verse for this unit is Proverbs 3:5–6. Take a few moments to review this verse, and then write it out from memory in the space below.

After God's Own Heart

An unexpected diagnosis. A letter of foreclosure from the bank. An email hinting at layoffs. A child who won't return your phone calls. An unwanted move to an unfamiliar place. Facing challenges like these is difficult. Facing them alone is impossible.

We tend to feel most alone when we receive the phone call, the email, or the news that we never wanted to get. This is when our trust is truly tested—in the shadow of Jericho's walls. Hardship convinces us we are alone. No one knows how we feel. No one can help.

But faith tells us otherwise. God isn't afraid of the shadows. He is not daunted by formidable walls. He meets us there. He knows how we feel, and he can help. We trust him when the battle is easy. Can we trust him when the battle feels impossible?

WEEKLY BIBLE STUDY

READ: JOSHUA 5:13–6:20 AND MATTHEW 28:1–10

1. Joshua asked the man if he was on the Israelites' side. How did the man respond (see Joshua 5:13–14)? How do you think his presence was an encouragement to Joshua in that moment?

2. What promise did the Lord give to Joshua (see 6:2)? How did Joshua respond to God's instructions to take the city—and what does that say about his trust in the Lord (see verses 6–7)?

3. Joshua trusted the Lord, and the Israelites trusted him. What was the result (see verse 20)?

4. How is the appearance of the angel at Jesus' tomb described in Matthew 28:2–4? How does this person compare to the commander of the Lord's army in Joshua 5:13–15?

5. Mary Magdalene and the "other Mary" were likely feeling grieved, alone, and scared after Jesus' death. How do you think the angel's message encouraged them (see Matthew 28:5–8)?

6. The women followed the angel's instructions and hurried away to tell the disciples what they had seen. Why do you think Jesus chose to appear to them along the way (see verses 9–10)?

7. What Jericho are you facing today—a challenge that feels insurmountable? How is God revealing to you that he is right there with you in that challenge?

Week 14: THE LAST LAUGH

God had promised Sarai and Abram a child. But now twenty-five years had passed since that promise had first been made. Abram is now ninety-nine, and Sarai is not much younger. She knits, he plays solitaire, and neither spends a lot of time lusting for the other.

Twenty-five years. A lot has happened during that time. The couple overcame scandal in Egypt. Their nephew Lot was captured and rescued. Then there was that whole Hagar-and-Ishmael ordeal. But still no son has been born. No promised heir. For Abram, whose name meant "exalted father," the conversations must have become dreadfully routine.

"Say, what is your name?"

"Abram."

"Oh, 'exalted father'! Wow, what a great title. Tell me, how many sons do you have?"

Abram would sigh. "None."

Occasionally, I'm sure he'd think of God's promise and give Sarai a wink. She'd give him a smile and think, Well, God did promise us a child, didn't he? And they'd both chuckle at the thought of bouncing a boy on their bony knees.

God was chuckling too. With the smile still on his face, he began getting busy doing what he does best—the unbelievable. But first he had to change a few things, beginning with their names. "I am changing your name from Abram to Abraham," he said, "because I am making you a father of many nations. . . . I will change the name of Sarai, your wife, to Sarah. I will bless her and give her a son, and you will be the father" (Genesis 17:5, 15–16 NCV).

Abram, the father of one, would now be Abraham, the "father of a multitude." Sarai, the barren one, would now be Sarah, the "mother of nations." It was another assurance from God that the promise would be fulfilled. The couple chose to trust and never give in to doubt.

Ah, *doubt.* He's a nosy neighbor. He's an unwanted visitor. He's an obnoxious guest. Just when you are all prepared for a weekend of relaxation . . . just when you pull off your work clothes and climb into your Bermuda shorts . . . just when you unfold the lawn chair and sit down . . . his voice interrupts your thoughts.

"Hey, Bob. Got a few minutes? I've got a few questions. I don't mean to be obnoxious, Bob, but how can you believe that a big God could ever give a hoot about you? Don't you think you are being presumptuous in thinking God wants you in heaven? How do you know God gives a flip about you anyway?"

Got a neighbor like this? He'll pester you. He'll irritate you. He'll criticize your judgment. He'll kick the stool out from under you and refuse to help you up. He'll tell you not to believe in the invisible yet offer no answer for the inadequacy of the visible.

He's a mealy-mouthed, two-faced liar who deals from the bottom of the deck. His aim is not to convince you but to confuse you. He doesn't offer solutions; he only raises questions. Don't let him fool you. Though he may speak the current jargon, he is no newcomer. His first seeds of doubt were sown in the garden of Eden in the heart of Eve. He undoubtedly worked hard to sow those same seeds in the hearts of Sarah and Abraham.

But Sarah and Abraham never gave up trusting God. Although their get-up-and-go had got up and gone, and all they had was a Social Security check and a promise from heaven, they decided to trust that promise rather than focus on the problems. As a result, the couple were the first to bring a crib into the nursing home.

In Hebrews 11:13, the author writes that the greatest biblical heroes "died in faith, not having received the promises" (NKJV). Sometimes we won't see God's promises unfold during our lifetime. Other times, it may take only a matter of minutes. Regardless, in seasons of doubt we must remember that God doesn't need an alarm clock. He hasn't dozed off or forgotten his plan for our lives. He is faithful, and his timing is perfect.

Sarah's name isn't the only thing God changes in her life. He soon changes her mind. He changes her faith. He changes the number of her tax deductions. He changes the way she defines the word impossible. But most of all, he changes her attitude about what it means to trust in him. It begins one day when three visitors arrive at her tent.

Abraham sees them first. He runs to greet them and then goes to find Sarah. "Quick," he says, "get some flour and bake some bread." Sarah does so, but as she kneads the dough in the tent, she does some eavesdropping as well. "I will surely return to you about this time next year," she hears one visitor say, "and Sarah your wife shall have a son" (Genesis 18:10 ESV).

When Sarah hears the news, a cackle escapes before she can contain it. Her shoulders shake, and she buries her wrinkled face in her bony hands. She knows she shouldn't laugh, for this visitor indeed is the Lord speaking to her. But just as she catches her breath and wipes away the tears, she thinks about it again—and a fresh wave of hilarity doubles her over.

Later on, after the visitors have left, Abraham looks over at Sarah—as fruitful as a pitted prune and just as wrinkled. And he cracks up. He tries to contain it, but he can't. He has always been a sucker for a good joke.

But one year later, it's God who has the last laugh. "The LORD visited Sarah as he had said, and the LORD did to Sarah as he had promised. And Sarah conceived and bore Abraham a son in his old age at the time of which God had spoken to him" (Genesis 21:1–2 ESV).

Even the heroes of the faith doubted at times. As you seek after a trusting heart today, God will meet you in your search.

THE HEART OF THE MATTER

- God's promises can be trusted even when the timing feels delayed.
- Refuse to give in to doubt while you wait on the Lord to fulfill his promises.
- God will often redefine what you view to be possible!
- As you seek a trusting heart, God will meet you in that search.

MEMORY VERSE

Your memory verse for this unit is Proverbs 3:5–6. Take a few moments to review this verse, and then write it out from memory in the space below.

After God's Own Heart

Nothing will chip away at your trust like waiting. Waiting for a child, waiting for reconciliation, waiting for healing. The longer you wait, the harder it is to trust and the easier it is to doubt.

The Bible is filled with characters who were called to wait. Abraham and Sarah waited to give birth to a nation. Hannah waited to conceive Samuel. David waited to be crowned king. Surely, these individuals doubted at times. But beneath the doubt was steady trust—a trust that God would do what he said he was going to do.

It's not wrong to doubt. But what is beneath your doubt? Perhaps you could let trust speak louder than that voice today. What God says he will do, he will do. Maybe not when you want. Maybe not how you want. But he will do it in in his way and in his time.

WEEKLY BIBLE STUDY

READ: GENESIS 12:1–7, 17:1–8, 21:1–7, AND PSALM 37:1–13

1. What promise did God make to Abram regarding his offspring (see Genesis 12:2–3) and the land they would receive (see verse 7)? How did he demonstrate he trusted God's promises?

2. What does God say to Abraham in Genesis 17:1–8 to assure him that the promise of an heir would come to pass? How much time had passed since God's original promise?

3. What does the author of Genesis say about the timing of God's promise to Abraham and Sarah (see 21:2)? How did Sarah react when God's promise to them was fulfilled (see verses 6–7)?

4. David wrote Psalm 37 when he was older (see verse 25). What had he learned over his lifetime about how God deals with evildoers (see verses 1–2)?

5. What does David say will happen to those who trust in the Lord and commit their way to him (see verses 4–6)? What specific instruction does David give in verse 7?

6. What reminder does David give about God's timing in verses 9–10 and 12–13? What does it mean that "the meek will inherit the land" (verse 11)?

7. Are you in a season of waiting for God to direct you to the next step? What truths do you take away from these passages that give you hope as you continue to wait?

Week 15: FOCUS ON THE FATHER

It's the expression of Jesus that puzzles us. We've never seen his face like this.

Jesus smiling? Yes.

Jesus weeping? Absolutely.

Jesus stern? Even that.

But Jesus anguished? Cheeks streaked with tears? Face flooded in sweat? Rivulets of blood dripping from his chin?

You remember the night:

> Jesus left the city and went to the Mount of Olives, as he often did, and his followers went with him. When he reached the place, he said to them, "Pray for strength against temptation." Then Jesus went about a stone's throw away from them. He kneeled down and prayed, "Father, if you are willing, take away this cup of suffering. But do what you want, not what I want." Then an angel from heaven appeared to him to strengthen him. Being full of pain, Jesus prayed even harder. His sweat was like drops of blood falling to the ground (Luke 22:39–44 NCV).

The Bible I carried as a child contained a picture of Jesus in the Garden of Gethsemane. His face was soft, hands calmly folded as he knelt beside a rock and prayed. Jesus seemed peaceful. One reading of the Gospels disrupts that image. Mark says, "Jesus fell to the ground" (Mark 14:35 NCV). Matthew tells us Jesus was "very sad and troubled . . . to the point of death" (Mattew 26:37–38 NCV). According to Luke, Jesus was "full of pain" (Luke 22:44 NCV).

Equipped with those passages, how would you paint this scene? Jesus flat on the ground? Face in the dirt? Extended hands gripping grass? Body rising and falling with sobs? Face as twisted as the olive trees that surround him?

What do we do with this image of Jesus?

Simple. We turn to it when we look the same. We read it when we feel the same. We go to it when we feel afraid. For isn't it likely that fear is one of the emotions Jesus felt? One might even argue that fear was the primary emotion. He saw something in the future so fierce, so foreboding that he begged for a change of plans. "Father, if you are willing, take away this cup of suffering" (Luke 22:42 NCV).

How remarkable that Jesus felt such fear. But how kind that he told us about it. We tend to do the opposite. Gloss over our fears. Cover them up. Keep our sweaty palms in our pockets, our nausea and dry mouths a secret. Not so with Jesus. We see no mask of strength. But we do hear a request for strength.

"Father, if you are willing, take away this cup of suffering." The first one to hear his fear is his Father. He could have gone to his mother. He could have confided in his disciples. He could have assembled a prayer meeting. All would have been appropriate, but none was his priority. He went first to his Father. The first one to hear his fear was his Father in heaven.

A millennium earlier David was urging the fear-filled to do the same.

> *Even though I walk*
> *through the darkest valley,*
> *I will fear no evil,*
> *for you are with me;*
> *your rod and your staff,*
> *they comfort me* (Psalm 23:4).

"I will fear no evil." How could David make such a claim? Because he knew where to look: "The LORD is my shepherd, I lack nothing. He makes me lie down in green pastures, he leads me beside quiet waters, he refreshes my soul" (verses 1–3).

Rather than turn to the other sheep, David turned to the Shepherd. Rather than stare at the problems, he stared at the rod and staff. Because he knew where to look, David was able to say, "I will fear no evil."

I knew a fellow who had a fear of crowds. When encircled by large groups, his breath grew short, panic surfaced, and he began to sweat like a sumo wrestler in a sauna. He received some help, curiously, from a golfing buddy. The two were at a movie theatre, waiting their turn to enter, when fear struck again. The crowd closed in like a forest. He wanted out and out fast. His buddy told him to take a few deep breaths. Then he helped manage the crisis by reminding him of the golf course.

"When you're hitting your ball out of the rough, and are surrounded by trees, what do you do?"

"I look for an opening."

"You don't stare at the trees?"

"Of course not. I find an opening and focus on hitting the ball through it."

"Do the same in the crowd. When you feel the panic, don't focus on the people; focus on the opening."

Good counsel in golf. Good counsel in life. Rather than focus on the fear, focus on the solution.

That's what Jesus did.

That's what David did.

How did Jesus endure the terror of the crucifixion? He went first to the Father with his fears. He modeled the words of Psalm 56:3: "When I am afraid, I put my trust in you."

Do the same with your fears. Don't avoid life's Gardens of Gethsemane. Enter them. Just don't enter them alone. And while there, be honest. Pounding the ground is permitted. Tears are allowed. And if you sweat blood, you won't be the first. Do what Jesus did; open your heart. And find what David found: "Surely your goodness and love will follow me all the days of my life, and I will dwell in the house of the LORD forever" (Psalm 23:6).

THE HEART OF THE MATTER

- Jesus' example shows that you should bring your worries and fears to God first.
- In Jesus we see no mask of strength but a request for strength.
- If you know where to look, you are able to honestly say, "I will fear no evil."
- Trust that God's goodness and love will sustain you through life's darkest moments.

MEMORY VERSE

Your memory verse for this unit is Proverbs 3:5–6. Take a few moments to review this verse, and then write it out from memory in the space below.

After God's Own Heart

What are your everyday prayer requests—the ones you know will quickly pass, but you still bring to God each day?

Lord . . . may I find a parking space.
may I pass this test.
may you take away this headache.

The everyday requests take no effort. You toss them up with hardly a thought! If God doesn't answer them, you aren't devastated.

But the major requests are different. These are your heart cries, your deepest fears, your deepest pain. Bringing these requests before God requires great vulnerability—you will be devastated if he doesn't answer them—and vulnerability requires trust.

Do you trust God with your major requests? David did and, more importantly, Jesus did. So do as David did and pray as Jesus prayed: with anguish and honesty, trust and vulnerability.

Your everyday requests and life-altering prayers matter to God. He is listening and responding. Every prayer matters to your heavenly Father.

WEEKLY BIBLE STUDY

READ: PSALM 23:1–6 AND LUKE 22:39–44

1. How does David describe God's character in Psalm 23:1–3? How do you think this understanding enabled him to trust God completely in spite of everything he was facing?

2. What allowed David to say "I will fear no evil" even though he was walking "through the darkest valley" (verse 4)? What would allow you to say the same in your darkest valleys?

3. The shepherd's *rod* was used to defend the sheep while the *staff* was used to guide or rescue them. How do you see God using both of those shepherd's tools in your life?

4. What does the picture that David paints in verses 5–6 reveal about his sense of peace in spite of being surrounded by enemies? How do you need that same kind of peace today?

5. Jesus went to the Mount of Olives the night before he was crucified. What do you think he was feeling (see Luke 22:44)? How does it help you to know that Jesus felt these emotions?

6. An angel appeared to strengthen Jesus (see verse 43). What does this reveal about how God responds when you are honest about your pain and present your full self to him?

7. What is something that you are reluctant to bring before the Father in prayer? Is your hesitation rooted in a lack of trust, fear of disappointment, or something else? Be honest with God.

Week 16: LIGHT IN THE DARKNESS

Long ago, or maybe not so long ago, there was a tribe in a dark, cold cavern.

The cave dwellers would huddle together and cry against the chill. Loud and long they wailed. It was all they did. It was all they knew to do. The sounds in the cave were mournful, but the people didn't know it, for they had never known joy. The spirit in the cave was death, but the people didn't know it, for they had never known life.

But then, one day, they heard a different voice. "I have heard your cries," it announced. "I have felt your chill and seen your darkness. I have come to help."

The cave people grew quiet. They had never heard this voice. Hope sounded strange to their ears. "How can we know you have come to help?"

"Trust me," he answered. "I have what you need."

The cave people peered through the darkness at the figure of the stranger. He was stacking something, then stooping and stacking more.

"What are you doing?" one cried, nervous.

The stranger didn't answer.

"What are you making?" one shouted even louder.

Still no response.

"Tell us!" demanded a third.

The visitor stood and spoke in the direction of the voices. "I have what you need." With that he turned to the pile at his feet and lit it. Wood ignited, flames erupted, and light filled the cavern.

The cave people turned away in fear. "Put it out!" they cried. "It hurts to see it."

"Light always hurts before it helps," he answered. "Step closer. The pain will soon pass."

"Not I," declared a voice.

"Nor I," agreed a second.

"Only a fool would risk exposing his eyes to such light."

The stranger stood next to the fire. "Would you prefer the darkness? Would you prefer the cold? Don't consult your fears. Take a step of faith."

For a long time no one spoke. The people hovered in groups, covering their eyes. The fire builder stood next to the fire. "It's warm here," he invited.

"He's right," one from behind him announced. "It's warmer." The stranger turned and saw a figure slowly stepping toward the fire. "I can open my eyes now," she proclaimed. "I can see."

"Come closer," invited the fire builder.

She did. She stepped into the ring of light. "It's so warm!" She extended her hands and sighed as her chill began to pass.

"Come, everyone! Feel the warmth," she invited.

"Silence, woman!" cried one of the cave dwellers. "Dare you lead us into your folly? Leave us. Leave us and take your light with you."

She turned to the stranger. "Why won't they come?"

"They choose the chill, for though it's cold, it's what they know. They'd rather be cold than change."

"And live in the dark?"

"And live in the dark."

The now-warm woman stood silent. Looking first at the dark, then at the man.

"Will you leave the fire?" he asked.

She paused, then answered, "I cannot. I cannot bear the cold." Then she spoke again. "But nor can I bear the thought of my people in darkness."

"You don't have to," he responded, reaching into the fire and removing a stick. "Carry this to your people. Tell them the light is here, and the light is warm. Tell them the light is for all who desire it."

And so she obeyed. She took the small flame and stepped into the shadows.

John wrote, "This is the verdict: Light has come into the world, but people loved darkness instead of light because their deeds were evil" (John 3:19).

I've always perceived John as a fellow who viewed life simply. "Right is right and wrong is wrong, and things aren't nearly as complicated as we make them out to be."

For example, defining Jesus would be a challenge to the best of writers, but John handles the task with casual analogy: "In the beginning was the Word, and the Word was with God" (1:1). The Messiah, in a word, was "the Word." A walking message. A love letter.

And life? Well, life is divided into two sections: light and darkness. If you are in one, you are not in the other, and vice versa.

> Everyone who does evil hates the light, and will not come into the light for fear that their deeds will be exposed. But whoever lives by the truth comes into the light, so that it may be seen plainly that what they have done has been done in the sight of God (3:20–21).

As you seek after the heart of God, take a risk. Trust in the Lord and step out of the shadows. Feel the warmth and forsake the darkness. And then tell the others in your world, "The light is here, and the light is warm. The light is here for all who desire it."

THE HEART OF THE MATTER

- Stepping into God's light requires faith but brings warmth and transformation.
- Sadly, many cling to the darkness because it feels familiar and safe.
- When you embrace God's light, you can share it with others.
- Trust in the Lord, step out of the shadows, and ask him to guide you.

MEMORY VERSE

Your memory verse for this unit is Proverbs 3:5–6. Take a few moments to review this verse, and then write it out from memory in the space below.

After God's Own Heart

Would you step toward the fire? It's easy to say yes. The cave dwellers seem ignorant in not trusting the stranger's gift when they obviously should have. Yet so many of us choose the dark because we are uncertain of light. We remain stuck in sin, shame, and addiction because we don't know what life would be like without it. Who would we be without our pain?

Obedience requires trust. We must trust Jesus if we're going to step into the light, and we must trust him if we're going to bring this light back to the others. Perhaps you are feeling called to accept the love of Christ, but you're afraid. Who will I become? Or perhaps you're being called to share the love of Christ, but you're afraid. What will people think? This is where obedience steps in and trust takes over. Trust the fire maker! He will lead you toward life.

WEEKLY BIBLE STUDY

READ: ISAIAH 9:1–7 AND JOHN 1:1–15

1. The Israelite people were living "in darkness" in the form of an impending Assyrian invasion that had come about because of their continued sin. What "light" would God send to them (see Isaiah 9:1–2)?

2. God promised to shatter "the yoke" that had burdened his people and break "the rod" of their oppressor (verse 4). How would this deliverance come (see verse 6)?

3. What is the significance of the names that would be given to this coming ruler (see verse 6)? What would characterize his reign on earth (see verse 7)?

4. Isaiah was describing the coming of Jesus as the Messiah. What does John reveal about the identity of this Messiah and his relationship with God the Father (see John 1:1–4)?

5. What is the significance of Jesus being "the light of all mankind" (verse 4)? Who chose *not* to receive this light—and why do you think they made that decision (see verses 10–11)?

6. What is the promise given to all who *do* make the choice to trust in Jesus and receive his light (see verses 12–13)? What is the importance of the "right" they receive?

7. God's light is meant to be shared with others. In what ways is God calling you to spread his light—whether that is through telling others about Jesus or through loving and serving them?

Week 17: TRAVELING LIGHT

I've never been one to travel light. I've tried. Believe me, I've tried.

But ever since I stuck three fingers in the air and took the Boy Scout pledge to be prepared, I've been determined to be exactly that—prepared. Prepared for a bar mitzvah, baby dedication, or costume party. Prepared to parachute behind enemy lines or enter a cricket tournament. And if, perchance, the Dalai Lama might be on my flight and invite me to dine in Tibet, I carry snowshoes. One has to be prepared.

I don't know how to travel light.

Fact is, there's a lot about travel I don't know. I don't know how to interpret the restrictions of a supersaver seat—half price if you leave on Wednesdays during duck-hunting season and return when the moon is full in a nonelection year. I don't know why they don't build the whole plane out of the same metal they use to build the little black box. I don't know how to escape the airplane toilet without sacrificing one of my extremities to the jaws of the folding door. And I don't know what to say to guys like the taxi driver in Rio who learned I was an American and asked me if I knew his cousin Eddie who lives in the U.S.

There's a lot about traveling I don't know.

But most of all, I don't know how to travel light.

I don't know how to travel without granola bars, sodas, and rain gear. I don't know how to travel without flashlights and a generator and a global tracking system. I don't know how to travel without an ice chest of wieners. What if I stumble upon a backyard barbecue? To bring nothing to the party would be rude.

I've got an iron that doubles as a paperweight, a hair dryer the size of a coach's whistle, and a Swiss Army knife that expands into a pup tent.

I need to learn to travel light.

You're wondering why I can't. Loosen up! you're thinking. You can't enjoy a journey carrying so much stuff. Why don't you just drop all that luggage?

Funny you should ask. I'd like to inquire the same of you. Haven't you been known to pick up a few bags?

Odds are, you did this morning. Somewhere between the first step on the floor and the last step out the door, you grabbed some luggage. Don't remember doing so? That's because you did it without thinking. Don't remember seeing a baggage terminal? That's because the carousel is not the one in the airport; it's the one in the mind. And the bags we grab are not made of leather; they're made of burdens.

The suitcase of guilt. A sack of discontent. You drape a duffel bag of weariness on one shoulder and a hanging bag of grief on the other. Add on a backpack of doubt, an overnight bag of loneliness, and a trunk of fear. You picked up the guilt of sins that have not been repented. No wonder you're so tired at the end of the day. Lugging luggage is exhausting.

What you were saying to me, God is saying to you. "Set that stuff down! You're carrying burdens you don't need to bear."

> Jesus said, "Come to me, all of you who are weary and carry heavy burdens, and I will give you rest" (Matthew 11:28 NLT).

Traveling light means trusting God with the burdens you were never intended to bear. So why don't you try traveling light? Do it for the sake of those you love.

And, for the sake of the God you serve, do the same. He wants to use you, you know. But how can he if you are exhausted? This truth came home to me one day when I was on a run. Preparing for a jog, I couldn't decide what to wear. The sun was out, but the wind was chilly. Jacket or sweatshirt? The Boy Scout within me prevailed. I wore both.

Of course, needing to stay in touch with my family, I carried my phone. So no one would steal my car, I pocketed my keys. As a precaution against thirst, I brought along some drink money in a pouch. I looked more like a pack mule than a runner! Within half a mile, I was peeling off the jacket and hiding it in a bush. That kind of weight will slow you down.

What's true in jogging is true in faith. God has a great race for you to run. But you have to drop some stuff. How can you share grace if you are full of guilt? How can you lift someone else's load if your arms are full with your own?

For the sake of those you love, travel light.

For the sake of the God you serve, travel light.

For the sake of your own joy, travel light.

There are certain weights in life you simply cannot carry. Your Lord is asking you to set them down and trust him. He is the father at the baggage claim. When a dad sees his five-year-old son trying to drag the family trunk off the carousel, what does he say? The father will say to his son what God is saying to you.

"Set it down, child. I'll carry that one."

What do you say you take God up on his offer? What do you say you seek after him with a trusting heart? You just might find yourself traveling a little lighter.

By the way, I may have overstated my packing problems. (I don't usually take snowshoes.) But I can't overstate God's promise: "Unload all your worries onto him, since he is looking after you" (1 Peter 5:7 PHILLIPS).

THE HEART OF THE MATTER

- We all travel through life with heavy burdens—regret, guilt, sin, and anxiety.
- We were never meant to bear our burdens alone.
- Traveling light means trusting God and experiencing his freedom.
- God can't use you if you're exhausted, so lay down your burdens!

MEMORY VERSE

Your memory verse for this unit is Proverbs 3:5–6. Take a few moments to review this verse, and then write it out from memory in the space below.

After God's Own Heart

When traveling through the airport, the goal is to bring as little as possible. A carry-on suitcase. Minimal clothing and accessories. A pair of shoes, a few other small personal items, and maybe a book. This should also be our goal when traveling through life.

Yet, for life's travels, we tend to select our largest suitcase. The old trunk in the attic where we can pack as much as possible: fear, worry, anger, resentment, guilt, shame, regret. When it comes to our burdens, there seems to be no limit to what we'll carry. Why? Because we don't trust Jesus with the things that weigh us down. We'd rather carry them ourselves. No wonder he was so adamant: Come to me, all you who are weary.

Stop packing and start praying. Stop ruminating and start resting. Accept the invitation to come to Jesus and receive his rest. And watch as your burdens float away.

WEEKLY BIBLE STUDY

READ: PSALM 25:1–22 AND MATTHEW 11:28–30

1. David opens this psalm by acknowledging, "In you, LORD my God, I put my trust" (25:1). What does he then say about releasing the burden of shame (see verses 2–3)?

2. What does David ask the Lord to "not remember" in verse 7? What does this reveal that David had learned about God's goodness (see verses 8–11)?

3. Traveling light means trusting God and experiencing his freedom. How does David reveal in verses 16–21 that he was trusting his burdens of fear and anxiety to the Lord?

4. Jesus invites those who are "weary" to come to him (Matthew 11:28). In his day, this weariness was often caused by the burdens of human-made rules the Jewish religious leaders were placing on the people. What is Jesus' promise to those who had been weighed down in this way?

5. Jesus' yoke represents a life of following after him and learning from him. What does Jesus say about his heart? How does he describe his yoke (see verses 29–30)?

6. Notice that Jesus repeats the promise that those who come to him and receive his instruction will receive rest. How does trust in Jesus play a part in receiving this promised rest?

7. What are some of the burdens you are currently carrying with you in life? What would it take for you to trust Jesus with those burdens so you could carry a lighter load?

Week 18: A LITTLE IMAGINATION

Thomas. He defies tidy summary.

Oh, I know we've labeled him. Somewhere in some sermon somebody called him "Doubting Thomas." And the nickname stuck. And it's true, he did doubt. It's just that there was more to it than that. There was more to his questioning than a simple lack of faith and trust. It was more due to a lack of imagination. You see it in more than just the resurrection story.

Consider, for instance, the time that Jesus was talking in all eloquence about the home he was going to prepare. Though the imagery wasn't easy for Thomas to grasp, he was doing his best. You can see his eyes filling his face as he tries to envision a big white house on St. Thomas Avenue. And just when Thomas is about to get the picture, Jesus assumes, "You know the way that I am going."

Thomas blinks a time or two, looks around at the other blank faces in the room, and then bursts out with candid aplomb, "Lord, we don't know where you are going, so how can we know the way?" (John 14:5).

Thomas didn't mind speaking his mind. If you don't understand something, say so! His imagination would only stretch so far.

And then there was the time that Jesus told his disciples he was going to go be with Lazarus even though Lazarus was already dead and buried. Thomas couldn't imagine what Jesus was referring to, but if Jesus was wanting to go back into the arena with those Jews who had tried once before to stone him, Thomas wasn't going to let him face them alone. So he patted his trusty sidearm and said, "Let's die with him!" (John 11:16, my paraphrase).

Thomas had spent his life waiting on the Messiah, and now that the Messiah was here, Thomas was willing to spend his life for him. Not much imagination, but a lot of loyalty.

Perhaps it is this trait that explains why Thomas wasn't in the Upper Room when Jesus appeared to the other apostles. I think Thomas took the death of Jesus pretty hard. Even though he couldn't quite comprehend all the metaphors that Jesus at times employed, he was still willing to go to the end with him. But he had never expected that the end would come so abruptly and prematurely. As a result, Thomas was left with a crossword puzzle full of unanswered riddles.

On the one hand, the idea of a resurrected Jesus was too far-fetched for dogmatic Thomas. His limited creativity left little room for magic or razzle-dazzle. Besides, he wasn't about to set himself up to be disappointed again. One disappointment was enough, thank you. Yet, on the other hand, his loyalty and trust made him yearn to believe. As long as there was the slimmest thread of hope, he wanted to be counted in.

His turmoil, then, came from a fusion between his lack of imagination and his unwavering loyalty. He was too honest with life to be gullible and yet was too loyal to Jesus to be unfaithful. In the end, it was this realistic devotion that caused him to utter the now-famous condition: "Unless I see the nail marks in his hands and put my fingers where the nails were, I will not believe it" (John 20:25, my paraphrase).

So, I guess you could say that he did doubt. But it was a different kind of doubting that springs not from timidity or mistrust but from a reluctance to believe the impossible and a simple fear of being hurt twice.

Most of us are the same way, aren't we? In our world of budgets, long-range planning, and computers, don't we find it hard to trust in the unbelievable? Don't most of us tend to scrutinize life behind furrowed brows and walk with cautious steps? It's hard for us to imagine that God can surprise us. To make a little room for miracles today, well, it's not sound thinking.

As a result, we, like Thomas, find it hard to believe that God can do the very thing that he is best at—replacing death with life. Our infertile imaginations bear little hope that the improbable will occur. We then, like Thomas, let our dreams fall victim to doubt.

We make the same mistake that Thomas made: We forget that "impossible" is one of God's favorite words.

How about you? How is your imagination these days? When was the last time you let some of your dreams elbow out your logic? When was the last time you imagined the unimaginable? When was the last time you dreamed of an entire world united in peace or all believers united in fellowship? When was the last time you dared dream of the day when every mouth will be fed and every nation will dwell in peace? When was the last time you dreamed about every creature on earth hearing about the Messiah? Has it been a while since you trusted God's promise to do "more than all we ask or imagine" (Ephesians 3:20)?

Though it went against every logical bone in his body, Thomas said he would believe if he could have just a little proof. And Jesus (who is ever so patient with our doubting) gave Thomas exactly what he requested. He extended his hands one more time. And was Thomas ever surprised. He did a double take, fell flat on his face, and cried, "My Lord and my God!" (John 20:28).

Jesus must have smiled. He knew he had a winner in Thomas. Anytime you mix loyalty with a little imagination, you've got a person of God on your hands.

You've got a person who is seeking after God with a trusting heart.

THE HEART OF THE MATTER

- Doubt doesn't disqualify faith—it can coexist with loyalty and a desire to believe.
- Jesus is patient with your doubts and meets you where you are.
- Trusting God means stretching beyond logic to imagine the possibilities.
- Jesus defeated death, and because of this, we can trust in the impossible!

MEMORY VERSE

Your memory verse for this unit is Proverbs 3:5–6. Take a few moments to review this verse, and then write it out from memory in the space below.

After God's Own Heart

A key part of a child's development is make-believe. Pretending, playing, imagining—these are natural activities for children. From the moment they wake to the moment they sleep, they're a race car driver or a dog or a princess.

So, if imagination is key to a child's development, some might say that losing one's imagination is key for adult development. The older we get, the less we pretend, play, and believe. The less we live in the world of imagination, the less we tend to trust the impossible is possible.

As Christians, we have the ultimate proof the impossible can happen: the resurrection. Jesus defeated death itself! Still, we find ourselves standing beside Thomas, asking for a little more proof, a little more evidence. But if we had the mind of a child, think of how it would change our belief in God's power over our lives. The reconciliation we thought impossible would become possible. The healing we thought out of reach would suddenly be in our grasp. There would be nothing we could imagine that is outside of God's power.

Why don't you do this today? Use your imagination . . . and see how your trust grows!

WEEKLY BIBLE STUDY

READ: JOHN 20:19–29 AND EPHESIANS 3:14–21

1. Jesus appeared to his disciples as they gathered behind locked doors. What did Jesus show to them? How do you think this bolstered their belief in his resurrection (see John 20:19–20)?

2. Thomas was not present at this event. What did he say he needed to see in order to believe in the risen Christ (see verses 24–25)? Do you find this demand reasonable? Why or why not?

3. Jesus offered the proof of his resurrection that Thomas had requested (see verses 26–27). What does this say about how Jesus will treat you when you have doubts?

4. How did Thomas respond when he saw Jesus' nail-marked hands and spear-struck side? What statement did Jesus then make about trust and belief in him (see verses 28–29)?

5. What is Paul's prayer for the believers in Ephesians 3:16–17? What comes to mind when you picture the "glorious riches" of God being poured out on your behalf?

6. Trusting God means stretching beyond logic to imagine the possibilities. How does Paul encourage you to do this when he describes the love that Jesus has for you in Ephesians 3:18–19?

7. What are you facing today that would require the impossible to be possible? How do Paul's words in Ephesians 3:14–21 encourage you to trust that God can make this happen?

Week 19: HOIST THE SAIL

I consider myself to be a bit of an expert on the force of wind. I was raised in windy country. Springtime winds average twelve miles per hour in my hometown.

Some enterprising entrepreneur thought a buck could be made off this wind. He set up a sailboat-for-rent business on the shore of the city lake. The sailboats were the length of a surfboard with a single mast and sail. My friend James and I were among the first customers. Neither of us knew how to sail, mind you. West Texas generates wind, not sailors.

We climbed aboard and shoved off. Or did we shove off, then climb aboard? Either way we floated out onto the lake and for a few delightful moments enjoyed life on the high seas. But then our momentum ceased. I looked at James, and James looked at me, and we shrugged. We had no clue how to untie the mast or hoist the sail. So we did the only thing we knew how to do. We jumped into the water, positioned ourselves behind the boat, and got to work.

The image of two clueless teens kicking their way to the dock might serve as a picture of many well-intentioned Christians. We spend every drop of energy self-propelling our way to shore. God invites us to hoist the sail. He empowers us to be what he calls us to be.

This was the promise Jesus made to a certain religious leader who paid him a late-night visit. "Now there was a man of the Pharisees named Nicodemus, a ruler of the Jews" (John 3:1 ESV). There were only six thousand Pharisees in Israel. Nicodemus was numbered among them. There were only seventy-one clerics on the high counsel; he was one of them. Jesus even called him "the teacher of Israel" (verse 10 ESV), implying a special status.

If religion were an academic enterprise, Nicodemus would have had a wall full of diplomas. Jesus was unimpressed with his credentials. He told Nicodemus, "You must be born again" (verse 7 ESV), as if to say, "Go back to the beginning and start over."

A bit radical for someone as finely frocked as Nicodemus. The Pharisee was taken aback. He questioned, "How can a person be born when he is old? He cannot enter a second time into his mother's womb a second time and be born, can he?" (verse 4 NASB).

Nicodemus was obsessed with what a person can and cannot do. He was all about human effort, human gumption, human achievement. In his view, the gate to heaven was greased with elbow grease.

Jesus, to the contrary, made four references to human inability. Absent the help of heaven, we "cannot see the kingdom of God," "cannot enter the kingdom of God," cannot be "born of the Spirit," and cannot "know where [the Spirit] is coming from and where it goes" (verses 3, 5, 6, 8 ESV).

This is a classic conversation. On one side Nicodemus, representing all well-meaning, God-fearing, Bible-toting, law-abiding, tax-paying, tithe-giving, candle-lighting, pew-sitting, scripture-memorizing, boat-rowing folk. On the other, Jesus Christ.

And what the latter says to the former is so uncanny that it sends shock waves through church pews and synagogues to this very day. "I assure you, no one can enter the Kingdom of God without being born of water and the Spirit. Humans can reproduce only human life, but the Holy Spirit gives birth to spiritual life" (verses 5–6 NLT).

The phrase "Kingdom of God" refers to a relationship with God in this life and entrance into heaven in the next. This is high stakes! How do we receive citizenship? Be born again.

In our first birth we become brand-new humans. In our second birth we become brand-new creations. And who oversees our second birth? The Holy Spirit![11] Indeed, were it not for the work of the Spirit, the new birth would be impossible! "No one can say, 'Jesus is Lord,' except by the Holy Spirit" (1 Corinthians 12:3).

If Nicodemus was having trouble keeping up with Jesus' comments, we can hardly fault him. He'd barely said, "Good evening," and Jesus, in rapid fire, told him about a new kingdom, a new birth, and the power to experience them both. But Jesus was just getting warmed up.

"The wind blows where it wishes, and you hear its sound, but you do not know where it comes from or where it goes. So it is with everyone who is born of the Spirit" (John 3:8 ESV). When it came to describing the Holy Spirit, Jesus had a universe of metaphors at his disposal. Comets. Galaxies. Ocean depths. Beluga whales. And out of the entire glossary, he chose this word picture to give to Nicodemus: wind. It's easy to see why.

The Spirit, like wind, is an unseen force.

He is wholly holy and unlike any being in our world. Which is such good news! We need alien assistance, a source of strength that is unbuffeted by that which buffets us, undisturbed by that which disturbs us, untethered to whatever ties us down. The Spirit is not subject to weather patterns, aging bodies, pandemics, stock market swings, or despots. He has never been sick. He will never be afraid. He does not worry, strive, or struggle. He is the Holy Spirit, marked by mystery and characterized by majesty.

Rowboat Christianity exhausts and frustrates. Those who attempt it are left depleted and desperate at the attempt. Those who let the Spirit do the work, on the other hand, find a fresh power. Life still has storms. The water grows rough. But they are not left to face the fury on their own.

Nicodemus was fixated on the word can. The Christian is fixated on the word done. The work of salvation is done. God helps those who admit they cannot help themselves.

Does that describe you? If so, can I urge you, if you have not done so already, to believe on him whom God has sent? Trust Jesus to do the work that only he can do. Rely upon the Holy Spirit to quicken within you a new spirit, a new creation.

No more ceremony. No more huffing and puffing. Gone is the endless list of dos and don'ts and the deadening thought that having done much, you haven't done enough. No more coming to Christ in the dark of the night in fear.

Come to him in the light of a new day! In the power of a new you.

THE HEART OF THE MATTER

- Salvation is not earned by effort but received through the Holy Spirit's power.
- The Holy Spirit, like the wind, is unseen yet brings strength, renewal, and guidance.
- You can let go of all the striving and simply embrace the freedom of God's grace.
- Life's storms persist, but relying on the Spirit provides the power to endure.

MEMORY VERSE

Your memory verse for this unit is Proverbs 3:5–6. Take a few moments to review this verse, and then write it out from memory in the space below.

After God's Own Heart

Imagine you just bought a new car. Its safety record is flawless, its engine sound, its brakes secure. You take the car home and then leave it in the driveway. For weeks.

Your neighbor finally asks, "When are you gonna take the new wheels for a spin?"

"Oh," you say, "I'm not going to drive it. I don't trust it."

Sounds absurd. Yet this is often how we trust Jesus. Only partially, not fully. Not enough to actually surrender our lives to him and trust him as our Savior. We leave our faith in the driveway but never test it on the open road. We're too flawed, too hurt, too broken—or at least that's what we tell ourselves. A good God could never love someone as flawed as I am.

But remember, a good God's love doesn't depend on our goodness. It depends on his. You are loved. Fully and completely. The only question is . . . do you believe it?

WEEKLY BIBLE STUDY

READ: JOHN 3:1–8 AND ROMANS 8:5–8

1. Jesus initiated his conversation with Nicodemus by saying he had to be "born again" to "see the kingdom of God" (John 3:3). How did Nicodemus interpret the comment (see verse 4)?

2. Jesus knew that Nicodemus, a prestigious Pharisee, had spent his life studying God's law and trying to follow it. So what did he mean when he said that Nicodemus must be born again?

3. Jesus describes the Holy Spirit as "the wind" that "blows wherever it pleases" (verse 8). How does this metaphor describe the way the Holy Spirit works in your life?

4. Jesus is clear that entrance into God's kingdom cannot be earned through any human effort. So what is required on your part to obtain salvation?

5. What does Paul say in Romans 8:5 distinguishes those who "live according to the flesh" from those who "live in accordance with the Spirit"?

6. What are the indications that a person's mind is truly being governed by the Holy Spirit? What is such an individual able to do (see verses 6–8)?

7. Is there a situation you are facing right now where you need to trust more in the Holy Spirit's power and less in your own strength? What will you do this week to initiate that trust?

Unit 4

Seeking A Prayerful Heart

David is on the lam, a wanted man in Saul's court. His young face decorates post office posters. His name tops Saul's to-kill list. He runs, looking over his shoulder, sleeping with one eye open, eating with his chair next to the restaurant exit.

Was it just two or three years ago that he was tending flocks in Bethlehem? Back then a big day was watching sheep sleep. Then came Samuel, a ripe old prophet with a fountain of hair and a horn of oil. As the oil covered David, so did God's Spirit. David went from serenading sheep to serenading Saul. The overlooked runt of Jesse's litter became the talk of the town, King Arthur to Israel's Camelot years, handsome and humble. Enemies feared him. Jonathan loved him. Michal married him.

But Saul hated him. David had to dash into the desert, where he found refuge among the caves near the Dead Sea. Several hundred loyalists followed him. So did Saul. Ever since, Saul has been getting the best of him. Over time, David's loyalists have grown to some six hundred men—who had wives and children. David, by now, had two wives of his own.

Running from a crazed king. Hiding in hills. Leading a ragtag group of soldiers. Feeding more than a thousand mouths. David feels like he is on his last stand. Just listen to him: "One of these days I will be destroyed by the hand of Saul" (1 Samuel 27:1). No hope and, most of all, no God. David immerses himself in his fear until his fear takes over.

He defects into the hands of the enemy. He strikes a deal with Achish, the king of Gath. Achish grants David a village, Ziklag, and asks only that David turn against his own people and kill them. As far as Achish knows, David does. But David actually raids the enemies of the Hebrews: "Now David and his men went up and raided the Geshurites, the Girzites and the Amalekites" (verse 8). Not David's finest hour.

Things get worse before they get better. The Philistines decide to attack King Saul. David and his men opt to switch sides and join the opposition. They journey three days to the battlefield, get rejected, and travel three days home. "The Philistine officers said . . . 'He's not going into battle with us. He'd switch sides in the middle of the fight!'" (29:4 MSG).

David leads his unwanted men back to Ziklag, only to find the village burned to the ground. The Amalekites had destroyed it and kidnapped all the wives, sons, and daughters. Venom flares in the soldiers' eyes. "David was now in great trouble, because his men were all very bitter about losing their children, and they were threatening to stone him" (30:6 GNT).

What had David failed to do during all this time? *He had failed to pray.* But that changed there in the smoldering ruins of Ziklag. After sixteen months in Gath, the Philistine rejection, the Amalekite attack, and the insurrection by his men, he remembered what to do: "David found strength in the LORD his God" (1 Samuel 30:6).

It's good to have you back, David. We missed you while you were away.

— PRAYER —

Father, you are my God and my king. You are holy and above all. I know you listen to me when I speak and take my prayers seriously. Still, I know I often neglect to pray. I look to other things when I need help or comfort. Please give me a prayerful heart—one that cries out to you first. Thank you for welcoming me to your temple. May I go there daily. In Jesus' name, amen.

— MEMORY VERSE —

Rejoice always, pray without ceasing, in everything give thanks; for this is the will of God in Christ Jesus for you.

1 THESSALONIANS 5:16–18 NKJV

Week 20: FIXED ON GOD

I can get lost anywhere. Seriously. Anywhere. The simplest map confuses me; the clearest trail bewilders me. If geese had my sense of direction, they'd spend winters in Alaska. I can relate to Columbus, who, as they say, didn't know where he was going when he left, didn't know where he was when he got there, and didn't know where he had been when he got back.

Can you relate?

Of course you can. We've all scratched our heads a time or two, if not at highway intersections, at least at the crossroads of life. *Do I . . .*

take the job or leave it?
accept the marriage proposal or pass?
leave home or remain there?
build or buy?

One of life's giant-size questions is: *How can I know what God wants me to do?* And David asked it. Before he stepped out, he would look up. He made a habit of running his options past God. And he did so with a fascinating tool: the ephod.

Trace its appearance to David's initial escape from Saul. David sought comfort from the priests of Nob. Saul accused the priests of harboring the fugitive and, consistent with Saul's paranoia, he murdered them. One priest by the name of Abiathar, however, was able to flee. He escaped to David with more than just his life—he escaped with the ephod.

When David learned of Saul's strategy to destroy him at a city called Keilah, he said to Abiathar, "Bring the ephod" (1 Samuel 23:9). David then prayed, "God of Israel, I've just heard that Saul plans to come to Keilah and destroy the city because of me. Will the city fathers of Keilah turn me over to him? Will Saul come down and do what I've heard?" (verse 10 MSG).

God's reply? "He will" (verse 11). The Lord also revealed that the citizens of Keilah would surrender David and his men to Saul. "So David and his men got out of there" (verse 13 MSG).

David dons the ephod, speaks to God, and receives an answer. Something similar occurs after the destruction of Ziklag. With his village in ruins and his men enraged, David says to Abiathar, "Bring me the ephod" (30:7). When Abiathar brings it to him, David prays, "Shall I go after these raiders? Can I catch them?" God's answer? "Go after them! Yes, you'll catch them! Yes, you'll make the rescue!" (verse 8 MSG).

What is this ephod? What made it so effective? And are they sold in department stores?

The ephod originated in the era of the wilderness wanderings. Moses presented the first one to Aaron, the priest. It was an ornate vest, woven of white linen, inwrought with threads of blue, purple, scarlet, and gold. A breastplate bearing twelve precious stones adorned the vest. The breastplate contained one or two, maybe three, resplendent diamonds or diamondlike stones. These stones had the names Urim and Thummim. No one knows the exact meaning of the terms, but *light* and *perfection* lead the list.

God revealed his will to the priests through these stones. How? Ancient writers have suggested several methods. It could be that the stones illuminated when God said *yes*. Or contained moving letters that gathered to form a response. Or were sacred lots that, upon being cast, would reveal an answer.[12] While we speculate on the technique, we don't need to guess at the value. Would you not cherish such a tool? When faced with a puzzling choice, David could, with reverent heart, make a request and God would answer.

Wouldn't you love to have an ephod? You could ask God a question and he would answer. You could cry out to him and he would reply. Well, who's to say you don't have one? God hasn't changed. He still promises to guide us:

> The LORD says, "I will guide you along the best pathway for your life. I will advise you and watch over you" (Psalm 32:8 NLT).
>
> Seek his will in all you do, and he will show you which path to take (Proverbs 3:6 NLT).
>
> Whether you turn to the right or to the left, your ears will hear a voice behind you, saying, "This is the way; walk in it" (Isaiah 30:21).

Maybe you have no Urim and Thummim stones. But you, like David, have prayer.

David's wisdom after the destruction at Ziklag came when he "strengthened himself in the LORD" (1 Samuel 30:6 NKJV). When Saul's soldiers tried to capture him, David turned toward God: "You have been my defense and refuge in the day of my trouble" (Psalm 59:16 NKJV).

How do you survive a fugitive life? David did with prayers like this one: "Be good to me, God—and now! I've run to you for dear life. I'm hiding out under your wings until the hurricane blows over. I call out to High God, the God who holds me together" (Psalm 57:1–2 MSG).

When David soaked his mind in God, he stood. When he didn't, he flopped. You think he spent much time in prayer the evening he seduced Bathsheba? Did he write a psalm the day he murdered Uriah? Doubtful. Mark well this promise: "[God] will keep in perfect peace all who trust in [God], whose thoughts are fixed on [God]" (Isaiah 26:3 NLT).

God promises not just peace but *perfect* peace. Undiluted, unspotted, unhindered peace. To whom? To those whose minds are "fixed" on God. Forget occasional glances. Dismiss random ponderings. Peace is promised to the one who fixes thoughts and desires on the king.

THE HEART OF THE MATTER

- We've all scratched our heads a time or two at the crossroads of life.
- Like David, you should make it a habit to run your options past God.
- Prayer is your "ephod"—how you directly receive guidance from God.
- God promises peace to those whose minds are fixed on him.

MEMORY VERSE

Your memory verse for this unit is 1 Thessalonians 5:16–18. Take a few moments to review this verse, and then write it out from memory in the space below.

After God's Own Heart

Tarot cards, Ouija boards, fortune cookies, horoscopes—people have questions and are always looking for answers (especially regarding the future). So they consult the latest woo-woo trend, online guru, or best friend to tell them what to do, where to go, and how to get there.

When you read David used an *ephod*, you may picture some ancient version of a Magic 8 Ball. Just shake it up and look at what answer comes up in the little window. But what David was actually doing was communicating with God. He was asking the Lord questions—and quite specific ones—about his next moves. "Go after them! You'll catch them! You'll rescue them!"

It's easy to assume that God isn't concerned about the specific questions in our lives—that he only cares about what we think are the big issues. David's story proves the opposite. The more specific your prayers, the more specifically God can respond to them. And those responses will build your trust in him so that the next time you have a question about your future, you will bypass everything else and take the matter straight to God in prayer.

WEEKLY BIBLE STUDY

READ: 1 SAMUEL 23:1–14, 30:1–8, AND 1 JOHN 5:14–15

1. What is the first thing David did when he heard the Philistines were attacking Keilah (see 1 Samuel 23:2)? What does this tell you about David's relationship with the Lord?

2. What was David's response when he learned that Saul was plotting to take his life (see verse 9)? If you received such dire news, what would you be tempted to turn to first for guidance?

3. David used the ephod to ask specific questions of God (see verses 10–12). Do you ask specific questions of God like this, or are your requests more general? Explain your response.

4. The Amalekites later destroyed Ziklag and kidnapped everyone in the town (see 1 Samuel 30:1–5). What did David do when he was confronted with that crisis (see verses 6–8)?

5. Prayer is how you receive direct guidance from God. What does John say you can be confident of receiving when you approach God and ask "according to his will" (1 John 5:14)?

6. What else does John say you can know for certain when you ask according to God's will (see verse 15)? What does this reveal about the need to align your requests with God's purposes?

7. God promises peace to those whose minds are fixed on him. What does it mean to "fix" your mind on God? How would this help you recognize his voice and know his will?

Week 21: THE *SOMEONE* OF GOD'S KINGDOM

I'd like you to think about someone. His name is not important. His looks are immaterial. His title is irrelevant. He is important not because of who he is but because of what he did.

He went to Jesus on behalf of a friend. His friend was sick, and Jesus could help, and someone needed to go to Jesus, so someone went. Others cared for the sick man in other ways. Some brought food; others provided treatment; still others comforted the family. Each role was crucial. Each person was helpful, but none was more vital than the one who went to Jesus.

He went because he was asked to go. An earnest appeal came from the family of the afflicted. "We need someone who will tell Jesus that my brother is sick. We need someone to ask him to come. Will you go?"

The question came from two sisters. They would have gone themselves, but they couldn't leave their brother's bedside. They needed someone else to go for them. Not just anyone, mind you, for not just anyone could. Some were too busy; others didn't know the way. Some fatigued too quickly; others were inexperienced on the path. Not everyone could go.

And not everyone would go. This was no small request the sisters were making. They needed a diligent ambassador, someone who knew how to find Jesus. Someone who wouldn't quit mid-journey. Someone who would make sure the message was delivered. Someone who was as convinced as they were that Jesus *must* know what had happened.

They knew of a trustworthy person, and to that person they went. They entrusted their needs to someone, and that someone took those needs to Christ. "So Mary and Martha sent *someone* to tell Jesus, 'Lord, the one you love is sick'" (John 11:3 NCV, emphasis added).

Someone carried the request. Someone walked the trail. Someone went to Jesus on behalf of Lazarus. And because someone went in trust, Jesus responded.

Let me ask you, how important was this person in the healing of Lazarus? How essential was his role? Some might regard it as secondary. After all, didn't Jesus know everything? Certainly he knew that Lazarus was sick. Granted, but he didn't respond to the need until someone came to him with the message. "When Jesus heard this, he said, 'This sickness will not end in death. It is for the glory of God, to bring glory to the Son of God'" (verse 4 NCV).

When was Lazarus healed? After *someone* made the request. Oh, I know the healing wouldn't unfold for several days, but the timer was set when the appeal was made in full trust in Jesus' power. All that was needed was the passage of time.

Would Jesus have responded if the messenger had not spoken? Perhaps, but we have no guarantee. We do, however, have an example: The power of God was triggered by prayer. Jesus looked down the very throat of death's cavern and called Lazarus back to life . . . all because someone prayed.

Think about how a furnace functions. You add some form of fuel to it, and it heats the whole house. Your prayers are like the fuel you add to a furnace. Your intercession is coal on the fire. Your pleadings are kindling to the flames. The furnace is sturdy, and the vents are ready; all that is needed is your prayer. Paul wrote, "Prayer is essential in this ongoing warfare. Pray hard and long" (Ephesians 6:18 MSG).

In the economy of heaven, the prayers of saints are a valued commodity. John the apostle would agree. He wrote the story of Lazarus and was careful to show the sequence: The healing began when *someone* made the request.

When this someone tells Jesus of the illness, he says, "Lord, the one you love is sick" (John 11:3). He doesn't base his appeal on the imperfect love of the one in need but on the perfect love of the Savior. He doesn't say, "The one *who loves you* is sick." He says, "The one *you love* is sick." The power of the prayer, in other words, does not depend on the one who makes the prayer but on the One who hears the prayer.

We can and must repeat the phrase in manifold ways. "The one you love is tired, sad, hungry, lonely, fearful, depressed." The words of the prayer vary, but the response never changes. The Savior hears the prayer. He silences heaven, so he won't miss a word. He hears the prayer. Remember the phrase from John's Gospel? "When he *heard* this, Jesus said, 'This sickness will not end in death'" (verse 4, emphasis added).

The Master heard the request. Jesus stopped whatever he was doing and took note of the man's words. This anonymous courier was heard by God.

John's message is critical. You can talk to God because God listens. Your voice matters in heaven. He takes you very seriously. When you enter his presence, the attendants turn to you to hear your voice. No need to fear that you will be ignored. Even if you stammer or stumble, even if what you have to say impresses no one, it impresses God—and he listens. He listens to the painful plea of the elderly in the rest home. He listens to the gruff confession of the death-row inmate. When the alcoholic begs for mercy, when the spouse seeks guidance, when the businessman steps off the street into the chapel, God listens.

Intently. Carefully. The prayers are honored as precious jewels. Purified and empowered, the words rise in a delightful fragrance to our Lord. "The smoke from the incense went up from the angel's hand to God with the prayers of God's people" (Revelation 8:4 NCV). Incredible. Your words do not stop until they reach the very throne of God.

"Then the angel filled the incense pan with fire from the altar and threw it on the earth" (verse 5 NCV). One call and heaven's fleet appears. Your prayer on earth activates God's power in heaven, and God's will is done in earth as it is in heaven.

You are the *someone* of God's kingdom. Your prayers move God to change the world. You may not understand the mystery of prayer. You don't need to. But this is clear: Actions in heaven begin when someone trusts enough to pray on earth.

What an amazing thought!

THE HEART OF THE MATTER

- Prayer is powerful. It activates God's work and brings his will to earth.
- God listens to every prayer and values your words as precious and significant.
- The effectiveness of prayer depends on God's power and not on your eloquence.
- You are the *someone* of God's kingdom. You have access to God through prayer.

MEMORY VERSE

Your memory verse for this unit is 1 Thessalonians 5:16–18. Take a few moments to review this verse, and then write it out from memory in the space below.

After God's Own Heart

Prayer is a mysterious mechanism beyond our human understanding. If millions are praying at once, how can one individual voice be heard? When there are so many concerns, trials, and fears being lifted to the Lord, how can we know that God cares about our fears and concerns? And why is my need or my request more urgent than someone else's? These questions can diminish our reliance on prayer. *I am just one voice. God is too far away.*

Lazarus's story suggests the opposite. Just like a child's cry immediately captures the attention of his mother, one word is all it takes to turn the Father's head. Why? Because he is hearing the cry of the one he loves. He is hearing the cry of his own child.

We won't fully understand the inner workings of prayer until we reach heaven. But in the meantime, we can have confidence that our voice is enough—more than enough—to captivate the ear of God and activate his power.

WEEKLY BIBLE STUDY

READ: PSALM 141:1–10 AND JOHN 11:1–16

1. Compare Psalm 141:2 to Revelation 8:4. What similarities do you find in these verses? How does the imagery in each verse depict the prayers of God's people?

2. God values our words as precious and significant. What does David ask of the Lord in verse 3? Why do you think he specifically asks God to "set a guard" over him in this way?

3. What does David say is the focus of his prayers in verses 5–6? What does he say is the focus of his life in verse 8—and how does that bring him peace and confidence?

4. Martha and Mary sent "someone" to inform Jesus of Lazarus's illness (see John 11:1–3). Why was this no small request that the sisters were making?

5. How did Jesus respond when the messenger finally reached him (see verses 4–7)? How do you think the messenger *expected* Jesus to answer the request?

6. What tend to be your expectations when you make requests of God? What does this story reveal about why God will often answer prayer in ways you don't expect?

7. You are the someone of God's kingdom. Who needs your intercessory prayers? Take a moment to bring that person's needs to Jesus and ask him to act in that person's life.

Week 22: TAKING THE PROPER PATH

"Give us today our daily bread" (Matthew 6:11). The first word in this phrase from Jesus' prayer seems abrupt. Wouldn't an "If you don't mind" be more appropriate? Perhaps a "Pardon me, but could I ask you to give . . ." be better? Am I not being irreverent if I simply say, "Give us today our daily bread"? Well, you are if that is where you begin. But if you follow Christ's model for prayer, your preoccupation has been his wonder rather than your stomach.

The first three petitions are God-centered, not self-centered. "Hallowed be your name . . . your kingdom come . . . your will be done" (verses 9–10).

Jesus first reminds you of your adoption: "Our *Father* in heaven." He then invites you ponder his permanence: "Our Father *who is* in heaven." Next you marvel at his handiwork: "Our Father who is in *heaven*." This is followed by worshiping his holiness: "Hallowed be your name." You touch the lowered scepter and pray the greatest prayer: "Your kingdom come." You submit your desires to him and pray, "Your will be done." And all of heaven is silent as you place your prayer like fuel in the furnace, saying, "On earth as it is in heaven."

Proper prayer follows such a path, revealing God to us before revealing our needs to God. (You might reread that one.) The purpose of prayer is not to change God but to change us. Aren't our hearts warmed when we call him Father? Aren't our fears stilled when we contemplate his constancy? Aren't we amazed as we stare at the heavens?

Seeing his holiness causes us to confess our sin. Inviting his kingdom to come reminds us to stop building our own. Asking God for his will to be done places our will in second place to his. And realizing that heaven pauses when we pray leaves us breathless in his presence.

By the time we get to "Give us today our daily bread," we're renewed! We've been comforted by our Father, conformed by his nature, convicted by his character, and constrained by his power. We've been commissioned by our Teacher and compelled by his attention to our prayers. The petitions encompass all the concerns of our lives. *Our daily bread* addresses the present. *Forgive our sins* addresses the past. *Lead us not into temptation* speaks to the future. (The wonder of God's wisdom: how he can reduce all our needs to three simple statements.)

First he addresses our need for bread. The term means all of a person's physical needs. Martin Luther defined bread as "everything necessary for the preservation of this life, including food, a healthy body, house, home, wife and children."[13] We are urged to talk to God about the necessities of life. God may also give us the luxuries of life, but he certainly will grant the necessities. Would he give the stars their glitter and not give us our food?

Of course not. Trust this: He has committed to care for us. We aren't wrestling crumbs out of a reluctant hand but, rather, confessing the bounty of a generous hand. The essence of the prayer is really a trusting affirmation of the Father's care. Our provision is his priority. God is committed to caring for our needs.

Paul wrote, "Anyone who does not provide for their relatives, and especially for their own household, has denied the faith and is worse than an unbeliever" (1 Timothy 5:8). How much more will a holy God care for his children? After all, how can we fulfill his mission unless our needs are met? How can we teach or minister or influence unless we have our basic needs satisfied? Will God enlist us in his army and not provide a commissary? Of course not.

"I pray that the God of peace will give you every good thing you need so you can do what he wants" (Hebrews 13:20 NCV). Hasn't that prayer been answered in our lives? We may not have had a feast, but haven't we always had food? Perhaps there was no banquet, but at least there was bread. And many times there was a banquet.

In fact, many of us in the United States have trouble relating to the phrase "give us this day our daily bread" because our pantries are so packed and our bellies so full we seldom ask for food. This doesn't negate the importance of this phrase, however. Just the opposite. For us, the blessed of belly, this prayer has double meaning.

We pray, only to find our prayer already answered! We are like the high school senior who decides to go to college and then learns the cost of tuition. He runs to his father and pleads, "I'm sorry to ask so much, Dad, but I have nowhere else to go. I want to go to college, and I don't have a penny." The father puts his arms around the son and smiles and says, "Don't worry, son. The day you were born I began saving for your education. I've already provided for your tuition."

The boy made the request only to find the father had already met it. The same happens to you. At some point in your life, it occurs to you that someone is providing for your needs. You take a giant step in maturity when you agree with David's words in 1 Chronicles 29:14: "Everything we have has come from you, and we only give you what is yours already" (TLB).

You may be writing a check and stirring the soup, but there's more to putting food on the table than that. What about the ancient symbiosis of the seed and the soil and the sun and the rain? Who created animals for food and minerals for metal? Long before you knew you needed someone to provide for your needs, God already had.

So the first rule is one of dependence. Ask God for whatever you need. He is committed to you. God lives with the self-assigned task of providing for his own, and so far, you've got to admit, he's done pretty well at the job.

THE HEART OF THE MATTER

- Prayer begins with remembering who God is before presenting your needs to him.
- The point of prayer is to change *you* and *your heart*—not God.
- God provided for your needs long before you knew you even had a need.
- God daily meets both your physical and spiritual needs in abundance.

MEMORY VERSE

Your memory verse for this unit is 1 Thessalonians 5:16–18. Take a few moments to review this verse, and then write it out from memory in the space below.

After God's Own Heart

The thought wakes you at night. Again and again, you are haunted by the same question: *Will I have enough* _____________? You fill in the blank. Will I have enough money? Will I have enough courage? Will I have enough work, time, energy? You do the math, the planning, that you hope will tell you, *yes, you will have enough*. But nothing assures you because the future is unknown.

It's in these lonely and uncertain moments that Jesus is waiting for you. He is hoping that you will call on him—hoping you will remember the words. "Give us today our daily bread." Not your bread for the month, week, or year. No, your bread for *today*. For that is all you are to think about. This day, this moment, this sleepless night.

Jesus is here. Ask him to provide. And know that he already has.

WEEKLY BIBLE STUDY

READ: MATTHEW 6:7–15 AND 2 CORINTHIANS 9:8–11

1. Jesus says "your Father knows what you need before you ask him" (Matthew 6:8). Why does God encourage you to make requests of him even though he already knows what you need?

2. What does praying to your "Father in heaven" (verse 9) reveal about your status before him? What are you doing when you pray for God's will to "be done on earth" (verse 10)?

3. What is encompassed by the term "daily bread" (verse 11)? What does it say about God's concern for you that he wants to meet even the most basic necessities of your life?

4. What do Jesus' words in verses 12–15 reveal about the need for you to not only seek forgiveness from God but also forgive others who have wronged you?

5. What does Paul proclaim in 2 Corinthians 9:8 about how God will meet your needs? What does God want you to "abound in" by meeting your needs abundantly?

6. Paul reminds you that God is one who "supplies seed to the sower" (verse 10). What does this say about the way God has anticipated your needs and is already working to meet them?

7. What do you need God to provide for you today? What is stopping you from asking him for it? Spend time praying the Lord's prayer this week and asking God for what you need.

Week 23: THE SHEPHERD'S VOICE

Many times the Bible calls us the flock of God. "We are his people, the sheep he tends" (Psalm 100:3 NCV). We needn't know much about sheep to know that the shepherd never leaves the flock. If we see a flock coming down the path, we know a shepherd is nearby. If we see a Christian ahead, we can know the same. The Good Shepherd never leaves his sheep.

God is as near to you as the vine is to the branch, as present within you as God was in the temple, as intimate with you as a husband with a wife, and as devoted to you as a shepherd to his sheep. God desires to be as close to you as he was to Christ—so close that when others sense the storm and worry, you hear his voice and smile.

Here is how David described this most intimate of all relationships: "I'm an open book to you; even from a distance, you know what I'm thinking. You know when I leave and when I get back; I'm never out of your sight. You know everything I'm going to say before I start the first sentence" (Psalm 139:1–4 MSG). Paul also testifies to the possibility of a constant sense of God's presence:

> "Pray without ceasing" (1 Thessalonians 5:17 KJV).
>
> "Be constant in prayer (Romans 12:12 RSV).
>
> "Continue steadfastly in prayer (Colossians 4:2 RSV)
>
> "In everything . . . let your requests be made known to God" (Philippians 4:6 NASB).

Does unceasing communion seem daunting, complicated? Are you thinking, *Life is difficult enough. Why add this?* If so, remind yourself that God is the burden-remover, not the burden-giver. God intends that unceasing prayer lighten—not heighten—our load. The more we search the Bible, the more we realize that unbroken communion with God is the intent and not the exception. Within the reach of *every* Christian is the unending presence of God.

How, then, do you live in God's presence? How do you detect his unseen hand on your shoulder and his inaudible voice in your ear? A sheep grows familiar with the voice of the shepherd. How can you grow familiar with the voice of God and respond in worship and prayer? Here are a few ideas.

Give God your waking thoughts. Before you face the day, face the Father. Before you step out of bed, step into his presence. I have a friend who makes it a habit to roll out of his bed onto his knees and begin his day in prayer. Personally, I don't get that far. With my head still on the pillow and my eyes still closed, I offer God the first seconds of my day. The prayer is not lengthy and far from formal. Depending on how much sleep I got, it may not even be intelligible. Often it's nothing more than, "Thank you for a night's rest. I belong to you today."

C. S. Lewis wrote, "The moment you wake up each morning. . . [all] your wishes and hopes for the day rush at you like wild animals. And the first job of each morning consists in shoving them all back; in listening to that other voice, taking that other point of view, letting that other, larger, stronger, quieter life come flowing in."[14]

Here is how the psalmist began his day: "Every morning, I tell you what I need, and I wait for your answer" (Psalm 5:3 NCV). Which leads to the second idea:

Give God your waiting thoughts. Spend time with him in silence. The mature married couple has learned the treasure of shared silence; they don't need to fill the air with constant chatter. Just being together is sufficient. Try being silent with God. "Be still, and know that I am God" (Psalm 46:10). Awareness of God is a fruit of stillness before God.

Journalist Dan Rather once asked Mother Teresa, "What do you say to God when you pray?" Mother Teresa answered quietly, "I listen." Taken aback, Rather tried again. "Well, then, what does God say?" Mother Teresa smiled. "He listens."[15]

Give God your whispering thoughts. Through the centuries Christians have learned the value of brief sentence prayers, prayers that can be whispered anywhere, in any setting. In the nineteenth century an anonymous Russian monk set out to live in unceasing communion with God. In a book titled *The Way of the Pilgrim*, he tells of how he learned to have one prayer constantly in his mind: "Lord Jesus Christ, Son of God, have mercy on me, a sinner." With time, the prayer became so internalized that he was constantly praying it, even while consciously occupied with something else.

Imagine considering every moment as a potential time of communion with God. By the time your life is over, you will have spent six months at stoplights, eight months opening junk mail, a year and a half looking for lost stuff (double that number in my case), and a whopping five years standing in various lines.[16] Why don't you give these moments to God?

By giving God your whispering thoughts, the common becomes uncommon. Simple worshipful phrases such as "Thank you, Father," "Be sovereign in this hour, O Lord," and "You are my resting place, Jesus" can turn a commute into a pilgrimage. You needn't leave your office or kneel in your kitchen. Just pray where you are. Let the kitchen become a cathedral or the classroom a chapel. Give God your whispering thoughts.

And last, *give God your waning thoughts.* At the end of the day, let your mind settle on him. Conclude the day as you began it: talking to God. Thank him for the good parts. Question him about the hard parts. Seek his mercy. Seek his strength. And as you close your eyes, take assurance in the promise: "He who watches over Israel will neither slumber nor sleep" (Psalm 121:4). If you fall asleep as you pray, don't worry. After all, what better place to doze off than in the arms of your Father?

THE HEART OF THE MATTER

- God, the Good Shepherd, is always near to those in his flock.
- Offer your waking, waiting, whispering, and waning thoughts to the Lord.
- Embrace stillness and silence to grow familiar with God's voice.
- Transform ordinary moments into sacred ones with simple prayers in your day.

MEMORY VERSE

Your memory verse for this unit is 1 Thessalonians 5:16–18. Take a few moments to review this verse, and then write it out from memory in the space below.

After God's Own Heart

Maybe you view your faith as something reserved for Sunday mornings in a particular building. Maybe it's an item on your to-do list. *Bible study? Check!* Maybe it's something you practice a couple of times a year on Christmas and Easter. You reserve moments for prayer and worship, but the majority of your day is what could be called secular—apart from God.

God has a better invitation for you than sporadic prayer and seasonal worship. He wants to be with you *all the time*. When you wake up and when you lie down. When you're in the car, at work, at the baseball game. The best way to commune with him? Prayer. Short or long. Thoughtful or rash. Words or no words.

What if you prayed as often as you texted or checked social media? What would happen? It's safe to say you would begin to experience his presence not just on the weekend but throughout your day . . . and throughout your life.

WEEKLY BIBLE STUDY

READ: PSALM 5:3, 46:10, 63:1, 121:3–4, AND JOHN 10:22–30

1. What does David say in Psalm 5:3 about giving your waking thoughts to God? What do you think David had learned about waiting "expectantly" for the Lord's response?

2. What does the psalmist write in Psalm 46:10 about giving your waiting thoughts to God? What are some practical ways that you have learned to be "be still" before the Lord?

3. Your prayers can be whispered to God anywhere and in any setting. What simple prayer do you find in Psalm 63:1? What is David "whispering" to God in this verse?

4. What does the psalmist acknowledge about God in Psalm 121:3–4? What practices do you have in place for trusting your waning thoughts to the Lord?

5. Jesus often referred to himself as a shepherd and to his followers as sheep (see John 10:11). What does Jesus say about the Jews who approached him at the temple (see verses 22–26)?

6. What does Jesus say are the traits of his sheep? What is the promise given to those of his flock who hear his voice and choose to follow him (see verses 27–29)?

7. How difficult is it for you to embrace stillness in God's presence—not saying anything but just listening for his voice? What might be the benefits of regularly doing this?

Week 24: PATHWAY TO PEACE

The airport atmosphere at Chicago O'Hare was anything but peaceful. Thunder was audible outside. The tension was palpable inside. The hour was late, and we passengers were not happy. Unless the sky cleared, we'd be searching for hotel rooms and next-day flights.

Oh, the grumbling. I was doing my share. Airport food again? Grrr.

Everyone was upset. Well, almost everyone. I heard someone singing. Seated a few feet away was a mother and her infant. A blanket covered the nursing child. It was clear to me that the calmest person in the sitting area was a baby, only a few months old.

The child had peace because the child had a mother. The baby had the peace of the mother—the warmth of the mother's body, the comfort of the mother's song, the assurance of the mother's presence. Yank the child from the arms of the mom, and fear would erupt. But since the child was near the mother, the baby was the calmest person in the airport.

God longs to give us what the mom gave that child. His warmth. His nourishment. His assurance. We can have the peace of Jesus. We can uproot thoughts of catastrophe and replace them with truths like this one: "The peace of God, which surpasses all understanding, will guard your hearts" (Philippians 4:7 NKJV). When your heart needs peace, trust God. But also, *tell* God.

Paul wrote, "Pray and ask God for everything you need, always giving thanks" (Philippians 4:6 NCV). Satan hates to see you pray. He does not scatter when you listen to a sermon. Demons do not backpedal when you perform acts of benevolence. The principalities of hell are not flustered when you open a Christian book (unless it's a Lucado book). But the walls of hell shake when, with an honest heart and faithful confession, you bow your head and pray.

Satan knows the power of prayer. He is aware of these promises:

> Come near to God, and God will come near to you (James 4:8 NCV).
>
> When a believing person prays, great things happen (James 5:16 NCV).
>
> The LORD is close to everyone who prays to him, to all who truly pray to him (Psalm 145:18 NCV).

Do you long for peace? Then pray. You cannot control events that are uncontrollable, so don't try. You cannot change the future as long as the future is in the future, so don't try. There is so much we cannot do. But there is one thing we must do. We must pray.

Anxiety happens when we think the world is spinning out of control. The untruth deceives us into believing the problem has no solution. The consequential false narrative says, "My life is nothing but a maelstrom of messes." An overreaction chimes in with a Chicken Little squawk of, "The sky is falling! The sky is falling!" Be on the alert for this downward spiral. Disarm these thoughts the moment they begin to grouse. Rather than heed them, heed him. Anxiety is calmed when we talk to the One in charge.

> God raised [Christ] from death and set him on a throne in deep heaven, in charge of running the universe, everything from galaxies to governments, no name and no power exempt from his rule. And not just for the time being, but forever. He is in charge of it all, has the final word on everything (Ephesians 1:20–22 MSG).

Christ runs the show. A meteor just streaked through a distant realm. Christ caused it to do so. A giraffe just took its first breath in the Congo. Jesus knows how many she'll take in her lifetime. The migration of the belugas through the oceans? Christ dictates their itinerary.

He has authority over the world, and he has authority over your world. Your date of birth. Your date of death. Your mood swings, sleep patterns, and eating habits. Your salary. The traffic on your commute. The arthritis in your joints. Christ reigns over all of these. He's never surprised. He's never caught off guard. He's never ever uttered the phrase: "How did that happen?" So uproot your fear of pandemonium and replant this assuring promise: "[God] makes everything work out according to his plan" (Ephesians 1:11 NLT).

Jesus is the Command Center of the cosmos. "What is the price of two sparrows—one copper coin? But not a single sparrow can fall to the ground without your Father knowing it" (Matthew 10:29 NLT). He, and only he, occupies the Oval Office. He called a coin out of the mouth of a fish. He stopped the waves with a word. He spoke and a tree became barren. He prayed and a basket became a banquet.

Economy. Meteorology. Biology. "All things have been handed over to me by my Father" (Matthew 11:27 ESV). Your greatest problem is nothing but two plus two for him. "What is impossible with man is possible with God" (Luke 18:27 ESV).

Satan does not want you to believe this. He wants you to think you're all alone; a mouse in a snake pit. Ignore him. Early detection is key. Take your fretful thoughts to Jesus. The sooner you pray, the sooner you find peace. The more you pray, the more you find peace. Mark well this promise: "[God] will keep in perfect peace all who trust in [God], whose thoughts are fixed on [God]!" (Isaiah 26:3 NLT).

Kneeling knees never knock.

Trust God. Tell God. And thank God.

Make a list of your blessings. You cannot be anxious and thankful at the same time. Write down the things you are thankful for. Write a thank-you note to a person who made a difference in your life. Be specific about the ways they helped you. Deliver it in person and prepare yourself for a flood of joy.

God's pathway to peace is paved with thoughts of appreciation.

THE HEART OF THE MATTER

- Peace comes from trusting in God's sovereignty and bringing your worries to him.
- Prayer calms anxiety, strengthens faith, and invites God's presence into your life.
- Fix your thoughts on God's promises and know he is in control of every detail.
- Focus on your many blessings and thank God for his continued faithfulness.

MEMORY VERSE

Your memory verse for this unit is 1 Thessalonians 5:16–18. Take a few moments to review this verse, and then write it out from memory in the space below.

After God's Own Heart

It's not just airport delays that cause us to grumble. We find all kinds of reasons to complain. *Traffic is too slow* (grumble). *People are driving too fast* (grumble). *Costs are too high* (grumble). *There's not enough places to eat* (grumble). *There's never enough time in the day to get all the things done I need to get done in the day* (grumble, grumble, grumble).

All the while, Jesus longs to give us his peace. Flight delays, traffic, economics, time—he controls it all. Nothing is impossible for him or out of his reach. All he asks us to do is bring our fretful worries to him, trust him to take care of our needs, and then respond with a heart of gratitude. When we do this—trust God, tell God, thank God—we will experience his peace and, in the process, find there are fewer and fewer things that cause us to grumble.

WEEKLY BIBLE STUDY

READ: PSALM 145:17–21 AND LUKE 11:9–13

1. Satan knows the power of prayer and is aware of God's promises to his people. What does David proclaim about the Lord's faithfulness in Psalm 145:17–18?

2. What does God promise to do for those "who fear him" (verse 19)? What does it mean to fear the Lord—and how do you incorporate that kind of fear into your prayers?

3. What else does the Lord promise to do for those who belong to him (see verse 20)? How does this promise from God bring you peace and security today?

4. Jesus often spoke with his disciples about the power of praying to their heavenly Father. What promise does he give in Luke 11:9–10 for those who seek after God in prayer?

5. What analogy does Jesus use to describe the way that God—as a good Father—responds to his children (see verses 11–12)? What is Jesus saying about God's nature?

6. Jesus states that earthly fathers, though flawed, know how to give good gifts to their children (see verse 13). What does this say about God's willingness to answer your prayers?

7. What causes you to be the most grateful to God as you consider all these promises? Take a few moments each day this week to express this gratitude to God in prayer.

Seeking A WORSHIPFUL HEART

The messenger is a breathless Amalekite with torn clothing and hair full of dirt. He stumbles into Camp Ziklag with the news: "The people have fled from the battle, many of the people are fallen and dead, and Saul and Jonathan his son are dead also" (2 Samuel 1:4 NKJV). When the man presents David with Saul's crown and bracelet, David has undeniable proof.

Jonathan, closer than a brother—dead. Saul, God's chosen king—dead.

Leaving David to face yet another giant—the giant of grief.

We've felt his heavy hand on our shoulders. Not in Ziklag, but in emergency rooms, in children's hospitals, and at car wrecks. And we, like David, have a choice in how we respond.

Many of us opt to flee grief. The grave stirs such unspeakable hurt and unanswerable questions that we're tempted to turn and walk. Change the subject, avoid the issue. Work hard. Drink harder. Stay busy. Stay distant. Leave town and don't look back. Yet we pay a high price when we do. Bereavement comes from the word *reave*. Look up *reave* in the dictionary, and you'll read "to take away by force, plunder, rob." Death robs you. The grave plunders moments and memories not yet shared: birthdays, vacations, lazy walks, talks over tea. You are bereaved because you've been robbed.

At some point, you need to make the choice that David made. Face your grief. Upon hearing of the deaths of Saul and Jonathan, "David lamented" (verse 17 NKJV). The commander buried a bearded face in calloused hands and cried. He "ripped his clothes to ribbons. All the men with him did the same. They wept and fasted the rest of the day, grieving the death of Saul and his son Jonathan, and also the army of GOD and the nation Israel, victims in a failed battle" (verses 11–12 MSG).

David refused to ignore his grief. "Then David sang this lament over Saul and his son Jonathan. . . . *The mighty warriors—fallen, fallen! . . . Women of Israel, weep for Saul. . . . O my dear brother Jonathan, I'm crushed by your death. Your friendship was a miracle-wonder, love far exceeding anything I've known—or ever hope to know*" (verses 17, 19, 24, 26–27 MSG).

David wept as creatively as he worshiped. He called the nation to mourning. He refused to gloss over or soft-pedal death. He faced it, fought it, challenged it. But he didn't deny it.

Do the same. Face your grief. Give yourself time. Permit yourself tears. God knows the sorrow of a grave. He buried his son. But he also knows the joy of resurrection. By his power, you will too. And on that day, you will say with David, "I will exalt you, my God the King; I will praise your name for ever and ever" (Psalm 145:1).

— PRAYER —

Dear God, you are worthy of all worship and praise. Give me a heart full of worship. My heart is often full of worry, fear, and guilt. But worship is the cure for these ailments. May your name be ever on my lips. May your song be ever on my heart. When I focus on your goodness, I forget all the bad in my life. So I worship you today, Father, in Spirit and in truth. Amen.

— MEMORY VERSE —

Therefore, I urge you, brothers and sisters, in view of God's mercy, to offer your bodies as a living sacrifice, holy and pleasing to God—this is your true and proper worship.

ROMANS 12:1

Week 25: GOD'S GREATEST GIFT

David has just learned of the deaths of Saul and Jonathan. Suddenly the throne is empty, and his options are open. The crown has scarcely been resized for his head when he sets his eyes on Jerusalem. "The king and his men went to Jerusalem against the Jebusites, the inhabitants of the land, who spoke to David, saying, 'You shall not come in here; but the blind and the lame will repel you," thinking, 'David cannot come in here'" (2 Samuel 5:6 NKJV).

David dismisses their words and goes about his work. Others focus on the obvious. David searches for the unusual. Where everyone else sees walls, he sees tunnels. "David said on that day, 'Whoever would strike the Jebusites, let him get up the water shaft to attack'" (verse 8 ESV). Since he did what no one expected, he achieved what no one imagined. "David then took up residence in the fortress and called it the City of David" (verse 9).

After the just-crowned David settles the city of Jerusalem, he makes the return of the ark of the covenant his top priority. The ark was a rectangular box commissioned by Moses. A trio of the most precious Hebrew artifacts indwelt it: a gold jar of unspoiled manna, Aaron's walking stick, and the stone tablets that had felt the engraving finger of God. The ark symbolized God's provision (the manna), God's power (the staff), God's precepts (the commandments), and, most of all, God's presence.

Stunningly, the Israelites had let it gather dust for thirty years in the house of a priest who lived seven miles west of Jerusalem. Neglected. Ignored. David determines to change that. He plans a Macy's-caliber parade and invites thirty thousand Hebrews to attend.

They gather near the home of Abinadab, the priest. His two sons, Uzzah and Ahio, are put in charge of the transport.[17] They load the ark on an ox-drawn wagon and begin the march. All goes well for the first two miles, until they hit a patch of rough road. The oxen stumble, the wagon shakes, and the ark shifts. Uzzah, thinking the holy chest is about to fall off the wagon, extends his hand to steady it . . . "and he died" (2 Samuel 6:7).

This will dampen a parade real quick. Everyone goes home. Deeply distressed, David returns to Jerusalem. The ark is kept at the home of Obed-Edom while David sorts things out. Apparently, he succeeds, because at the end of three months David returns, reclaims the ark, and resumes the parade. This time there is no death. There is dancing. David enters Jerusalem with rejoicing, and he "danced before the LORD with all his might" (verse 14 NKJV).

Two men. One dead. The other dancing. What do they teach us? Specifically, what do they teach us about invoking the presence of God? Should we light a candle, sing chants, build an altar? Uzzah and David blend death and dancing to reveal an answer.

Uzzah's tragedy teaches this: *God comes on his own terms.* He gave specific instructions as to the care and transport of the ark. Only the priests could draw near it. And then only after they had offered sacrifices for themselves and their families (see Leviticus 16). The ark would be lifted, not with hands, but with acacia poles (see Numbers 4:15; 7:9).

Uzzah should have known this. He was a priest, a Kohathite priest, a descendant of Aaron himself. The ark had been kept in the house of his father, Abinadab. He had grown up with it. Which may be the best explanation for his actions. The holy had become humdrum. So he exchanges commands for convenience, using a wagon instead of poles and bulls instead of priests. We see no reverence or sacrifice.

The image of a dead Uzzah sends a sobering and shuddering message: *Don't grow lax before the holy.* God won't be loaded on convenient wagons or toted about by dumb animals. God comes, mind you. But he comes on his own terms. He comes when commands are revered, hearts are clean, and confession is made.

But what of the second figure—of the man dancing?

David's initial response to the slaying of Uzzah is anything but joyful. He retreats to Jerusalem, confused and hurt, "angry because the LORD had punished Uzzah in his anger" (1 Chronicles 13:11 NCV). Three months pass before he returns for the ark.

David does so with a different protocol. Priests replace bulls. Sacrifice replaces convenience. Levites prepare "themselves for service to the LORD." They use "special poles to carry the Ark of God on their shoulders" (15:14–15 NCV).

No one hurries. When David realizes God is not angry, he offers a sacrifice and then dances "before the LORD with all his might" (2 Samuel 6:14 NKJV). This is no tapping of the feet. The Hebrew term portrays David rotating in circles, hopping and springing. And, if that's not enough, he strips down to the ephod, the linen prayer vest. Right there in front of God and the altar and everyone else, David removes all but his holy skivvies.

David dances . . . and we hold our breath. We know what God does to the irreverent. But did God tell David to behave? No. He let him dance. Scripture doesn't portray David dancing at any other time. He did no death dance over Goliath. He didn't inaugurate his term as king with a waltz. But when God came to town, he couldn't sit still.

Maybe God wonders how we do. Do we not enjoy what David wanted? The presence of God. Jesus promised, "I am with you always, even to the end of the age" (Matthew 28:20 NKJV). Yet how long since we rolled back the rug and celebrated the night away because of it?

What did David know that we don't? In a sentence, it might be this: *God's present is his presence.* His greatest gift is himself. Not sunsets, newborn babies, or Caribbean seas. Himself.

God hasn't left you alone with your fears, your worries, your disease, or your death. So kick up your heels for joy. And party! David "blessed the people in the name of the LORD Almighty. Then he gave a loaf of bread, a cake of dates and a cake of raisins to each person in the whole crowd of Israelites" (2 Samuel 6:18–19). God is with us. That's reason to celebrate!

THE HEART OF THE MATTER

- Seek God intentionally and prioritize his presence in your life.
- Approach God with reverence and fully seek to obey his ways.
- Don't hold back—worship the Lord God with all your heart!
- God's presence offers you comfort, strength, and a reason to rejoice.

MEMORY VERSE

Your memory verse for this unit is Romans 12:1. Take a few moments to review this verse, and then write it out from memory in the space below.

After God's Own Heart

When is the last time you threw your hands in the air in sheer delight? Whooped with happiness? Did a little jig? Maybe it was when your team won the big game, or when you found out you were going to be a grandparent, or when you watched your best friends say *I do*. What makes your body physically react with joy?

For David, it was the moment God entered Jerusalem. He was so overwhelmed with joy that he couldn't sit still. He danced in worship. He didn't take God's holiness for granted. The God who had created the universe, formed human beings, parted the Red Sea, and performed so many miracles for his people was right there beside him!

He's right beside you as well. His peace, his healing power, his comfort, his wisdom, his kindness, his compassion—it's all with you. David had the ark. You have the Holy Spirit. So lift your hands! Whoop and holler! Dance like no one's watching. The Lord is near.

WEEKLY BIBLE STUDY

READ: 2 SAMUEL 6:1–23 AND PSALM 150:1–6

1. What was King David's error in how he had the ark transported (see 2 Samuel 6:1–7)? What does this reveal about how you should approach God?

2. How did David react when Uzzah was struck dead? How did he know when it was time to renew the effort to bring the ark to Jerusalem (see verses 8–12)?

3. What did David do on this second attempt to show that he was honoring the Lord? How did David express his worship to God at this joyous event (see verses 13–15)?

4. What was Michal's complaint when she saw the way that David was worshiping? What does David's response reveal about his heart for the Lord (see verses 16–22)?

5. What does the psalmist recognize about God in Psalm 150:1? What reasons does he state in verse 2 as to why you can celebrate God's presence?

6. What do the psalmist's words in verses 3–5 reveal about the ways you can worship God? Which of these ways most inspires you—and why?

7. When is the last time God's presence inspired you to worship? How could you invite God's presence into your life today and give yourself space to just worship him?

Week 26: WORSHIP WORKS WONDERS

Worship does to the soul what a spring rain does to a thirsty field. It soaks down, seeps in, and stirs life. Are you stressed? Worship God, who could store the universe in his pocket. Are you bereaved? Your Shepherd will lead you through the valley of sorrow. Do you feel small? A few moments in front of the throne of your loving King will evaporate any sense of insignificance. Are you fearful? Draw courage from the one who calms your storms.

Worship works wonders. So for your own sake, do what the angels did when Jesus arrived on earth in Bethlehem: Make a big deal about the arrival of the King.

Worship verbally. "Through Jesus, therefore, let us continually offer to God a sacrifice of praise—the fruit of lips that openly profess his name" (Hebrews 13:15). In the early eighties, there was a popular country song called "Always on My Mind."[18] The singer tells his sweetheart that even though he seldom expressed his feelings through words or actions, she was always on his mind. I'm not sure where the songwriter learned the secret of romance, but he didn't consult women. No sweetheart would accept that excuse. "You never told me, never gave me flowers or compliments, but I was always on your mind? Yeah, right."

God doesn't buy it either. He wants to hear our affection. It is "out of the abundance of the heart the mouth speaks" (Matthew 12:34 NKJV), and when the mouth is silent, the heart is in question. Do you love God? Let him know. Tell him! Out loud. In public. Unashamed. "Make a joyful shout to God, all the earth!" (Psalm 66:1 NKJV).

Satan cannot tolerate Christ-centered worship. Unlike God, he is not omniscient. He is not moved by what you think, only by what you say. So have courage and say it! "Yell a loud *no* to the Devil and watch him make himself scarce" (James 4:7 MSG). Do you want your city to be free from Satan's grip? Worship! Do you want your home to be loosed from the devil? Worship! Do you want nations to be places of peace and prosperity? Then let the church assault Satan's strongholds with joy-filled praise. Worship verbally. And . . .

Worship in community. "There was . . . a *multitude* of the heavenly host praising God" (Luke 2:13 NKJV, emphasis added). The presence of Christ deserves an abundant chorus. Every generation has its share of "Jesus, yes; church, no" Christians. For a variety of reasons, they turn away from church attendance. They do so at a great loss. Something happens in corporate worship that does not happen in private worship. When you see my face in the sanctuary and I hear your voice in the chorus, we are mutually edified.

Granted, congregational worship is imperfect. We often sing off-key. Our attention wanders. The preacher stumbles over words. Even so, let us worship. The sincerity of our worship matters more than the quality. "Let's see how inventive we can be in encouraging love and helping out, not avoiding worshiping together as some do but spurring each other on, especially as we see the big Day approaching" (Hebrews 10:24–25 MSG).

Finally . . .

Worship demonstrably. Let your body courageously express what your heart is feeling. And let your heart be awakened by your body. "May the lifting up of my hands be like the evening sacrifice" (Psalm 141:2). "Because your love is better than life, my lips will glorify you. I will praise you as long as I live, and in your name I will lift up my hands" (Psalm 63:3–4).

Yes, outward expressions of worship can be used inappropriately. People show off. They worship to be seen. But don't let potential abuse preclude appropriate use. Lift your hands. Clap your hands. Bend your knees. Bow your head. Fall down on your face.

Something powerful happens when we worship.

Something powerful happened the day the soldiers did. It was Christmas Eve 1915 near the village of Laventie in northern France. World War I was raging. Bombs shook the soil of Europe. Frigid temperatures shook the bones of the fighters. Germans were entrenched on one side and the Royal Welsh Fusiliers on the other. Most of the soldiers were only a few years removed from boyhood. They were young, homesick, and longing to be with loved ones. Christmas seemed far away from this blood-soaked land.

At one point, from the German side of the field, came a chorus of voices singing a Welsh holiday hymn in German: "Sleep my child and peace attend thee, all through the night guardian angels God will send thee, all through the night soft the drowsy hours are creeping hill and vale in slumber sleeping, I my loving vigil keeping, all through the night."[19]

Soldiers on both sides set down their weapons. For a moment, there was no war; there was just the song. What happened next could only be described as a miracle. The night was spent in carol singing. Around dawn the feelings of goodwill emboldened the soldiers to step out of their trenches and greet their foes. Shouting such greetings as "Hello, Tommy" and "Hello, Fritz," they shook hands in no-man's-land and exchanged gifts. German beer, sausages, and spiked helmets from one side. Canned corned beef and biscuits from the other.

Then, of all things, a game broke out. A form of soccer. It was disjointed and unorganized with perhaps as many as fifty players on each side. For half an hour or so, the battlefield became a soccer field and enemies enjoyed time together.[20]

And it all began with worship.

We can only pray that an armistice would happen again—that warriors would become worshipers, that we would lay down our weapons of pride and vengeance, and that we would join hearts to thank the One who came to bring peace on earth. Someday that peace will come. Conflict will give way to an eternal chorus. Until then, we can practice.

THE HEART OF THE MATTER

- Worship refreshes your soul in times of fear, anxiety, or sadness.
- Express your praise to the Lord boldly and unashamedly.
- Satan cannot hear your thoughts—but he can hear your praise!
- Worship verbally, worship in community, and worship demonstrably.

MEMORY VERSE

Your memory verse for this unit is Romans 12:1. Take a few moments to review this verse, and then write it out from memory in the space below.

After God's Own Heart

When your arms are weak, lift them to the Lord. When your heart is grieved, turn it over to the Lord. When your eyes are red from a night of tears, lift up your gaze to the Lord. When your mouth is regretful of the things you said, sing a song of praise to the Lord. When your head is full of fear and worry, set your mind on the Lord.

In other words, *worship*.

Do it when you feel like it and when you don't. Do it when you're weary and when you're joyful. Do it when you feel brave and when you feel weak. Sing to God. Speak of his goodness. Declare what the Lord has done for you and what he will do for you.

Worship in the morning and the evening. Worship in your car and at the dinner table. Worship at church, in the park, and at the game. Worship with the ones you love. Worship with the ones you don't. Worship the Lord . . . because that's what you were made to do.

WEEKLY BIBLE STUDY

READ: LUKE 2:1–21 AND HEBREWS 13:15–16

1. How did God announce that Jesus, the Savior, had been born (see Luke 2:8–14)? What is the significance of God choosing to reveal this to shepherds?

2. What was the shepherds' initial response to the angel (see verse 9)? What did they feel inspired to do after they witnessed the angelic host (see verse 15)?

3. How does this story display worship that is verbal, demonstrative, and communal? When have you experienced this type of worship—and what impact did it have on you?

4. What does this story tell you about Jesus' presence and how it can inspire worship? How do you respond when you find yourself unexpectedly in the presence of Jesus?

5. What type of praise are we instructed to offer to God in Hebrews 13:15? How comfortable do you feel verbally professing your praise to God in your worship?

6. We are to offer up to God a "sacrifice of praise" (verse 15). What other sacrifice does the author mention in verse 16 that also pleases God?

7. Of the three types of worship discussed this week—verbal, communal, demonstrable—which do you struggle with the most? Why?

Week 27: PREPARED FOR WORSHIP

The day Jesus went to worship, his very face was changed. "You're telling me that Jesus went to worship?" I am. The Bible speaks of a day when Jesus took time to stand with friends in the presence of God. "Jesus took Peter, James, and John, the brother of James, up on a high mountain by themselves. While they watched, Jesus' appearance was changed; his face became bright like the sun, and his clothes became white as light" (Matthew 17:1–2 NCV).

Matthew presupposes a decision on Jesus' part to stand in the presence of God. The simple fact he chose his companions and went up on a mountain suggests this was no spur-of-the-moment action. He didn't awaken one morning, look at the calendar and then at his watch, and say, "Oops, today is the day we go to the mountain." No, he made preparations. He suspended ministry to people so ministry to his heart could occur. Since his chosen place of worship was some distance away, he had to select the right path and stay on the right road. By the time he was on the mountain, his heart was ready. Jesus prepared for worship.

Let me ask you, do you do the same? Do you prepare for worship? What paths do you take to lead you up the mountain? The question may seem foreign, but my hunch is that many of us simply wake up and show up. We're sadly casual when it comes to meeting God.

Would we be so lackadaisical with, let's say, the President? Suppose you were granted a Sunday morning breakfast at the White House. How would you spend Saturday night? Would you get ready? Would you collect your thoughts? Would you think about your questions? Of course you would. Should we prepare any less for an encounter with the holy God?

Let me urge you to come to worship prepared to worship. Pray before you come so you will be ready to pray when you arrive. Sleep before you come so you'll stay alert when you arrive. Read the Word before you come so your heart will be soft when you worship. Come hungry. Come willing. Come asking. Come expecting God to speak.

As you do, you'll discover the purpose of worship—to change the face of the worshiper. This is exactly what happened to Christ on the mountain. Jesus' appearance was changed: "His face became bright like the sun" (verse 2 NCV).

The connection between the face and worship is more than coincidental. Our faces are the most public parts of our bodies. They are also the most recognizable parts of our bodies. We don't fill a school yearbook with photos of people's feet but with photos of faces. God desires to take our faces—these exposed and memorable parts of our bodies—and use them to reflect his goodness. Paul wrote, "Our faces, then, are not covered. We all show the Lord's glory, and we are being changed to be like him. This change in us brings ever greater glory, which comes from the Lord, who is the Spirit" (2 Corinthians 3:18 NCV).

God invites us to see his face so he can change our faces. He uses our uncovered faces to display his glory. The transformation isn't easy. The sculptor of Mount Rushmore faced a lesser challenge than does God. But our Lord is up to the task. He loves to change the faces of his children. By his fingers, wrinkles of worry are rubbed away. Shadows of shame and doubt become portraits of grace and trust. He relaxes clenched jaws and smooths furrowed brows.

His touch can remove the bags of exhaustion from beneath the eyes and turn tears of despair into tears of peace. How? Through worship.

We would expect something more complicated or more demanding. A forty-day fast or the memorization of the book of Leviticus perhaps. No. God's plan is simpler. He changes our faces through worship.

Exactly what is worship? I like King David's definition: "Exalt the LORD with me, and let us exalt His name together" (Psalm 34:3 NASB). Worship is the act of magnifying God. Enlarging our vision of him. Stepping onto the flight deck to see where he sits and observe how he works. Of course, his size doesn't change, but our perception of him does. As we draw nearer, he seems larger. Isn't that what we need? A *big* view of God? Don't we have *big* problems, *big* worries, *big* questions? Of course we do. Hence we need a big view of God.

Worship offers that. How can we sing "Holy, Holy, Holy" and not have our vision expanded? Or what about the lines from "It Is Well with My Soul"?

> My sin—O the bliss of this glorious thought,
> My sin—not in part but the whole,
> Is nailed to the cross and I bear it no more,
> Praise the Lord, praise the Lord, O my soul![21]

Can we sing those words and not have our countenance illuminated?

A vibrant, shining face is the mark of one who has stood in God's presence. After speaking to God, Moses had to "put a covering over his face" (Exodus 34:33 NCV). After seeing heaven, Stephen's face "looked like the face of an angel" (Acts 6:15 NCV).

God is in the business of changing the face of the world.

Let me be very clear. This change is his job, not ours. Our goal is not to make our faces radiant. Not even Jesus did that. Matthew says, "Jesus' appearance was changed," not "Jesus changed his appearance." Moses didn't even know "his face was shining" (Exodus 34:29 NCV).

Our goal is not to conjure up some fake, frozen expression. Our goal is simply to stand before God with a prepared and willing heart and then let God do his work.

And he does. He wipes away the tears. He mops away the perspiration. He softens our furrowed brows. He touches our cheeks. He changes our faces as we worship.

THE HEART OF THE MATTER

- Prepare your heart, mind, and schedule to worship the Lord.
- Allow worship to "change your face" and transform your heart.
- Worship changes your view of God—he gets bigger, holier, and mightier.
- Remember that *God* is the one who changes you through worship.

MEMORY VERSE

Your memory verse for this unit is Romans 12:1. Take a few moments to review this verse, and then write it out from memory in the space below.

After God's Own Heart

Who doesn't love a good makeover show? A designer is tasked with transforming a dilapidated house with buried charm. Or a stylist transforms the wardrobe, hair, and makeup of a hesitant subject. Whether the makeover subject is a person or a house, don't we love a before-and-after? The messiness of the *before* contrasted with the pristine of the *after* is satisfying.

Worship can be a powerful makeover experience. As we prepare ourselves to enter God's sanctuary, we are ridden with guilt, worry, and fear. But through song and scripture, we are reminded of exactly who God is. How *big* he is. That he is greater than whatever it is causing our guilt, fear, and worry. We leave feeling made over from the inside out. What was heavy now feels lighter. What was impossible now feels possible with God.

We entered the sanctuary with a frown. We emerge with a smile, ready to spread God's love to others. A truly satisfying before-and-after!

WEEKLY BIBLE STUDY

READ: EXODUS 33:12–23, 34:26–32, AND MATTHEW 17:1–5

1. Moses made preparations for worship. What request did he make to the Lord in Exodus 33:12–13 to ensure that he would find favor in God's sight?

2. What reasons did God provide in verse 17 as to why he would do what Moses asked? What does it say about Moses' heart that God knew him "by name"?

3. Moses' close relationship with God allowed him to make a bold request. What was that request? What was God's response (see verses 18–23)?

4. How was Moses changed by spending time in God's presence in a way that others could see (see Exodus 34:26–32)?

5. Matthew writes that Jesus led Peter, James, and John up "a high mountain" (17:1). How does this demonstrate that Jesus prepared for worship?

6. What was the result of Jesus spending time in God's presence (see verse 2)? What did God say to Jesus that he had also said to Moses (see verse 5)?

7. How has God changed your "face" as you've worshiped him? In what ways have you sensed that he is pleased with you as you've come before him?

Week 28: WORSHIP CONQUERS WORRY

When a father leads his four-year-old son down a crowded street, he takes him by the hand and says, "Hold on to me." He doesn't say, "Let's see if you can find your way home." The good father gives the child one responsibility: "Hold on to my hand."

God does the same with you. Your goal is not to know every detail of the future. Your goal is to hold the hand of the One who does and never, ever, let go.

This was the choice of Kent Brantly, a medical missionary in Liberia who waged a war on the cruelest of viruses: Ebola. The epidemic was killing people by the thousands. Kent, more than anyone, knew the consequences of the disease. He had treated dozens of cases. He was aware of the symptoms—soaring fever, severe diarrhea, and nausea. He had seen the results of the virus. And for the first time, he was feeling the symptoms himself.

His colleagues drew blood and began the tests, but it would be at least three days before they knew the results. On a Wednesday evening, Kent quarantined himself and waited. His wife and family were across the ocean. His coworkers could not enter his residence. He was, quite literally, alone with his thoughts. He opened his Bible and meditated on a passage from the book of Hebrews. Then he wrote in his journal, "The promise of entering his rest still stands, so let us never give up. Let us, therefore, make every effort . . . to enter that rest."[22]

Kent considered the phrase "make every effort" (Hebrews 4:11). He knew he would have to do exactly that. He then turned his attention to another verse from the same chapter in Hebrews: "Let us then approach the throne of grace with confidence, so that we may receive mercy and find grace to help us in our time of need" (verse 16). He copied the scripture into his prayer journal and wrote the words "with confidence" in italics.[23]

The test results confirmed what they feared: He had contracted Ebola. Kent called his wife, Amber, with the diagnosis the following Saturday afternoon. He went straight to the point. "The test results came back. It's positive." Amber began to cry. They talked for a few moments before Kent said that he was tired and would call again soon.

Now it was Amber's turn to process the news. She and her parents sat on the edge of her bed and wept for several minutes. After some time, Amber excused herself, went outside, walked across a field toward a large mesquite tree, and took a seat on a low-hanging branch. She found it difficult to find words to formulate her prayers, so she used the lyrics of hymns she had learned as a young girl: "There is no shadow of turning with Thee; Thou changest not. Thy compassions, they fail not. As Thou hast been Thou forever wilt be."[24]

The words lifted her spirits, so she sang aloud another song she treasured: "I need Thee every hour, in joy or pain; come quickly and abide, or life is in vain."[25] She later wrote, "I thought my husband was going to die. I was in pain. I was afraid. Through those hymns, though, I was able to connect with God in a meaningful way when I couldn't find my own words to pray."[26]

Kent was transported to Atlanta. His caregivers chose to risk an untested treatment. Little by little, his condition improved. Within a few days, his strength began to return. The entire world, it seemed, rejoiced when he was able to exit the hospital, cured of Ebola.

We can applaud the Brantlys for their victory over another disease—a virus that is every bit as deadly and contagious: the unseen contagion of anxiety. Kent and Amber were prime candidates for panic, yet they reacted with the same resolve that enabled them to battle Ebola. They resolved to abide in Christ. Kent opened his Bible. Amber meditated on hymns. They filled their minds with the truth of God.

Jesus taught us to do the same. He tells us, "Do not worry about your life, what you will eat or drink; or about your body, what you will wear" (Matthew 6:25). He then says to "look at the birds of the air" (verse 26). When we do, we notice how happy they seem to be. They aren't frowning, cranky, or grumpy. They don't appear sleep-deprived or lonely. They sing, whistle, and soar. Yet they do not "sow or reap or store away into barns" (verse 26). They don't drive tractors or harvest wheat, yet Jesus asks us, do they appear well cared for?

Jesus then turns our attention to the flowers of the field: "Consider the lilies" (verse 28 NKJV). By the same token, they don't do anything. Even though their life span is short, God dresses them up for red-carpet appearances. Even Solomon, the richest king in history, "was not arrayed like one of these" (verse 29 NKJV). How do we disarm anxiety? We stockpile our minds with God-thoughts. Draw the logical implication: If birds and flowers fall under the category of God's care, won't he care for us as well? Saturate your heart with the goodness of God. "Set your mind on things above, not on earthly things" (Colossians 3:2).

How might you do this?

A friend recently described to me her daily ninety-minute commute. "Ninety minutes!" I commiserated. "Don't feel sorry for me," she smiled. "I use the trip to think about God." She went on to describe how she fills the hour and a half with worship and sermons. She listens to entire books of the Bible. She recites prayers. By the time she reaches her place of employment, she is ready for the day. "I turn my commute into my chapel."

Do something similar. Is there a block of time you can claim for God? Perhaps you could turn off the news and open your Bible. Set the alarm for fifteen minutes earlier. Listen to an audio version of a Christian book as you fall asleep.

"If you abide in my word, you are truly my disciples, and you will know the truth, and the truth will set you free" (John 8:31–32 ESV). Free from fear. Free from dread. And, yes, free from anxiety. So . . . what can you turn into your "chapel" today to worship the Lord?

THE HEART OF THE MATTER

- Trust God to guide you through uncertainly—and never let go of his hand.
- Jesus calls you to look at God's care for the birds and lilies when you are anxious.
- Disarm anxiety by stockpiling your mind with God-thoughts.
- Create your own "chapel moments" where you contemplate God's goodness.

MEMORY VERSE

Your memory verse for this unit is Romans 12:1. Take a few moments to review this verse, and then write it out from memory in the space below.

After God's Own Heart

Where do you look when you're anxious? Do you look at your phone, doomscrolling the latest news? Do you look at your TV, bingeing the latest hit? Do you look at your friends, whose lives seem to be better than your own? When you're anxious, the places you tend to fix your gaze may distract you for a time, but, in the end, they will only make you more anxious.

Try this instead. The next time you feel overwhelmed by anxiety, *go outside*. Walk into your backyard or to a park—any outdoor space will do. Notice what you see. Trees, grass, flowers? Notice what you hear. Birdsong, wind rustling the branches, crickets? Then notice what you feel and smell. Dew on the grass, the coming rain, a neighbor's chimney?

Take a deep breath. A few minutes in God's creation can do wonders for your anxiety. The God who made everything you can see, touch, smell, and hear is taking care of you.

WEEKLY BIBLE STUDY

READ: MATTHEW 6:25–34 AND HEBREWS 4:1–16

1. Jesus tells you, as his follower, to "not worry about your life" (Matthew 6:25). How does trusting God to provide for your needs reflect a heart of worship?

2. What does Jesus say about God's care for creation (see verses 26–30)? How does this inspire you to trust in his provision and worship him for the way he cares for you?

3. What does it mean to seek God's kingdom first (see verse 33)? What does this say about the importance of prioritizing worship over worry and material concerns?

4. How does a person actively enter into God's promised rest (see Hebrews 4:1–3)? Have you experienced the rest that only God can give?

5. What does the author of Hebrews mean when he says to "make every effort" to enter into God's rest (verse 11)? How does choosing to do so reflect a heart of worship and trust?

6. What is significant about the way in which you can approach God's throne (see verse 16)? What would it look like to approach God's throne in that way today?

7. Think about a block of time you can claim in your schedule to spend time with the Lord. What will you turn into your "chapel" today so you can worship him?

Week 29: JOIN WITH THE ANGELS

The poet John Milton wrote, "Millions of spiritual creatures walk the Earth unseen, both when we wake, and when we sleep."[27] Angels occupy an unquestioned role in the Bible. If you believe in God's Word, you have to believe in angels. At the same time, you have to be puzzled by them. Angel study is biblical whale watching. Angels surface just long enough to grant a glimpse and raise a question but then disappear before we have a full view.

One thing is certain: Biblical and contemporary portrayals of angels don't match up. Tabloids present angels as Thumbelina fairies with see-through wings. They exist to do us favors—heaven's version of bottled genies who find parking places, lost keys, and missing cats. Snap your finger and *poof*—they appear. Snap again and they vanish.

Not quite a biblical image. Two adjectives capture the greater truth about angels: *many* and *mighty*. Multitudes of angels populate the world. The author of Hebrews speaks of "thousands of angels in a joyful gathering" (12:22 NLT). Jude declared, "The Lord is coming with thousands and thousands of holy angels to judge everyone" (verses 14–15 CEV). An inspired King David wrote, "The chariots of God are twenty thousand, even thousands of angels: the Lord is among them, as in Sinai, in the holy place" (Psalm 68:17 KJV).

Thousands of angels awaited the call of Christ on the day of the cross: "Do you think that I cannot appeal to My Father, and He will at once put at My disposal more than twelve legions of angels?" (Matthew 26:53 NASB). One legion equated to six thousand soldiers. Quick math reveals that seventy-two thousand hosts of heaven stood poised to rescue their Master. The book of Revelation, brimming as it is with glimpses into the soon-to-be world, refers to angels around the heavenly throne, "and the number of them was ten thousand times ten thousand, and thousands of thousands" (Revelation 5:11 NKJV).

You need an adjective to describe angels? Start with *many*. Continue with *mighty*. Chiffon wings and meringue sweetness? God's angels are marked by indescribable strength. Paul says Christ "will come with his mighty angels" (2 Thessalonians 1:7 NLT). The Greek word translated "mighty" (*dunatos*) is the root of our English word *dynamic*. Angels pack dynamic force. It took only one angel to slay the firstborn of Egypt and only one angel to close the mouths of the lions to protect Daniel. David called angels "mighty ones who carry out [God's] plans, listening for each of his commands" (Psalm 103:20 NLT).

No need for you to talk to angels. They won't listen. Their ears incline only to God's voice. They are "spirits who serve God" (Hebrews 1:14 NCV), responding to his command and following only his directions. Jesus said they "always see the face of my Father in heaven" (Matthew 18:10). Only one sound matters to angels—God's voice. Only one sight enthralls angels—God's face. They know that he is Lord of all.

As a result, they worship him. "When God brings his firstborn Son into the world, he says, 'Let all God's angels worship him'" (Hebrews 1:6 NCV). They did . . . and they do. Remember the earlier reference to the ten thousand times ten thousand angels encircling the throne of heaven? Guess what they are doing? "All the angels stood around the throne . . . saying: 'Amen! Blessing and glory and wisdom, thanksgiving and honor and power and might, be to our God forever and ever. Amen'" (Revelation 7:11–12 NKJV).

Doesn't their worship proclaim volumes about God's beauty? Angels could gaze at the Grand Canyon, Picasso paintings, and the Sistine Chapel, but they choose to fix their eyes on the glory of God. They can't see enough of him and can't be silent about what they see.

At the very moment you read these words, God's sinless servants are offering unceasing worship to their Maker. He is, remember, their creator. So, they worship him, and—here is a drink for thirsty hearts—they protect us. "All the angels are spirits who serve God and are sent to help those who will receive salvation" (Hebrews 1:14 NCV).

Just look at Peter, sleeping on a pallet in a Jerusalem prison's death row. One word from Herod and his head would roll. All earthly efforts to save him had expired. But heavenly efforts had not. An angel not only woke Peter up but also walked him out! "Suddenly an angel of the Lord appeared and a light shone in the cell. He struck Peter on the side and woke him up. 'Quick, get up!' he said, and the chains fell off Peter's wrists" (Acts 12:7).

Angels minister to God's people. "[God] has put his angels in charge of you to watch over you wherever you go" (Psalm 91:11 NCV). You are beneath the care of celestial beings. Let that truth lower your anxiety level! The wealthiest of the world don't have the protection God's servants give you. And angels love to give it! Angels not only serve you; they are stunned by you. "Do you realize how fortunate you are? Angels would have given anything to be in on this!" (1 Peter 1:12 MSG). Amazed angels behold the gifts God has given you.

Does the Holy Spirit indwell angels? No. But he dwells in you. Do angels thank God for salvation? No, they've never been lost. But you have. Did Christ become an angel? No. But he became a human. And angels stood in awe when he did. Worshiping angels attended his birth. Awaiting angels witnessed his death. Excited angels announced his resurrection. Attentive angels watch the work of the church. "Through followers of Jesus like yourselves gathered in churches, this extraordinary plan of God is becoming known and talked about even among the angels!" (Ephesians 3:10 MSG). God's work in you leaves angels wide-eyed and applauding.

What can you do in response to these wondrous things? You can join with the angels in worshiping God, proclaiming, "'Holy, holy, holy is the Lord God Almighty'" (Revelation 4:8).

THE HEART OF THE MATTER

- Angels in the Bible, unlike modern portrayals, are many and mighty.
- Angels stand in awe of the salvation, Spirit, and gifts that God has given you.
- Angels worship God without ceasing—they are forever enthralled by his glory.
- Angels remind us how we are to respond to God's glory: in worship.

MEMORY VERSE

Your memory verse for this unit is Romans 12:1. Take a few moments to review this verse, and then write it out from memory in the space below.

After God's Own Heart

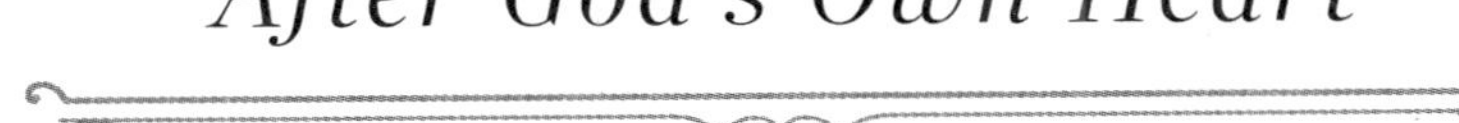

A beautiful sunset stops us in our tracks. Our love for our children fills us with awe. Our own salvation causes us to rejoice. These are life's miracles we can grasp. Things we can see or feel.

But angels? If we've never encountered them, it can be hard for us to believe in them. Maybe they were metaphorical in the Bible. Maybe they're a thing of the past, no longer among us. Maybe they occasionally show up but only at the bedside of the dying.

The Bible would beg to differ. Angels are mentioned often. Angels rescue Lot and his family. They shut the mouths of lions when Daniel is in their den. They await the Savior as he hangs on a cross. They appear to Jesus' followers to guide them and save them. In John's vision, they surround God's throne and worship him and the Lamb who was slain.

In Scripture, there is no question that angels are real. And while they differ from us, we humans have one thing in common with them: We were also made to worship the Lord.

WEEKLY BIBLE STUDY

READ: PSALM 91:9–16 AND REVELATION 5:6–14

1. What is the promise in Psalm 91:9–10 if you make the Lord your refuge? What are some practical ways that you choose to "make the Most High your dwelling"?

2. What do you learn in verses 11–12 that God's angels are doing on your behalf? How does this lower your anxiety levels today?

3. What other promises are given in verses 14–16 to those who acknowledge God's name and seek to follow after him with a heart of worship?

4. The word angel comes from a Greek word that means "messenger." What are some of the ways that angels in the Bible served as God's messengers?

5. In the apostle John's vision, what do the four living creatures and the twenty-four elders say about Jesus, the Lamb who was slain (see Revelation 5:8–10)?

6. What do the "thousands upon thousands" of angels say about the Lamb (see verses 11–12)? What does this picture reveal about worship in the heavenly realms?

7. Revelation 5:6–14 paints a picture of heaven's hosts praising Jesus. How do these verses inspire your worship today? How do they encourage you to trust in Jesus wholeheartedly?

Week 30: WORSHIP IN THE STORM

"Immediately Jesus made his disciples get into the boat and go on ahead of him to Bethsaida, while he dismissed the crowd. After leaving them, he went up on a mountainside to pray. Later that night, the boat was in the middle of the lake, and he was alone on land. He saw the disciples straining at the oars, because the wind was against them" (Mark 6:45–48).

Mark is specific about the order of events. Jesus sent the disciples to the boat and had them go on ahead to the other side. Then he dismissed the crowd and ascended a mountainside. It was evening, probably around 6:00 PM. The storm struck immediately. The sun had scarcely set before typhoon-like winds began to roar.

Note that Jesus sent the disciples out into the storm *alone*. Even as he was ascending the mountainside, he could feel and hear the gale's force. Jesus was not ignorant of the storm. He was aware that a torrent was coming that would carpet-bomb the sea's surface. But he didn't turn around. The disciples were left to face the storm . . . alone.

Imagine the incredible strain of bouncing from wave to wave in a tiny fishing vessel. One hour would weary you. Two hours would exhaust you.

Surely Jesus will help us, they thought. They'd seen him still storms like this before. On this same sea, they had awakened him during a storm, and he had commanded the skies to be silent (see 4:35–41). They'd seen him quiet the wind and soothe the waves.

Surely he will come off the mountain. But he doesn't. Their arms begin to ache from rowing. Still no sign of Jesus. Three hours. Four hours. The winds rage. The boat bounces. Still no Jesus. Midnight comes. Their eyes search for God—in vain.

By now the disciples have been on the sea for as long as six hours. All this time they have fought the storm and sought the Master. And, so far, the storm is winning. And the Master is nowhere to be found.

Peter, Andrew, James, and John have seen storms like this. They are fishermen; the sea is their life. They know the havoc the gale-force winds can wreak. They've seen the splintered hulls float to shore. They've attended the funerals. They know, better than anyone, that this night could be their last. "Why doesn't he come?" they sputter.

Finally, he does. "Now about the fourth watch of the night [3:00 to 6:00 AM.] He came to them, walking on the sea" (6:48 NKJV).

"A ghost!" someone in the boat screamed. Fear of the sea was eclipsed by a new terror. Thoughts raced as the specter drew near. Was it a figment of their imagination? Was it a vision? A flash of lightning illuminated the sky. For a second the disciples could see its face . . . his face. A second was all they needed. It was the Master!

He spoke: "Take courage! It is I. Don't be afraid" (verse 50). Before they knew it, Jesus was in the boat with them. The sea stilled as silk. The winds hushed. A canyon opened in the clouds; soft moonlight fell over the water. From chaos to calm. From panic to peace.

The disciples looked at the water, and then looked at each other, and then looked at Jesus. And they did the only thing they could have done. With the stars as their candles and the stilled boat as their altar, they fell at his feet and worshiped. As Matthew writes in his account of the story, "Then those who were in the boat worshiped him, saying, 'Truly you are the Son of God'" (14:33). After the storm, they worshiped him.

They had never, as a group, done that before. Never. Check it out. Open your Bible. Search for a time when the disciples corporately praised him. You won't find it.

You won't find them worshiping when he heals the leper, forgives the adulteress, or preaches to the masses. They were willing to follow, willing to leave family, willing to cast out demons. But only after the incident on the sea did they worship him.

Why? Simple. This time, they were the ones who were saved. This time, their necks were removed from the noose. Their bodies were plucked from the deep. One minute they were dangling over the edge of the abyss, staring into the throat of the slack-jawed canyon. The next they were bottom-plopped and wide-eyed on the deck of a still boat on a placid sea. So they worshiped. They did what anyone would do if a death sentence were stayed at the eleventh hour: They looked to the Eternal Governor who gave the pardon and thanked him.

When you recognize God as Creator, you will admire him. When you recognize his wisdom, you will learn from him. When you discover his strength, you will rely on him. But only when he saves you will you worship him.

It's a "before and after" scenario. Before your rescue, you could easily keep God at a distance. Comfortably dismissed. Neatly shelved. Sure, he was important, but so was your career. Your status. Your salary. God was high on your priority list, but he shared the spot with others. Then came the storm . . . the fight . . . the ripped moorings . . . the starless night. Despair fell like a fog. Your bearings were gone. In your heart, you knew there was no exit.

Turn to your career for help? Only if you want to hide from the storm, not escape it. Lean on your status for strength? A storm isn't impressed with your title. Rely on your salary for rescue? Many try . . . many fail.

Suddenly you are left with one option: *God*. And when you ask—genuinely ask—he will come. And from that moment on, he is not just a deity to admire, a teacher to observe, or a master to obey. He is the Savior. The Savior to be worshiped.

I think the disciples would climb into that boat again. I'm sure they would. They would endure the storm another night, or a thousand other nights, if that's what it took. Why? Because through the storm they saw the Savior.

THE HEART OF THE MATTER

- Even when God feels distant, he knows your situation and will come to you.
- The proper response to God's salvation is worship and gratitude.
- It is in the storms that you experience God's strength, peace, and presence.
- Storms bring you closer to God and will transform your view of him.

MEMORY VERSE

Your memory verse for this unit is Romans 12:1. Take a few moments to review this verse, and then write it out from memory in the space below.

After God's Own Heart

The disciples had *followed* Jesus, put their *faith* in him, and *participated* with him in ministry. But it was only after he rescued them that they truly *worshiped* him. This time, they were the ones who had been saved. So they fell at the feet of Jesus in that boat and worshiped him.

The storms of life have a way of stripping away our self-reliance. When it's just us against the sea—and the odds of survival aren't looking good—we are left with only one option: God. When we then witness the Lord intervene and save us from that dire situation, he suddenly becomes not a deity to admire but a Savior to be worshiped.

Let it be your prayer today to cultivate a heart of worship that sees the mighty hand of God not only in the dramatic rescues but also in the quiet moments of everyday life. Let your worship flow from a heart that acknowledges him as your Savior. Choose to worship him in his sovereignty through every season—whether that is the calm or the storm.

WEEKLY BIBLE STUDY

READ: PSALM 18:1–15 AND MARK 6:45–52

1. What does David acknowledge about the Lord in Psalm 18:1–3? How did this understanding help him worship God during trials?

2. What difficult situation was David facing at this point in his life? What happened when he chose to turn to the Lord in this time of distress (see verses 4–6)?

3. What does the imagery used in verses 7–15 reveal about God's power, authority, and intervention in our lives? How does this inspire you to worship him?

4. Why do you think Jesus sent the disciples out into the storm alone while he went up on a mountainside to pray (see Mark 6:45–46)?

5. How did Jesus calm his disciples' fears when they thought he was a ghost (see verses 47–50)? How has Jesus calmed your fears in your storms?

6. Matthew adds that when Jesus' presence calmed the storm, the disciples "worshiped him" (14:33). Why was worship an appropriate response at that moment?

7. How do you stay focused on God and recognize him as your rock, fortress, deliverer, refuge, shield, and stronghold during the storms of life?

Week 31: THE BETTER OPTION

Satan peddles in fear. I'm convinced he runs a school dedicated to one topic: the Language of Anxiety. Somewhere in the bowels of hell, classrooms of demons are taught the dialect of dread and doubt. Were you to sit in on this class (not recommended), you would see the professor of advanced panic stalking about the room, parlaying the fine art of fear distribution.

He points a bony finger in the air. "You must sow seeds of distress in the minds of these children of God," he says through a snarl. "Exaggerate, overstate, and amplify. Wake them up in the middle of the night. Better still, keep them awake so they cannot rest. Make sure they assume the worst. Urge them to envision a world of no escape, no solution, and no hope."

Were you to eavesdrop on a class (again, not recommended), you would hear his mousy minions rehearsing the declarations of trepidation.

No one will ever help me!
It's all over!
Everyone is against me!
I'll never get through this!

The demons graduate with one assignment: to stir faith-robbing, nail-biting, sleep-stealing unease.

Are they whispering in your ear?

Our stress-laden society has developed many skills for dealing with anxiety. We have breathing exercises and meditation techniques. We have medications and seminars. These tools have their place. But the person in whom the Spirit dwells has the greatest of resources. Turn to him for help. The next time a wave of anxiety begins to roll over you, go immediately to the Spirit in worship. As Paul said, "Do not get drunk on wine, which leads to debauchery. Instead, be filled with the Spirit" (Ephesians 5:18).

The apostle contrasts two strategies for facing inner chaos: inebriation and celebration. Many people numb themselves, if not with liquor, then with long weeks of work, bouts of shopping, or hours of playing. Anyone who has tried this approach knows its falsehood. Happy hours do not make us happy. We may forget our troubles for a moment, but they are awaiting us as we leave the bar. The better option? Celebration. "Speak to each other with psalms, hymns, and spiritual songs" (verse 19 NCV).

Paul used a verb tense in Ephesians 5:18 that caused one translator to write, "Ever be filled and stimulated with the [Holy] Spirit" (AMPC). Constant worship clears the debris from our hearts. Praise is the cleansing element that flushes the trash of worry and anxiety.

Rather than panic, we can choose to praise. The Holy Spirit will give us the power; we just have to use it. In worship, we stand firm against the forces of hell: "For God has not given us a spirit of fear, but of power and of love and of a sound mind" (2 Timothy 1:7 NKJV).

Let me show you how this works. It's midnight. You've been trying to get to sleep since ten o'clock, but you cannot. You have a big meeting tomorrow. You need some rest. You try the different sleep-inducing strategies: slow breaths, counting sheep, listening to a Lucado sermon, but nothing works. Your mind won't shut off.

You begin to envision worst-case scenarios. You will forget your notes. You'll call your boss by the wrong name. Your thoughts spin around in descending circles, taking you down, down, down until you are in a pit. You pound your pillow, and your heart pounds in your chest. The old version of you might have spent the night staring into the dark. But a new version of you is taking shape. A version that has received the fullness of the Holy Spirit. A version that does not face challenges alone but turns quickly to worship.

So here is what happens. You climb out of bed and find a quiet place where you can open your Bible and pray. You read the verses that promise peace from the Holy Spirit.

"God met me more than halfway, he freed me from my anxious fears. . . . When I was desperate, I called out, and God got me out of a tight spot. God's angel sets up a circle of protection around us while we pray" (Psalm 34:4–7 MSG).

You select a favorite song, either to listen to or to sing. Maybe both. If one isn't enough, you sing some more. Then you pray. You pray in the Spirit, and the Spirit prays in you. You surrender tomorrow to the care of your loving God. And then, to make sure the devil knows he has failed, you tell him to leave you alone. *I belong to Jesus Christ, thank you very much. So you must depart from here.* Indeed, he must. And he will.

Will you fall fast asleep? Probably. But if not, stay at it.

The Holy Spirit will do for you what my daughter did for her son.

It was a big day for little Max. His first haircut. Everyone was excited. Everyone, that is, except Max. His sixteen months of life had yet to prepare him for this moment.

It did not matter that he got to sit in a miniature fire truck. It did not matter that he was promised a piece of candy. He was undistracted by the cartoons on the TV. All he saw was a woman he did not know coming at him with a pair of scissors.

He began to cry. His daddy tried to comfort him. His grandma did the same. I told him he would someday wish he had hair to cut. Made no difference. But then came Mama. She leaned down and whispered in his ear words that the rest of us could not hear. He still was unhappy, but he calmed down enough to complete the event.

The Spirit, the mother heart of God, will soothe you as well. He calmed the creation. He descended as a dove. Take a deep breath and relax. The Spirit of God is here to help.

THE HEART OF THE MATTER

- Fear and anxiety are tools that Satan uses to steal your peace.
- Choose *celebration* over *inebriation* when it comes to your anxious thoughts.
- Trust the Holy Spirit to equip you with peace, love, and a sound mind.
- Surrender your fears to God, trust his care, and stand firm against the enemy.

MEMORY VERSE

Your memory verse for this unit is Romans 12:1. Take a few moments to review this verse, and then write it out from memory in the space below.

After God's Own Heart

Our best moments don't reveal our true selves. It's during the difficult, overwhelming, anxious moments that who we are on the *inside* comes out on the *outside*. Consider the case of Paul and Silas in Acts 16. Even after being thrown into a Philippian prison, where they were flogged and beaten, what came out of their mouths? Prayers and hymns to God.

What would come out of yours? Is your heart so full of worship that even during your darkest moments the praise couldn't help but escape your lips? Or, if you were in the missionaries' shoes, would you curse, lament, blame, and allow anxiety to rule your heart?

Paul and Silas weren't worshiping in this moment for the first time. Worship was their way of life. It was always on their lips. So when life got hard—as it often did in their ministry—what they turned to was worship. Do the same. Start worshiping today! Practice now so that when life gets hard tomorrow, you can also respond to God with prayer and hymns.

WEEKLY BIBLE STUDY

READ: JOHN 10:7–13 AND EPHESIANS 5:15–20

1. Jesus says that he is the gate for his sheep (see John 10:7, 9). What is he communicating through this metaphor about his ability to guide and protect his followers?

2. How does this contrast with the intentions of the thief (see verses 8, 10)? What enables followers of Christ to avoid the traps of the enemy?

3. What is different about the way Jesus watches over his flock (see verses 11–13)? What is Jesus saying here about the importance of heeding his voice?

4. What is Paul's warning to believers in Ephesians 5:15–17? What does it mean to live "not as unwise but as wise" when it comes to living in this world?

5. What two contrasting strategies does Paul present for dealing with inner turmoil? What is the danger in numbing yourself to your troubles?

6. What is the better course that Paul recommends? How does having a worship-filled heart enable a follower of Jesus to put their trials in perspective?

7. What passages from the Bible give you peace during stress-filled times? How is the Holy Spirit helping you to keep your mind fixed on Christ?

Week 32: LAY DOWN YOUR CROWN

"And when the Chief Shepherd appears, you will receive the crown of glory that will never fade away" (1 Peter 5:4).

Peter was speaking to persecuted Christians. They had suffered much for their faith. He wanted them to see that their sufferings were worthwhile. Paul made the same point: "We have small troubles for a while now, but they are helping us gain an eternal glory that is much greater than the troubles" (2 Corinthians 4:17 NCV).

To be crowned in glory, then, is to be crowned in victory: a final, ultimate victory over persecution. Scoffers will be silent, and the martyrs will be honored. Those mocked on earth will be praised in heaven. Those belittled on earth will be crowned in heaven.

Does your family criticize your faith? Don't be discouraged. Your day is coming.

Are you the source of jokes at work? Be patient. Your day is coming.

Are you the only believer in your class? Hang in there. Your day is coming.

Sooner than you can imagine, your Father will bless you.

"Good work! You did your job well" (Matthew 25:23 MSG).

That phrase reminds me of a story Joe Stowell told me about a time he met the President at the White House. Joe was president of Moody Bible Institute at the time. He and a dozen or so other leaders were invited to the White House to meet George W. Bush. They each waited in line for their turn to walk across the room and shake his hand.

While Joe waited, he rehearsed his greeting: "Hello, Mr. President, my name is Joe Stowell, president of Moody Bible Institute in Chicago . . ." Joe planned to go on to tell the president that they were praying for him.

Finally his turn came. When he reached the President, he extended his hand and began: "Hello, Mr. President, my name is Joe Stowell, president of Moody Bible Institute—"

He got no further. The President smiled, slapped him on the shoulder, and said, "Way to go, Joe." He then turned his attention to the next guest as aides escorted a bewildered Joe away. Later in the day he shared the story with his secretary. By the time he returned to Chicago, she'd ordered a T-shirt and hung it on his chair.

It read, *"Way to go, Joe"— George W. Bush.*[28]

When he shared the story, we laughed, and then I offered this thought: "You know, Joe, you'll someday hear similar words from the Supreme Commander of the universe. And they won't be spoken casually or quickly. He will look in your eyes and say, 'Way to go, Joe, you've done well.'"

Such is the promise from the pen of Paul. "[The Lord] will bring to light things that are now hidden in darkness, and will make known the secret purposes of people's hearts. Then God will praise each one of them" (1 Corinthians 4:5 NCV). What an incredible sentence. "God will praise each one of them." Not "the best of them" or "a few of them" or "the achievers among them." But God will praise *each* of them.

God does not delegate the job. The angel Michael doesn't hand out the crowns. Moses doesn't speak on behalf of the throne. God himself does the honors.

That day is coming. God will put a crown on your head and a hand on your shoulder and bless you. "God is fair; he will not forget the work you did and the love you showed for him by helping his people" (Hebrews 6:10 NCV).

Each child you hugged, he will praise you for it. Every time you forgave, he will praise you for it. Every penny you offered, truth you taught, prayer you prayed, he will praise you for it. He'll praise you for the day you refused to give in and the season you refused to give up. But most of all, he'll praise you for saying yes to Jesus.

One day, you will see what the apostle John saw when he was given a vision of Paradise. He saw the One who sits on the throne. "Around the throne there were twenty-four other thrones with twenty-four elders sitting on them. They were dressed in white and had golden crowns on their heads" (Revelation 4:4 NCV).

The number twenty-four is double twelve, probably representing the twelve Hebrew tribes and the twelve apostles. The Old Israel and the new covenant. The twenty-four are the proxy presence of all the faithful. Those under the commandments and those under the cross. Those who looked toward the Messiah and those who look back to the Messiah.

All are represented. Anyone who has desired to kneel before the throne is there. And since the elders represent us, what they do is what we will do.

"Then the twenty-four elders bow down before the One who sits on the throne, and they worship him who lives forever and ever. They put their crowns down before the throne and say: 'You are worthy, our Lord and God, to receive glory and honor and power, because you made all things'" (verses 10–11 NCV).

Yes, there will come a day when you will be crowned. Your Maker will praise what you have done. He will bless you. But he will have hardly finished before you fall on your face and lay your crown at his feet.

How gracious of him to give us a crown. For if he didn't, what would we have to give him? As joyfully as you receive it, you will surrender it. As freely as he gave it, you will offer it.

I can't wait to see you there. I want to see the look on your face when you see the look on his. One glance into the eyes of the King and you will know the elders were right. Heaven has only one head worthy of a crown. And it's not yours, and it's not mine.

THE HEART OF THE MATTER

- God sees your faithfulness in trials and one day will reward you.
- He will honor your love, sacrifices, and perseverance with a crown of victory.
- However, you will lay that crown at his feet and worship him!
- Stay faithful through trials and remember your day of blessing is coming.

MEMORY VERSE

Your memory verse for this unit is Romans 12:1. Take a few moments to review this verse, and then write it out from memory in the space below.

After God's Own Heart

"You will receive the crown of glory that will never fade away" (1 Peter 5:4). What a promise! For those who endure trials—who remain faithful to Jesus in spite of the criticism, mockery, and persecution—there is a reward beyond imagination. Your struggles are *not* in vain. Every act of faith, every moment of perseverance, is seen and cherished by God.

Just imagine the day when the Creator of the universe will place a crown on your head and say, "Well done, good and faithful servant!" (Matthew 25:21). In that moment, as the twenty-four elders reveal, you will lay that crown at Jesus' feet. Why? Because you will recognize that Jesus *alone* is worthy of all glory, honor, and power.

Your worship of God is not just for today but for all eternity. So let every trial you face now serve as a reminder: a great day is coming. And on that day, all glory will belong to him.

WEEKLY BIBLE STUDY

READ: HEBREWS 6:7–12 AND REVELATION 4:1–11

1. What are the two kinds of lives contrasted in Hebrews 6:7–8? What does this say about the importance of living for eternal rewards?

2. What will God remember when your time on this earth is over (see verses 9–10)? How does it encourage you to know that he "will not forget your work"?

3. What does it mean for followers of Jesus to "become lazy" (verse 12)? What part does perseverance and faithfulness play in receiving God's eternal rewards?

4. Who does John, in his vision of heaven, see seated around God's throne (see Revelation 4:1–4)? Who do these individuals represent?

5. What do these individuals do when the four living creatures give glory, honor, and thanks to the One who sits on the throne (see verses 9–11)?

6. What is the significance of these individuals taking the crowns they received from Christ and laying them down before his throne?

7. Heaven has only one head worthy of a crown. How does keeping Jesus front and center in your worship help you remember that truth in your everyday life?

Unit 6

Seeking AN HONEST HEART

King David's life couldn't be better. Just crowned. His throne room smells like fresh paint, and his city architect is laying out new neighborhoods. God's ark indwells the tabernacle; gold and silver overflow the king's coffers; Israel's enemies maintain their distance. The days of ducking Saul are a distant memory. But something stirs one of them.

In the midst of his new life, David remembers a promise from his old one. "Is there still anyone who is left of the house of Saul, that I may show him kindness for Jonathan's sake?" (2 Samuel 9:1 NKJV). Confusion furrows the faces of David's court. Why bother with the children of Saul? This is a new era, a new administration. Who cares about the old guard?

David does.

He does because he remembers the covenant he made with Jonathan. When Saul threatened to kill him, Jonathan sought to save him. Jonathan succeeded and made this request: "If I make it through this alive, continue to be my covenant friend. And if I die, keep the covenant friendship with my family—forever" (1 Samuel 20:14–15 MSG). Jonathan does die. But David's covenant does not. No one would have thought twice had he let it. But to David, a covenant was no small matter.

Finding a descendant of Jonathan wasn't easy. No one in David's circle knew one. Advisers summoned Ziba, a former servant of Saul. Did he know of a surviving member of Saul's household? Look at Ziba's answer: "Yes, one of Jonathan's sons is still alive. He is crippled in both feet" (2 Samuel 9:3 NLT). The person in question is Mephibosheth, the son of Jonathan.

When the boy was five, his father and grandfather died at the hands of the Philistines. Knowing their brutality, the family of Saul headed for the hills. Mephibosheth's nurse snatched him up and ran, then tripped and dropped the boy, breaking both his ankles, leaving him incurably lame. Servants carried him across the Jordan River to an inhospitable village called Lo Debar. The name means "without pasture." Mephibosheth hid there, first for fear of the Philistines, then for fear of David.

Servants are soon driving a stretch limousine across the Jordan River and knocking on the door of the shack. They explain their business, load Mephibosheth into the car, and carry him into the palace. The boy assumes the worst. But David calls in Ziba and tells him, "Everything that belonged to Saul and his family, I've handed over to your master's grandson. . . . from now on [he] will take all his meals at my table" (verses 8–10 MSG). Faster than you can say *Mephibosheth* twice, he gets promoted from Lo Debar to the king's table.

Why is David so loyal? *How* is he so loyal? Were you able to ask David how he fulfilled his promise, he would take you from his story to God's story. God sets the standard for covenant keeping. He makes—and never breaks—his promises. David was a walking parable of God's loyalty. You are called to do the same. Illustrate stubborn love. Incarnate fidelity. God is giving you a Mephibosheth-sized chance to show your children and your neighbors what real love does. So embrace it. And who knows? Maybe someone one day will tell your story of loyalty to illustrate the loyalty of God.

— PRAYER —

Dear God, you love the truth. You despise lies and dishonesty. I confess that I am not always honest and do not always honor my promises. Put an honest heart within me, God. Purify me of my lies and dishonesty and keep me from others who practice deceit. May I seek your truth above all else. In the name of Jesus I pray. Amen.

— MEMORY VERSE —

The LORD detests lying lips, but he delights in people who are trustworthy.

PROVERBS 12:22

Week 33: THE POISON OF SIN

You can climb too high for your own good. It's possible to ascend too far, stand too tall, and elevate too much. Which is exactly where David is. He has never been higher. The wave of his success has crested at age fifty. Israel is expanding. The country is prospering. In two decades on the throne, he has distinguished himself as a warrior, musician, statesman, and king.

His cabinet is strong and his boundaries stretch for sixty thousand square miles. No defeats on the battlefield. No blemishes on his administration. Loved by the people. Served by the soldiers. Followed by the crowds. David is at an all-time high. Never higher, yet never weaker. He stands at the highest point of his life, in the highest position in the kingdom, at the highest place in the city—on the balcony overlooking Jerusalem.

He should be with his men, at battle, astride his steed and against his foe. But he isn't. He is at home. "In the spring, when the kings normally went out to war, David sent out Joab, his servants, and all the Israelites. They destroyed the Ammonites and attacked the city of Rabbah. But David stayed in Jerusalem" (2 Samuel 11:1 NCV).

It's springtime in Israel. The nights are warm and the air is sweet. David has time on his hands, love on his mind, and people at his disposal. His eyes fall upon a woman as she bathes. We'll always wonder if Bathsheba was bathing in a place where she shouldn't bathe, hoping David would look where he shouldn't look. We'll never know. But we know that he looks and likes what he sees. So he inquires about her. A servant returns with this information: "That woman is Bathsheba daughter of Eliam. She is the wife of Uriah the Hittite" (verse 3 NCV).

The servant laces his information with a warning. He gives not only the woman's name but her marital status and the name of her husband. Why tell David she is married if not to caution him? And why give the husband's name unless David is familiar with it?

The servant hopes to deftly dissuade the king. But David misses the hint. The next verse describes his first step down a greasy slope: "So David sent messengers to bring Bathsheba to him. When she came to him, he had sexual relations with her" (verse 4 NCV).

David "sends" many times in this story. He *sends* Joab to battle. He *sends* the servant to inquire about Bathsheba. He *sends* for Bathsheba to have her come to him. When David later learns of her pregnancy, he *sends* word to Joab to *send* Uriah back to Jerusalem. David *sends* him to Bathsheba to rest, but Uriah is too noble. So David opts to *send* Uriah back to a place in the battle where he is sure to be killed. Thinking his cover-up is complete, "after the time of mourning was over" (verse 27), David *sends* for Bathsheba and marries her.

We don't like this sending, demanding David. We prefer the pastoring David, caring for the flock; the dashing David, hiding from Saul; the worshiping David, penning psalms; the honest David, keeping his covenant with Jonathan. We aren't prepared for the David who has lost control of his self-control, who sins as he sends.

What has happened to him? Simple. Altitude sickness. He's been too high too long. The thin air has messed with his senses. He can't hear as he used to. He can't hear the warnings of the servant or the voice of his conscience.

Nor can he hear his Lord. The pinnacle has dulled his ears and blinded his eyes. Did David see Bathsheba? No. He saw Bathsheba bathing. He saw Bathsheba, the conquest. But did he see Bathsheba, the human being? The wife of Uriah? The daughter of Israel? The creation of God? No. David had lost his vision. Too long at the top will do that to you. Too many hours in the bright sun and thin air will leave you breathless and dizzy.

The story of David and Bathsheba is less a story of lust and more a story of power. A story of a man who rose too high for his own good. A man who needed to hear these words: "Come down before you fall." Don't make the same mistake. It is far wiser to descend the mountain than to fall from it. How do you do this?

Start by *pursuing humility*. God hates to see his children fall. He hates to see his Davids seduce and his Bathshebas be victimized. God hates what pride does to his children. He doesn't just dislike arrogance . . . he *hates* it. Could he state it any clearer than Proverbs 8:13: "I hate pride and arrogance"? And then a few chapters later: "GOD can't stomach arrogance or pretense; believe me, he'll put those braggarts in their place" (16:5 MSG)?

You don't want God to do that. So practice humility. This doesn't mean you think less of yourself but that you think of yourself less. As Paul wrote, "Don't cherish exaggerated ideas of yourself or your importance, but try to have sane estimate of your capabilities by the light of the faith that God has given to you all" (Romans 12:3 PHILLIPS).

Next, *embrace your poverty*. We're all equally broke and blessed. "People come into this world with nothing, and when they die they leave with nothing" (Ecclesiastes 5:15 NCV).

Also, resist the place of celebrity. Take Jesus' words to heart: "Go sit in a seat that is not important. When the host comes to you, he may say, 'Friend, move up here to a more important place.' Then all the other guests will respect you" (Luke 14:10 NCV). Wouldn't you rather be invited up than put down?

Finally, *seek an honest heart*. David lied and then schemed to cover up his sin. Unconfessed sin does this. It sits on our hearts like festering boils . . . poisoning, expanding. And God, with gracious thumbs, applies the pressure. He will not rest until we are honest with ourselves and our failings. He will not sit idly by as sin poisons his children.

This was a lesson that David would soon learn for himself.

THE HEART OF THE MATTER

- It is when you, like David, are at your highest that you can fall the farthest.
- Pursue humility by thinking of yourself less to resist pride's destructive pull.
- Power without accountability leads to poor decisions and harm to others.
- Seek honesty with yourself and God to prevent sin from festering in your heart.

MEMORY VERSE

Your memory verse for this unit is Proverbs 12:22. Take a few moments to review this verse, and then write it out from memory in the space below.

After God's Own Heart

Altitude sickness. Climb too high and you risk suffering its effects: confusion and disorientation. Ascending the summit of earthly life can cause your perspective to change. It can compel you, like David, to take on a view of yourself that is not accurate or honest.

There are two steps to take in dealing with altitude sickness. First, you have to *recognize your condition*. You have to honestly assess your situation and realize that you are in trouble. Second, you must *descend to a lower elevation*. Humility is the key to staying grounded. It enables you to see that everything you have in life is dependent on God and God alone.

An honest heart is essential for your spiritual health. When you humbly come before God and present your failings, he will forgive, restore, and strengthen you. So let David's cautionary tale remind you to heed God's voice and keep your heart honest before him.

WEEKLY BIBLE STUDY

READ: 2 SAMUEL 11:1–27 AND JAMES 1:13–18

1. David had experienced success after success in battle. How might this have led him to stay behind in Jerusalem "at the time when kings go off to war" (2 Samuel 11:1)?

2. What did the messenger say about Bathsheba when David sent him to inquire about her? What was the significance of the messenger saying she was the wife of Uriah (see verses 2–3)?

3. Sadly, David failed to heed the warning. What plan did he contrive when he learned that Bathsheba was pregnant? How did he compound his sin (see verses 4–15)?

4. How does David's story show that God does not tempt anyone but "each person is tempted when they are dragged away by their own evil desire" (James 1:14)?

5. What was the end result of David's sin (see 2 Samuel 11:16–25)? How does this support what you read about the consequences of sin in James 1:15?

6. According to James 1:16–18, how can you know when you are being deceived by the enemy? What should you cling to so that you are not deceived?

7. What does David's story reveal about the dangers of allowing success to go to your head? How might things have been different if David had demonstrated humility?

Week 34: NOTHING BUT THE TRUTH

A woman stands before judge and jury, places one hand on the Bible and the other in the air, and makes a pledge. For the next few minutes, with God as her helper, she will "tell the truth, the whole truth, and nothing but the truth."

She is a witness. Her job is neither to expand upon nor dilute the truth. Her job is to tell the truth. Leave it to the legal counsel to interpret. Leave it to the jury to resolve. Leave it to the judge to apply. The witness speaks the truth. Let her do more or do less, and she taints the outcome. But let her do that—let her tell the truth—and justice has a chance.

Christians, too, are witnesses. We, too, make a pledge. Like the witnesses in court, we are called to tell the truth. The bench may be absent, and the judge unseen, but the Bible is present, the watching world is the jury, and we are the primary witnesses. We are subpoenaed by no less than Jesus himself: "You will be my *witnesses*—in Jerusalem, in all of Judea, in Samaria, and in every part of the world" (Acts 1:8 NCV, emphasis added).

We are witnesses. And like witnesses in a court, we are called to testify, to tell what we have seen and heard. And we are to speak truthfully. Period.

There is, however, one difference between the witness in court and the witness for Christ. The witness in court eventually steps down from the witness chair, but the witness for Christ never does. For the Christian, deception is never an option.

It wasn't an option for Jesus. One of the most astounding prophecies about Christ is this summary: "He had done nothing wrong, and he had never lied" (Isaiah 53:9 NCV). Jesus was staunchly honest. His every word accurate, his every sentence true. No cheating on tests. No altering the accounts. Not once did Jesus stretch the truth. Not once did he shade the truth. Not once did he avoid the truth. He simply told the truth. No deceit was found in his mouth.

And if God has his way with us, none will be found in ours. He longs for us to be just like Jesus. His plan is to shape us along the lines of his Son. He seeks not to decrease or minimize our deception but to eliminate our deception. God is blunt about dishonesty: "No one who is dishonest will live in my house" (Psalm 101:7 NCV).

Our Master has a strict honor code. From Genesis to Revelation, the theme is the same: God loves the truth and hates deceit. "Lying lips are an abomination to the LORD, but those who deal truthfully are His delight" (Proverbs 12:22 NKJV). Why? Why the hard line? Why the tough stance? For one reason: Dishonesty is absolutely contrary to the character of God.

God always speaks truth. When he makes a covenant, he keeps it. When he makes a statement, he means it. And when he proclaims the truth, we can believe it.

Satan, on the other hand, finds it impossible to tell the truth. According to Jesus, the devil is "the father of lies" (John 8:44 NCV). Deceit was the first tool out of the devil's bag. In the garden of Eden, Satan didn't discourage Eve. He didn't sneak up on her. He just lied to her: "God says you'll die if you eat the fruit? You will not die" (see Genesis 3:1–4).

Big fat liar. But Eve was suckered, and the fruit was plucked, and it's not more than a few paragraphs before husband and son are following suit and the honesty of Eden seems a distant memory. It still does. Daniel Webster was right when he observed, "There is nothing so powerful as the truth—and often nothing so strange."[29]

Perhaps the question shouldn't be "Why does God demand such honesty?" but rather "Why do we tolerate such dishonesty?" Never was Jeremiah more the prophet than when he announced: "The heart is deceitful above all things" (Jeremiah 17:9). How do we explain our dishonesty? What's the reason for our forked tongues and greasy promises?

The plain fact is that we don't like the truth. Our credo is, *You shall know the truth, and the truth shall make you squirm.* Our dislike for the truth began at the age of three when Mom walked into our rooms and asked, "Did you hit your little brother?" We knew then and there that honesty had its consequences. So we learned to cover things up.

"Did I hit baby brother? It depends on how you interpret the word *hit.* I mean, sure, I made contact with him, but would a jury consider it a hit? Everything is relative, you know."

"Did I hit baby brother? Yes, Dad, I did. But it's not my fault. Had I been born with nonaggressive chromosomes, and had you not permitted me to watch television, it never would have happened. So you can say I hit my brother, but the fault isn't mine."

The truth, we learn early, is not fun.

Not only do we not like the truth, but we also *don't trust the truth.* If we are brutally honest (which is advisable in a discussion on honesty), we have to admit that the truth seems inadequate to do what we need done.

We want our boss to like us, so we flatter. We call it polishing the apple.

God calls it a lie.

We want people to admire us, so we exaggerate. We call it stretching the truth.

God calls it a lie.

If you are ever in a dilemma, wondering if you should tell the truth or not, the questions to ask in such moments are, *Will God bless my deceit? Will he, who hates lies, bless a strategy built on lies? Will the Lord, who loves the truth, bless the business of falsehoods? Will God come to the aid of the cheater? Will God bless my dishonesty?*

I don't think so either.

Examine your heart. Ask yourself some tough questions. Do you tell the truth . . . always? If not, start today. The ripple of today's lie is tomorrow's wave and next year's flood. Start today to be just like Jesus. Tell the truth, the whole truth, and nothing but the truth.

THE HEART OF THE MATTER

- Christians, like the witnesses in a court, are called to tell the whole truth.
- The Bible is clear about lying: the Lord *hates* a lying tongue.
- The first tool that Satan, the father of lies, used against humanity was deceit.
- The ripple of today's lie is tomorrow's wave and next year's flood.

MEMORY VERSE

Your memory verse for this unit is Proverbs 12:22. Take a few moments to review this verse, and then write it out from memory in the space below.

After God's Own Heart

Adam and Eve lived in harmony with God in the garden. They felt no shame, guilt, or worry. Peace filled their days. Until Satan came along. He told a lie. Eve believed it. And what came next? First, shame. Then, more deceit. Then, more shame.

It's a cycle that ever since we've been unable to break. It's like the three-year-old who lies about hitting his little brother. Instead of the truth setting us free, it often makes us feel ashamed. And so we avoid it by telling more lies, which creates more shame.

If only we could be free from the cycle. If only a Savior could break our chains. A Savior who never lied, exaggerated, or told a half-truth. A perfect Savior willing to dwell among imperfect liars afraid of the truth. We have such a Savior! He poured out his life to intercede for our transgressions. In Jesus, we can know the truth, and the truth *will* set us free.

WEEKLY BIBLE STUDY

READ: GENESIS 2:16–17, 3:1–7, AND JOHN 8:42–47

1. Deceit was the first tool out of the devil's bag. What did he say to Eve to begin to lead her down the path of doubting God's word (see Genesis 3:1)?

2. Read God's command to Eve about the tree of the knowledge of good and evil in Genesis 2:16–17. What did Eve add when she spoke of this command (see 3:2)?

3. How did Satan use Eve's words to cause her to doubt God's good intentions (see verses 4–5)? What role do you think pride played in her decision to sin?

4. Notice that Adam "was with her" when all this was happening (see verse 6). What did the two of them experience as a result of their sin (see verse 7)?

5. In John 8:42, how did Jesus explain his mission to the Jews who were questioning him? Why were they not able to "hear" his truth (see verse 43)?

6. What did Jesus say about those who choose to peddle the devil's lies (see verse 44)? How does the story in Genesis 3:1–7 show that Satan was a liar from the beginning?

7. Are your words and actions revealing to the people in your life that you value God's truth? If not, what do you need to change to have an honest heart?

Week 35: HONESTY IN THE MIRROR

It happened this morning. Right after you awoke. Right there in your house. Did you miss it? Let me recreate the scene.

The alarm rings. Your wife pokes you or your husband nudges you or your mom or dad shakes you. And you wake up.

You've already hit the sleeper button three times; hit it again and you'll be late. You've already asked for five more minutes . . . five different times; ask again and you'll get water poured on your head.

The hour has come. Day has broken. So, with a groan and a grunt, you throw back the covers and kick a warm foot out into a cold world. It's followed by a reluctant companion.

You lean up and sit on the edge of the bed and stare at the back of your eyelids. You tell them to open, but they object. You pry them apart with your palms and peek into the room.

(The moment isn't holy yet, but it's almost here.)

You stand. At that moment, everything that will hurt during the course of the day hurts. It's as if the little person in your brain who's in charge of pain needs to test the circuits before you make it to the bathroom.

Back pain? *Check*. Stiff neck? *Check*. High school football knee injury? *Still hurting.* Hay fever reaction? *Achoo!*

With the grace of a pregnant elephant, you step toward the bathroom. You wish there were some way to turn on the light slowly, but there isn't. So you slap on the spotlight, blink as your eyes adjust, and step up to the bathroom sink.

You are approaching the sacred. You may not know it, but you have just stepped on holy tile. You are in the inner sanctum. The burning bush of your world.

The holiest moment of your life is about to occur. Listen. You'll hear the fluttering of angels' wings signaling their arrival. Trumpets are poised on heaven's lips. A cloud of majesty encircles your bare feet. Heaven's hosts cease all motion as you raise your eyes and . . .

(Get ready. Here it comes. The holy moment is nigh.)

Cymbals clash. Trumpets echo in sacred halls. Heaven's children race through the universe scattering flower petals. Stars dance. The universe applauds. Trees sway in choreographed adulation. And well they should, for the child of the King has awakened.

Look in the mirror. Behold the holy one. Don't turn away. The image of perfection is looking back at you. The holy moment has arrived.

I know what you are thinking. *You call that holy? You call that perfect? You don't know what I look like at 6:30* AM.

No, but I can guess. Hair matted. Pajamas or nightgown wrinkled. Chunks of sleep stuck in the corners of your eyes. Belly bulging. Dried-out lips. Pudgy eyes. Breath that could stain a wall. A face that could scare a dog.

"Anything but holy," you say. "Give me an hour and I'll look holy. Give me some coffee, some makeup. Give me a toothbrush and a hairbrush, and I'll make this body presentable. Then take me into the holy of holies. Then I'll make heaven smile."

Ah, but there's where you're wrong. You see, what makes the morning moment so holy is its honesty. What makes the morning mirror hallowed is that you are seeing exactly who God sees. And who God loves.

No makeup. No pressed shirts. No power ties. No matching shoes. No layers of images. No status jewelry. Just unkempt honesty. Just you.

If people love you at 6:30 in the morning, one thing is sure: they love *you*. They don't love your title. They don't love your style. They don't love your accomplishments. They just love you. "Love," wrote one forgiven soul, "covers over a multitude of sins" (1 Peter 4:8).

Sounds like God's love.

"He has made perfect forever those who are being made holy," wrote another (Hebrews 10:14). Underline the word *perfect*. The word is not *better*. Not *improving*. Not *on the upswing*. God doesn't improve; he perfects. He doesn't enhance; he completes. What does the perfect person lack?

Now I realize that there's a sense in which we're imperfect. We still err. We still stumble. We still do exactly what we don't want to do. And that part of us is, according to the verse, "being made holy."

But when it comes to our position before God, we're perfect. When he sees each of us, he sees one who has been made perfect through the One who is perfect—Jesus Christ. "All of you who were baptized into Christ have clothed yourselves with Christ" (Galatians 3:27).

This morning, I "put on" clothing to hide the imperfections I'd rather not display. When you see me, fully clothed, you can't see my moles, scars, or bumps. Those are hidden. When we choose to be baptized, by lifestyle as much as by symbol, into Christ, the same shielding occurs. Our sins and faults are lost beneath the sheer radiance of his covering.

"For you died, and your life is now hidden with Christ in God" (Colossians 3:3). Please don't miss the impact of this verse. When God sees us, he also sees Christ. He sees perfection! Not perfection earned by us, mind you, but perfection paid for by him.

Go ahead and get dressed. Go ahead and put on the rings, shave the whiskers, comb the hair, and cover the moles. Do it for yourself. Do it for the sake of your image. Do it to keep your job. Do it for the benefit of those who have to sit beside you. But don't do it for God.

He has already seen you as you really are. And in his book, you are perfect.

THE HEART OF THE MATTER

- When we look in the mirror, we see all the flaws that are worth hiding.
- Our sins and faults are hidden in Christ, who has covered us with his blood.
- When God looks at us, he sees his beloved child being made perfect through Christ.
- God sees us just as we really are—and in his book we are perfect.

MEMORY VERSE

Your memory verse for this unit is Proverbs 12:22. Take a few moments to review this verse, and then write it out from memory in the space below.

After God's Own Heart

Who is allowed to see you first thing in the morning? In your makeup-less, puffy-eyed, wild-haired, dried-drool state? Maybe you're willing to let that person see what you really look like on the outside. But would you be willing to let that person see who you are on the inside?

What makes the morning mirror hallowed is that you are seeing exactly who God sees—and who God loves. Yes, he knows your thoughts. Yes, he knows the sin pattern you can't shake. Yes, "he knows the secrets of the heart" (Psalm 44:21)—the secrets you want to hide. Still, he sees you for who you truly are. A heart being made new . . . a heart being made *perfect.*

You can be honest with God because he already knows your heart. He knows you inside and out. So be your full, honest self—if not with anyone else, then at least with him.

WEEKLY BIBLE STUDY

READ: PSALM 139:13–18 AND HEBREWS 10:11–18

1. Having an honest heart means seeing yourself as God sees you. What does David say in Psalm 139:13 about the way in which God created you?

2. What does it mean that you are "fearfully and wonderfully made" (verse 14)? How easy or difficult is it for you to believe this about yourself?

3. God saw your "unformed body" (verse 16) and knows all the days that lie ahead of you. What does this say about how much he values you?

4. God loved you so much that he sent his only Son to die for your sin (see Hebrews 10:12). What did Jesus' sacrifice allow you to become (see verse 14)?

5. The Holy Spirit also testifies that you have been made perfect through Christ's sacrifice. What is "the covenant" that God has now made with you (see verses 15–16)?

6. What does the Holy Spirit testify about all the former "sins and lawless acts" (verse 17) you've committed—those sins that you have confessed to Christ?

7. When you look in the mirror, what God sees is the reflection of his perfect Son. How should this profound truth affect the way you see yourself?

Week 36: FINE-SOUNDING WORDS

"The Jewish leaders sent some Pharisees and Herodians to Jesus to trap him in saying something wrong. They came to him and said, 'Teacher, we know that you are an honest man. You are not afraid of what other people think about you, because you pay no attention to who they are. And you teach the truth about God's way. Tell us: Is it right to pay taxes to Caesar or not?'" (Mark 12:13–14 NCV).

Chances are that when a man slaps you on the back, he wants you to cough up something. This is no exception. The Pharisees are doing some heavy backslapping in this verse. Though their question is valid, their motive is not. Of all the texts that drip with manipulation, this is the worst. The Pharisees appear gentle, but under the surface, they are not honest.

God has made it clear that flattery is never to be a tool of the sincere servant. Flattery is nothing more than fancy dishonesty. It wasn't used by Jesus, nor should it be used by his followers. "May the LORD cut off all flattering lips," affirmed the psalmist (Psalm 12:3 NKJV).

"Those who correct others will later be liked more than those who give false praise," agreed Solomon (Proverbs 28:23 NCV).

"Beware of the man with sweet words and wicked deeds," learned Lucy.

The psalmist you've read. Solomon you've admired. But Lucy? She learned about flattery the hard way. Here's her story: It's Washington, DC, in the 1860s. The nation is ravaged by war. The country is divided with strife. But for young Lucy, the greatest war is in her heart.

Lucy Lambert Hale was the youngest daughter of John P. Hale, one of New Hampshire's Civil War senators. She was one of the most ravishing bachelorettes in our nation's capital. The long list of those aspiring to her heart was not only long but was also historical. More than one of her young loves grew to be national figures.

Oliver Wendell Holmes, for instance, never won her hand but did win a seat on the Supreme Court. Robert Todd Lincoln, eldest son of Abraham Lincoln, was also among her admirers—and her father hoped they would marry. Lucy, however, ultimately married William Chandler, who became Secretary of the Navy and eventually a United States senator.

But there was another man who, for a time, did occupy a place in Lucy's heart. And it is this man whose legacy in history is one of kind words and deadly deeds. His name was John.

While the war was raging in the nation, their love was raging in Washington. And while the nation was at odds, they, too, were often at odds. What confused Lucy about John was his inconsistency. He would state one thing and live another. He would woo her with his words and bewilder her with his actions.

In his first love letter to her on Valentine's Day 1862, he flattered her beauty, gentleness, and amiability. He sent her a thousand wishes for future happiness, signing his letter, "a Stranger." With words as sweet as molasses and determination as fierce as a bull, John did not remain a stranger. And with time, he and Lucy became engaged. That's when the war broke out—not in the country, but between John and Lucy.

He was insanely jealous. They quarreled incessantly. They argued as they listened to President Lincoln's second inaugural address. They quarreled when the president appointed Lucy's father as ambassador to Spain. And John exploded when Lucy decided to break the engagement and go with her father to Spain.

John was kind with words but jealous with actions. For that reason, she left him. As I said, she eventually married William Chandler. But though she lived a long and happy life, she would never forget the stormy romance with the man of kind words and harsh deeds. Nor would the rest of the world forget John Wilkes Booth—the man who assassinated Abraham Lincoln.[30]

I'm sure there was more to this story than a romance with a young girl, but both the similarity and the lesson are significant. The words Jesus heard from the Pharisees that day were just as kind. Who would have imagined they came from the lips of murderers? But therein lies the lesson of flattery. Treat it as cautiously as you would a jewel-embedded scabbard, for within both are found a sword.

Enter: the Sadducees. This small band of leaders loved Greek philosophy and discounted traditional Torah teaching as too rigid and conservative. They were pro-Roman. The Pharisees were not—they were country club. The Sadducees were common—they thought there was no afterlife. The Pharisees could tell you what you were going to wear in the afterlife. Normally, these two never would have been on the same side. But their fear of Jesus united them.

The Sadducees used another trick of the tongue: hypothetical meandering. "If this and that happen with this occurring before that . . ." Their ploy was to create an extreme version of an unlikely incident and trap Jesus in his response.

If you want the long version of their question, read Matthew 22:24–28. If you want the short version and my interpretation, here it is: "Teacher, Moses said if a married man dies without having children, his brother must marry the widow and have the children for him. Once there were seven brothers among us, blah, blah, blah, blah, blah . . ."

Jesus' response is worth underlining: "You are way off." Now, your translation doesn't use those words, and neither does mine. But it could. A fair translation of the Greek would be: "You are off base. You are missing the point. You are chasing a rabbit down a dead-end trail."

Jesus left a clear message: Misuse of the mouth is noticed by God. The religious leaders thought they could manipulate Jesus with their words. They were wrong. God is not trapped by trickery, flattered by flattery, or fooled by hypotheses. He wasn't then, and he isn't now.

THE HEART OF THE MATTER

- God has made it clear that flattery is never to be a tool of the sincere servant.
- He values honesty and sees through attempts to manipulate with words.
- Misuse of the mouth, whether flattery or trickery, is noticed by God.
- God is not trapped by, nor fooled by, insincere or deceptive speech.

MEMORY VERSE

Your memory verse for this unit is Proverbs 12:22. Take a few moments to review this verse, and then write it out from memory in the space below.

After God's Own Heart

Flattery and manipulation are the sneaky cousins of lying. On the surface, they don't appear dishonest, but beneath the smooth talk, that's exactly what they are. Flattery is a compliment with an ulterior motive. Manipulation is talking *around* something—or someone—until we get what we want in an indirect way.

Jesus' response to the Pharisees' flattery and the Sadducees' manipulation tells us that he isn't a fan of these tactics. Yet they are so easy to use. Direct communication requires honesty and vulnerability, so we default to indirect means of getting what we want or hearing what we want to hear.

The next time you're tempted to pay a compliment you don't mean or ask a leading question to get a specific answer . . . stop and ask yourself, *Am I being honest? Is this direct communication? Would Jesus appreciate my words?* If the answer to any of these questions is no, pause before you speak and ask Jesus to give you an honest heart.

WEEKLY BIBLE STUDY

READ: MATTHEW 22:15–22 AND MARK 12:18–27

1. What did the Pharisees say to Jesus to try and manipulate him (see Matthew 22:15–16)? Why might they have chosen these particular flatteries?

2. The Herodians supported King Herod Antipas, who was backed by Rome. Why is this significant given the question that Jesus was asked (see verse 17)?

3. How did Jesus respond to the question (see verses 18–22)? How should you respond when you sense flattery is being used in an attempt to deceive you?

4. What detail do you find in Mark 12:18 about the beliefs of the Sadducees? Why is this important given the question they asked Jesus (see verses 19–23)?

5. How is the situation the Sadducees described an example of "hypothetical meandering"? What was their real intent in asking Jesus their question?

6. Jesus didn't respond to the Sadducees by addressing each point of the hypothetical situation. Instead, he got to the heart of the matter. How did he do this (see verses 24–27)?

7. Why is it critical for followers of Jesus to avoid using flattery and deceptive speech? What precautions do you take to guard your words in this way?

Week 37: AN HONEST ANSWER

Her eyes squint against the noonday sun. Her shoulders stoop under the weight of the water jar. She keeps her eyes down so she can dodge the stares of the others.

She is a Samaritan; she knows the sting of racism. She is a woman; she's bumped her head on the ceiling of sexism. She's been married to five men. *Five.* Five different marriages. Five different beds. Five different rejections. She knows the sound of slamming doors.

On this day, she comes to the well at noon. Why hadn't she gone in the early morning with the other women? Maybe she had. Maybe she just needed an extra draw of water on a hot day. Or maybe not. Maybe it was the other women she was avoiding. A walk in the hot sun was a small price to pay to escape their sharp tongues.

So she came at noon. She expected solitude. Instead, she found one who knew her better than she knew herself. She looked at him. He was obviously Jewish. What was he doing here? His eyes opened and hers ducked in embarrassment. She went quickly about her task.

Jesus asked her for water, but she was too streetwise to think that all he wanted was a drink. She wanted to know what he really had in mind. Her intuition was partly correct. He was interested in more than water. He was interested in her heart.

He told her about a spring of water that would quench not the thirst of the throat but of the soul. That intrigued her. "Sir, give me this water so that I won't get thirsty and have to keep coming here to draw water" (John 4:15).

"Go, call your husband and come back" (verse 16).

Her heart must have sunk. Here was a Jew who didn't care if she was a Samaritan. Here was a man who didn't look down on her as a woman. But now he was asking her about . . . *that.*

Anything but that. Maybe she considered lying. "Oh, my husband? He's busy." Maybe she wanted to change the subject. Perhaps she wanted to leave—but she stayed. And she told the truth. "I have no husband" (verse 17). Kindness has a way of inviting honesty.

You probably know the rest of the story. I wish you didn't. I wish you were hearing it for the first time. For if you were, you'd be wide-eyed as you waited to see what Jesus would do next. Why? Because you've wanted to do the same thing.

You've wanted to take off your mask. You've wanted to stop pretending. You've wondered what God would do if you opened your cobweb-covered door of secret sin. This woman wondered what Jesus would do. She must have wondered if the kindness would cease when the truth was revealed. *He will be angry. He will leave. He will think I'm worthless.* If you've had the same anxieties, then get out your pencil. You'll want to underline Jesus' answer.

"You are right when you say have no husband. The fact is, you have had five husbands, and the man you now have is not your husband" (verses 17–18).

No criticism? No anger? No lectures?

No. It wasn't perfection that Jesus was seeking; it was honesty.

The woman was amazed. "I can see that you are a prophet" (verse 19). Translation? "There is something different about you. Do you mind if I ask you something?"

Then she made a statement that revealed the gaping hole in her soul: "Our ancestors worshiped on this mountain, but you Jews claim that the place where we must worship is in Jerusalem" (verse 20). Translation? "Where is God? I don't know where he is."

I'd give a thousand sunsets to see the expression on Jesus' face as he heard those words. Did he smile? Did he look up into the clouds and wink at his father?

Of all the places to find a hungry heart—Samaria? Of all the Samaritans to be searching for God—a woman? Of all the women to have an insatiable appetite for God—a five-time divorcée? And of all the people to be chosen to personally receive the secret of the ages, an outcast among outcasts? The most "insignificant" person in the region?

Remarkable. Jesus didn't reveal the secret to King Herod. He didn't request an audience of the Sanhedrin and tell them the news. It wasn't within the colonnades of a Roman court that he announced his identity. No, it was in the shade of a well in a rejected land to an ostracized woman. His eyes must have danced as he whispered the secret. *"I am the Messiah."*

The most important phrase in the chapter is one easily overlooked: "The woman left her water jar beside the well and ran back to the village, telling everyone, 'Come and see a man who told me everything I ever did! Could he possibly be the Messiah?'" (John 4:28–29 NLT).

Don't miss the drama of the moment. Watch as she scrambles to her feet, takes one last look at this grinning Nazarene, and hotfoots it toward her hometown.

Did you notice what she forgot? Her water jar. She left behind the jug that had caused the sag in her shoulders. She left behind the burden she had brought. Suddenly the shame of the tattered romances disappeared. Suddenly the insignificance of her life was swallowed by the significance of the moment. "God is here! God has come! God cares . . . for me!"

That is why she forgot her water jar. That is why she ran to the city. That is why she grabbed the first person she saw and announced her discovery: "I just talked to a man who knows everything I ever did . . . and he loves me anyway!"

The disciples offered Jesus some food. He refused it—he was too excited! He had just done what he does best. He had taken a life that was drifting and given it direction. "Look!" he announced to the disciples, pointing at the woman who was running to the village. "Vast fields of human souls are ripening all around us, and are ready now for reaping" (John 4:35 TLB).

Who could eat at a time like this?

THE HEART OF THE MATTER

- Jesus seeks *honesty*. He meets you where you are without judgment.
- His love reaches the outcast and the broken, offering acceptance and purpose.
- Jesus can transform your shame (your "water jar") into joy and significance.
- Share your encounter with Jesus—for your story can inspire others to seek him.

MEMORY VERSE

Your memory verse for this unit is Proverbs 12:22. Take a few moments to review this verse, and then write it out from memory in the space below.

After God's Own Heart

Have you ever hidden something from a friend or loved one for fear that if that person found out, it would change your relationship? How did it feel to hide it? What happened once the truth came out (as it inevitably does)? Were you met with shame or were you embraced? The embrace of the one you love after sharing a dark truth is life-changing. The kindness can erase your shame and restore your hope—hope in yourself and in the relationship.

This must have been how the Samaritan woman felt. One minute she was hiding from her community, the next she was running toward them, shouting excitedly about meeting the Messiah. What changed? The kindness of Jesus. She shared her darkest truth, and he accepted her. Even loved her. This is a lesson for us all—the truth-tellers and the ones on the receiving end of that truth. Tell the truth. And be kind to others when they're honest with you.

WEEKLY BIBLE STUDY

READ: JOHN 4:1–42 AND 2 CORINTHIANS 5:16–19

1. The Samaritan woman was skeptical of Jesus' intentions when he asked for a drink of water. What did she say to get Jesus to reveal his motives (see John 4:7–9)?

2. Kindness has a way of inviting honesty. How did the Samaritan woman demonstrate honesty when Jesus asked about her husband (see verses 15–18)?

3. What did the Samaritan woman's question in verses 19–20 reveal about the gaping hole in her soul? What truth about God did she want to know?

4. The Samaritan woman left behind the burden she had brought. What was the result of her encounter with Jesus and the truth she received (see verses 39–42)?

5. What does it mean to be a "new creation" in Christ (2 Corinthians 5:17)? What are you able to put behind you when you accept Jesus as your Savior?

6. Jesus said, "My food . . . is to do the will of him who sent me" (John 4:34). According to 2 Corinthians 5:18–19, why should that be your "food" as well?

7. What does the story of the Samaritan woman reveal about the benefits of being honest with Christ? How have you witnessed these benefits in your life?

Week 38: THE SPIRIT OF TRUTH

I can't recall the fellow's name. It was an Italian name, for he was an Italian. He had that rugged Mediterranean look about him: dark hair, olive skin, and a handsome smile. He wore loose-fitting slacks, a silk shirt, and loafers. Pretty classy clothes. Then again, he was Italian.

He studied history in the university and made a living by leading tours through Rome. When our family had the opportunity to see the city, a friend of a friend of a friend gave us his name. He asked us what we wanted to see. Catacombs? Colosseum? Statues of Caesar?

We wanted to see all of those. But the site at the top of my list was the Sistine Chapel. His eyes lit up. Do you know that classic Italian gesture of kissing the tips of the fingers as if something is of exquisite taste? He did it and said, "The Sistine Chapel. I will take you there."

He knew everything: the quickest route to the Vatican, the shortest lines in the Vatican, the names of the guards of the Vatican. He talked the entire time, all about the Sistine Chapel. The story of Michelangelo, the scaffolding, and the painting on the ceiling that forever changed the way we see Western art.

By the time we arrived, I wondered if the chapel would live up to its billing. It most certainly did. We craned our necks and looked up at the ceiling. After a few moments I glanced in his direction. He was smiling. He was thrilled that we were thrilled. He had this see-I-told-you expression on his face. For a few moments he said nothing. But then he scurried over next to me and in a whispered voice appropriate to the location pointed out details I would never have noticed without him. He walked me over to the corners to get a better view. He used Italian terms, but he was so enthused I didn't ask him to translate.

He changed the way I saw the chapel. I had admired it from afar. I had appreciated it from a distance. But on that day I was thrilled by it in person.

Wouldn't it be great if someone could do for the story of Jesus what this Italian did for the chapel? If only we had an expert to teach us. Someone who knows Christ the way my friend knew the Sistine Chapel. Well, that Someone is alive and well. While I cannot recall the name of the fellow in Rome, Jesus made sure we would learn the name of the Helper he left in charge. He called him the *Paraclete*. The word appears only five times in Scripture, and of those five times, Jesus used it four, and he did so on the night before his crucifixion.[31]

"I will ask the Father, and he will give you another Helper [*Paraclete*], to be with you forever, even the Spirit of truth, whom the world cannot receive, because it neither sees him nor knows him. You know him, for he dwells with you and will be in you" (John 14:16–17 ESV).

So much in this passage deserves our attention. Look at the unity of the Trinity. The Son will ask the Father, and the Father will send the Spirit. There is a happy cooperation at work here as if to say all of heaven sends help in the direction of the disciples of Jesus.

Also take note of the pronoun. Jesus doesn't want us to think of the Holy Spirit as an *it* or a thing. The Spirit is a person, and, like a person, the Spirit has intellect, emotions, and will. The

Spirit led and commanded the disciples and intercedes for the believer.[32] The Spirit appoints elders, searches all things, knows the mind of God, and teaches the content of the gospel to us.[33] The Spirit dwells among and within believers, distributes spiritual gifts, and gives life to those who believe.[34] He helps us in our weaknesses, works all things together for our ultimate good, and strengthens believers.[35]

This list would surprise most people. According to one study, only four people in ten believe that the Spirit is a divine person. The rest of those surveyed either don't have an opinion or choose to believe the Spirit is more like a power surge than a divine being who empowers and teaches us.[36] That's regretful. How does one have a friendship with electricity?

The Spirit is a person. And Jesus calls him the *Paraclete*. Translators land on different, yet similar, translations for this Greek word: "Comforter" (KJV), "Counselor" (ESV), "Advocate" (NEB), "Intercessor" (margin of the NASB). The renderings may vary, but the central message is the same. We are not alone. Yet to what end?

The Spirit has a specific, overarching mission. His task is to teach us about Jesus. "*He will teach you* all things and *bring to your remembrance* all that I have said to you. . . . When the Helper comes, whom I will send to you from the Father, the Spirit of truth, who proceeds from the Father, *he will bear witness about me*. . . . When the Spirit of truth comes, *he will guide you into all the truth*, for he will not speak on his own authority, but *whatever he hears he will speak, and he will declare to you the things that are to come*. He will glorify me, for he will take what is mine and *declare it to you*" (John 14:26; 15:26; 16:13–14 ESV, emphasis added).

The chief aim of the Spirit is to escort you into the Sistine Chapel of Jesus and watch you grow wide-eyed and slack-jawed. He will enchant you with the manger, empower you with the cross, embolden you with the empty tomb. He will infect you with his love for the Savior.

He is the "Spirit of truth." So invite him into your world. Make it your aim to walk in the Spirit by inviting him into each day. "Since we live by the Spirit, let us keep in step with the Spirit" (Galatians 5:25). Let this prayer be quick to come to your mind: "In this moment what are you teaching me?" Or, "How am I to respond to this challenge, Lord?" Or, "Show me how to be honest, Lord." Pause and listen. Keep an ear inclined toward the Spirit.

Follow him into the Sistine Chapel of Jesus Christ. Listen as he whispers wonders in your ear. Be assured that, as you smile, the Spirit smiles with you. After all, he is your teacher.

THE HEART OF THE MATTER

- Jesus did not leave you alone after his ascension. He left you with the Holy Spirit.
- The Holy Spirit's mission is to teach and reveal the wonders of Jesus Christ.
- The Holy Spirit will show you the truth of Jesus so you can live in the truth.
- Whenever you don't know what is right or wrong, you can ask the Holy Spirit.

MEMORY VERSE

Your memory verse for this unit is Proverbs 12:22. Take a few moments to review this verse, and then write it out from memory in the space below.

After God's Own Heart

We've been talking about honesty and truth . . . but what about when you can't *discern* the truth? When you've been lied to so many times, you don't know who to trust? Or when you've been living in dishonesty for so long, you no longer know what's true? Enter the Holy Spirit.

This is the good news about an honest heart: God does not expect you to develop one on your own. He has left you his Holy Spirit to dwell within you. He will guide you and reveal to you the truth. Don't know who to trust? Ask the Spirit. Don't know if this person is telling the truth? Ask the Spirit. Unsure of your own truth versus your own lies? Ask the Spirit to show you.

Some call it a gut feeling. Others call it intuition. But it's the Spirit working within you. When you feel the nudge, stop and notice. The Spirit is likely speaking to you.

WEEKLY BIBLE STUDY

READ: JOHN 14:15–27 AND 1 CORINTHIANS 2:6–16

1. How does Jesus describe the Holy Spirit in John 14:16–17? What makes it possible for believers in Christ to accept the Holy Spirit?

2. What instruction does Jesus repeat in this passage (see verses 15, 21, 23)? How does the presence of the Holy Spirit enable a person to follow this instruction?

3. What else does Jesus say the Holy Spirit will do in the lives of his followers (see verses 26–27)? When have you sensed the Holy Spirit doing these things in your life?

4. What kind of wisdom does Paul say he is proclaiming in 1 Corinthians 2:6–7? What does he mean when he says this wisdom has been "hidden" until now (see verses 7–8)?

5. What role does the Holy Spirit play in revealing God's wisdom to people? What kind of thoughts and words is the Holy Spirit able to reveal (see verses 9–13)?

6. Why is it necessary for a person to be indwelt by the Holy Spirit to understand the things of God? What do believers in Christ possess (see verses 14–16)?

7. What is a situation you are facing today in which you need God's wisdom? What specific prayer will you pray this week to receive that wisdom from the Spirit of truth?

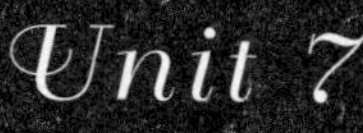

Seeking
A Repentant Heart

WEEK 39: INTO THE LIGHT
WEEK 40: BEAUTY AND THE BEAST
WEEK 41: THE CANYON OF GUILT
WEEK 42: HOPE FOR HEAVY HEARTS
WEEK 43: THEY CAME BACK
WEEK 44: COMING CLEAN
WEEK 45: THE LIST OF YOUR FAULTS
WEEK 46: AMAZING GRACE
WEEK 47: A GRACE-SHAPED HEART

The handwriting was shaky. The stationery was lined paper. The ink was black and the tone desperate. The note was dated February 6, 1974, and addressed to the U.S. government. "I am sending ten dollars for blankets I stole while in World War II. My mind could not rest. Sorry I'm late." It was signed, "an ex-GI." The postscript read, "I want to be ready to meet God."

This recruit was not alone in his guilt. His letter is one of literally tons of letters that have been sent to the U.S. government since it began collecting and storing the letters in 1811. Known as the Conscience Fund, it received more than $5.7 million in contributions during its first one hundred and seventy-five years of existence.[37]

One man writing from Brazil sent $50 to cover the cost of two pairs of cavalry boots, two pairs of trousers, one case of KC rations, and thirty pounds of frozen meat he stole from the army between 1943 and 1946. One Colorado woman sent in two eight-cent stamps to make up for having used one stamp twice (which, for some reason, had not been canceled). A former IRS employee mailed in $1 for four ballpoint pens she had never returned to the office. If the struggle to have a clean conscience weren't so common, the letters would be funny. But the struggle is common.

King David had seduced and impregnated Bathsheba, murdered her husband, and deceived his general and soldiers. His cover-up appeared to be complete. The casual observer detects no cause for concern. David has a new wife and a happy life. All seems well on the throne. But all is not well in David's heart. Guilt simmers. He will later describe this season of secret sin in vivid terms: "When I kept it all inside, my bones turned to powder, my words became daylong groans. The pressure never let up; all the juices of my life dried up" (Psalm 32:3–4 MSG).

David's soul resembles a Canadian elm in winter. Barren. Fruitless. Gray-shrouded. His harp hangs unstrung. His hope hibernates. The guy is a walking wreck. His sin stalks him like a pack of wolves. He can't escape it. Why? Because God keeps bringing it up.

Underline the last verse of 2 Samuel chapter 11: "But the thing David had done displeased the LORD" (verse 27). With these words, the narrator introduces a new character into the drama: *God.* Thus far, he's been absent from the text, unmentioned in the story.

David seduces—no mention of God. David plots—no mention of God. Uriah buried, Bathsheba married—no mention of God. God is not spoken to and does not speak. The first half of verse 27 lures the reader into a faux happy ending: "[Bathsheba] became David's wife and gave birth to his son" (NCV). They decorate the nursery and pick names out of a magazine. Nine months pass. A son is born. And we conclude: David dodged a bullet. God turned a blind eye.

But just when we think so, someone steps from behind the curtain and takes center stage. "The thing David had done displeased the LORD." God will be silent no more.

— PRAYER —

Lord, every day I battle with doing things I don't want to do and failing to do what is pleasing to you. Forgive my sins. Give me a heart of repentance. I know by the power of Jesus' blood, you can create a clean heart within me. May I never stop confessing, and may I never stop marveling at the miracle of your grace. In my Savior's name I pray. Amen.

— MEMORY VERSE —

Therefore confess your sins to each other and pray for each other so that you may be healed. The prayer of a righteous person is powerful and effective.

JAMES 5:16

Week 39: INTO THE LIGHT

God's name, not mentioned until the end of 2 Samuel 11, dominates the next chapter of David's story. The king of Israel sits while the King of the universe takes control.

God *sends* Nathan to David. Nathan is a prophet, a preacher, a White House chaplain of sorts. The man deserves a medal for going to the king. He knows what happened to Uriah. David had killed an innocent soldier. What will he do with a confronting preacher?

Still, Nathan goes. Rather than declare the deed, he relates a story about a poor man with one sheep. David instantly connects. He shepherded flocks before he led people. He knows poverty. He was the youngest son of a family too poor to hire a shepherd.

Nathan tells David how the poor shepherd loved this sheep—holding the lamb in his own lap, feeding her from his own plate. She was all he had. Enter, as the story goes, the rich jerk. A traveler stops by his mansion, so a feast is in order. But rather than slaughter a sheep from his own flock, the rich man sends his bodyguards to steal the poor man's animal:

> "Now a traveler came to the rich man, but the rich man refrained from taking one of his own sheep or cattle to prepare a meal for the traveler who had come to him. Instead, he took the ewe lamb that belonged to the poor man and prepared it for the one who had come to him" (12:4).

As David listens, the hair rises on his neck. He grips the arms of the throne. He renders a verdict without a trial: "The man who did this must die! He must pay for that lamb four times over, because he did such a thing and had no pity" (verses 5–6).

Oh, David. You never saw it coming. You never saw Nathan erecting the gallows or throwing the rope over the beam. You never felt him tie your hands behind your back, lead you up the steps, and stand you over the trap door. Only when he squeezes the noose around your neck do you gulp. Only when Nathan tightens the rope with four three-letter words:

"You are the man!" (verse 7).

David's face pales. A bead of sweat forms on his forehead. He slinks back in his chair. He makes no defense. He utters no response. He has nothing to say. God, however, is just clearing his throat. Through Nathan he proclaims:

> "I made you king over Israel. I freed you from the fist of Saul. I gave you your master's daughter and other wives to have and to hold. I gave you both Israel and Judah. And if that hadn't been enough, I'd have gladly thrown in much more. So why have you treated the word of God with brazen contempt, doing this great evil? You murdered Uriah the Hittite, then took his wife as your wife. Worse, you killed him with an Ammonite sword!" (verses 7–9 MSG).

God's words reflect hurt, not hate. They express bewilderment, not belittlement. David's flocks filled the hills. Why rob? Beauty populated his palace. Why take from someone else? Why would the wealthy steal? David has no excuse.

So God levies a sentence:

> "Now, therefore, the sword will never depart from your house, because you despised me and took the wife of Uriah the Hittite to be your own. . . . Out of your own household I am going to bring calamity on you. Before your very eyes I will take your wives and give them to one who is close to you, and he will sleep with your wives in broad daylight. You did it in secret, but I will do this thing in broad daylight before all Israel" (verses 10–12).

From this day forward, turmoil and tragedy will mark David's family. Surrounding nations now question the holiness of God. David had soiled God's reputation and blemished his honor. And God, who jealously guards his glory, punishes David's public sin in a public fashion. The infant perishes. The king of Israel discovers the harsh truth of Numbers 32:23: "You can be sure that your sin will track you down" (MSG).

God won't leave us alone with our unconfessed sin. He will take away our sleep, our peace, our rest. Why? Because he wants to take away our sin. He will not stop until we do what David did: confess our fault. It took a surprise pregnancy, the death of a soldier, the persuasion of a preacher, and the probing and pressing of God, but David's hard heart finally softened and he confessed: "I have sinned against the LORD" (2 Samuel 12:13).

Read what happened next: "Then David said to Nathan, 'I have sinned against the LORD.' Nathan replied, 'The LORD has taken away your sin. You are not going to die'" (2 Samuel 12:13).

Interesting. David sentenced the imaginary sheep stealer to death. God was more merciful. He lifted up David's sin and put it away. "As far as the east is from the west, so far has he removed our transgressions from us. As a father has compassion on his children, so the LORD has compassion on those who fear him" (Psalm 103:12–13).

God did with David's sin what he does with yours and mine—he put it away.

It's time for you to bring your unconfessed sins to light. Assemble a meeting of three parties: you, God, and your memory. Place the mistake before the judgment seat of God. Let him condemn it, let him pardon it, and let him put it away.

THE HEART OF THE MATTER

- God uses conviction to lead you toward repentance and restoration.
- Confession softens the heart and opens the door to God's mercy and forgiveness.
- God did with David's sin what he does with yours—he puts it away.
- It's time for you to bring your unconfessed sins to light.

MEMORY VERSE

Your memory verse for this unit is James 5:16. Take a few moments to review this verse, and then write it out from memory in the space below.

After God's Own Heart

It lurks in every corner. It visits you in the night, keeping you from sleep. It stalks you on your way to work, while you're playing with your kids, when you're cleaning your house. Nothing will haunt you like undealt-with sin.

You know the consequences of an unrepentant heart. Still, confession to God, others, and (especially) the one you wronged brings up the type of shame most of us run from. We will confess the small deeds—the mistakes made when we were too young to know better. But the truly raw, shame-inducing memories? We bury them. We hide them. Until the unconfessed sin is bigger and more daunting than it was when we first committed it.

We are the source of our own suffering. But God does not want us to suffer. He simply wants us to confess. When we do, the sin—along with our shame and suffering—disappear.

WEEKLY BIBLE STUDY

READ: 2 SAMUEL 12:1–25 AND JOHN 16:7–15

1. What did the parable that Nathan told in 2 Samuel 12:1–4 reveal to David about his sin? What was David's reaction to the story (see verses 5–6)?

2. What was the message that God gave to David (see verses 7–9)? Why do you think the Lord reminded David of all the blessings he had received?

3. What was God's response when David repented (see verses 13–14)? What does this reveal about the consequences that always accompany sin?

4. What did David do after the child born to him and Bathsheba died (see verses 18–20)? How does this show that David had a heart that sought after God?

5. Jesus promised to send the Holy Spirit to his disciples (see John 16:7). What did he say the Holy Spirit would prove to the world (see verses 8–11)?

6. Jesus said the Holy Spirit would guide his followers "into all the truth" (verse 13). How has the Holy Spirit guided you in truth when it comes to revealing your sin?

7. What do this week's passages reveal about how God convicts you of sin? How might the Holy Spirit be convicting you today?

Week 40: BEAUTY AND THE BEAST

What would have happened to the Beast if the Beauty hadn't appeared?

You know the story. There was a time when his face was handsome and his palace pleasant. But that was before the curse fell on the castle of the prince—before the shadows fell on his heart. And when the darkness fell, he hid. Secluded in his castle, he was left with a glistening snout and a bad mood.

But all that changed when the Beauty came. What would have happened if she hadn't appeared? Better yet, what would have happened if she hadn't cared? Who would have blamed her if she hadn't? He was such a . . . well, a beast. And she was such a beauty. If ever two people lived up to their names, didn't the Beauty and the Beast? But she did care. And because Beauty loved the Beast, the Beast became more beautiful himself.

The story is familiar not just because it's a fairy tale. It's familiar because it reminds us of ourselves. There is a beast within each of us.

It wasn't always so. There was a time when humanity's face was beautiful and the palace pleasant. But that was before the curse, before the shadow fell across the garden of Adam, before the shadow fell across the heart of Adam. And ever since the curse, we've been different. Beastly. Ugly. Defiant. Angry. As Paul explained it, "I do not do what I want to do, and I do the things I hate" (Romans 7:15 NCV).

Ever felt like saying those words? If so, you're in good company. Just consider the day Christ died. The disciples were first fast asleep, then fast afoot. Herod wanted a show. Pilate wanted out. And the soldiers? They wanted blood.

So they scourged Jesus. The legionnaire's whip consisted of leather straps with lead balls on each end. His goal was singular: Beat the accused within an inch of his death and then stop. Thirty-nine lashes were allowed but seldom needed. A centurion monitored the prisoner's status. No doubt Jesus was near death when he slumped to the ground.

The whipping was the first deed of the soldiers. The crucifixion was the third. (No, I didn't skip the second. We'll get to that in a moment.) Though his back was ribboned with wounds, the soldiers loaded the crossbeam on Jesus' shoulders and marched him to the Place of a Skull and executed him. We don't fault the soldiers for these two actions. After all, they were just following orders. But what's hard to understand is what they did in between.

The soldiers' assignment was simple: Take the Nazarene to the hill and kill him. But they had another idea. They wanted to have some fun first. Strong, rested, armed soldiers encircled an exhausted, nearly dead Galilean carpenter and beat up on him. The scourging was commanded. The crucifixion was ordered. But who would draw pleasure out of spitting on a half-dead man? They felt big by making Christ look small.

Ever done that? Maybe you've never spit on anyone. But have you gossiped? Slandered? Made someone feel bad so you would feel good? That's what the soldiers did to Jesus. When we do the same, we do it to Jesus too. "I tell you the truth, when you did it to one of the least of these my brothers and sisters, you were doing it to me!" (Matthew 25:40 NLT).

We have to face the fact there is something beastly within each and every one of us. Something beastly that makes us do things that surprise even us. Haven't you reflected on an act and wondered, "What got into me?" The Bible has an answer to the question: *sin*. As David said, "I was born a sinner—yes, from the moment my mother conceived me" (Psalm 51:5 NLT).

Could any of us say any less? Each one of us was born with a tendency to sin. Depravity is a universal condition. Scripture says it plainly: "There is none righteous, no, not one. . . . All have sinned and fall short of the glory of God" (Romans 3:10, 23 NKJV).

Our deeds are ugly. Our actions are harsh. We don't do what we want to do, we don't like what we do, and what's worse—yes, there is something worse—we can't change.

Think the assessment is too harsh? If so, accept this challenge. For the next twenty-four hours, lead a sinless life. I'm not asking for a perfect decade or year or even a perfect month. Just one perfect day. Can you do it? Can you live without sin for one day?

No? How about one hour? Could you promise that for the next sixty minutes you will have only pure thoughts and actions? Still hesitant? Then how about the next five minutes? Five minutes of worry-free, anger-free, unselfish living—can you do it? No? Nor can I.

Then we have a problem. We are sinners, and "the wages of sin is death" (Romans 6:23). What can we do? Repent. Allow the spit of the soldiers to symbolize the filth in our hearts. And then observe what Jesus does with our filth. He carries it to the cross.

God could have deemed otherwise. Jesus was offered wine for his throat, so why not a towel for his face? Simon carried the cross of Jesus, but he didn't mop the cheek of Jesus. Angels were a prayer away. They could have taken away the spittle, but Jesus never commanded them to. The One who chose the nails also chose the saliva. He bore the spit of man. Why? Could it be that he sees the beauty within the beast?

But here the correlation with Beauty and the Beast ends. In the fable, the Beauty kisses the Beast. In the Bible, the Beauty does much more. He becomes the beast so the beast can become the Beauty. Jesus changes places with us. We, like Adam, were under a curse, but Jesus "changed places with us and put himself under that curse" (Galatians 3:13 NCV).

What if the Beauty had not come? What if the Beauty had not cared? Then we would have remained a beast. But the Beauty did come, and the Beauty did care. The sinless One took on the face of a sinner so that we sinners could take on the face of a saint.

THE HEART OF THE MATTER

- The beast of sin lives within us. We have all fallen short of the glory of God.
- We don't do what we want to do, and we do what we don't want to do.
- The sinless Christ became cursed so we could be redeemed and made beautiful.
- Jesus, through his sacrifice, has transformed us from beasts into saints.

MEMORY VERSE

Your memory verse for this unit is James 5:16. Take a few moments to review this verse, and then write it out from memory in the space below.

After God's Own Heart

What got into me? How could I have done that? Our sin can baffle us. We do what we don't want to do . . . and don't do what we want to do. We choose the office over family time. We tell *that* story about *that* person that we know we shouldn't share. We tell a "little" fib. Most of the time, we don't *want* to sin, but we do. Then we're left looking at the rubble of sin's consequences, wondering what came over us and how we're going to clean up the mess.

The bad news is that as long as we live, we will keep sinning (even when we don't want to). The good news is that we don't have to clean up the mess on our own. Jesus is the "Beauty" to our beastly natures. He actually *became* the beast so that we—the beast—could become the Beauty. Jesus is the antibody to our sin . . . the cure to our incurable disease.

WEEKLY BIBLE STUDY

READ: PSALM 51:1–19 AND ROMANS 7:14–25

1. David wrote Psalm 51 after the prophet Nathan confronted him about his sin. What does David acknowledge about his sinful nature in verses 3–6?

2. What is David's request of the Lord regarding his "heart" and "spirit" (see verse 10)? What does he desire the Lord to restore to him (see verses 11–12)?

3. What does David say in verse 13 that he will do after he is restored by God? What does this say about how God can use your testimony of what he has done?

4. What does the apostle Paul write about his sinful nature in Romans 7:14–16? In what ways can you relate with the situation that he is describing?

5. What does Paul mean when he says it is the sin living in him that causes him to do wrong? How does this hamper his desire to do good (see verses 17–20)?

6. What are the two kinds of laws that Paul describes in verses 21–23? What is the only remedy for this quandary that all humans face (see verses 24–25)?

7. What are you willing to admit about your beastly nature to God in prayer? Reflect on this and then, like David, write out your own psalm of confession.

Week 41: THE CANYON OF GUILT

Few of us have been in a pit deeper than Peter's. Which is ironic, for just an hour or two before, he was high on the pinnacle and far from the pit. "Simon Peter, who had a sword, drew it and struck the high priest's servant, cutting off his right ear" (John 18:10).

Smugly, Peter stands next to Jesus, flashing his sword. "Step aside, Jesus, I'll take care of this one for you." My hunch is Peter was stunned when Jesus told him to put away his sword. Next thing Peter knows, the Savior and the soldiers are headed down the hill and Peter is alone with his decision. Does he stick close to Jesus or duck into the shadows? He opts to do neither.

Luke tells us that Peter followed Jesus and his captors "at a distance" (Luke 22:54). Not too close, yet not too far. Near enough to see him, but not near enough to be seen with him. Love made Peter ashamed to run; fear made him ashamed to draw near. The disciples chose the left side of the road and ran. Jesus chose the right side of the road and obeyed. But Peter chose the yellow stripe down the middle. BIG mistake.

He would have been better off in the shadows with the disciples. He would have been better off in the courtyard with his master. But instead Peter is warming his hands on the devil's hearth. A young girl recognizes him and says, "You also were with Jesus of Galilee."

"I don't know what you're talking about," Peter defies.

Moments later he is recognized by another servant. "This fellow was with Jesus of Nazareth," she says. For a second time, Peter denies his Lord. Then he is recognized by others: "Surely you are one of them; your accent gives you away." This time Peter begins to "call down curses" and swears to them, "I don't know the man!" (Matthew 26:69–74).

With each denial Peter inches closer to the edge of the canyon . . . until the ground gives way and he falls. Have you been there? Have you felt the ground of conviction give way beneath your feet? The ledge crumbles and down you go. *Poof!*

Now what do you do? You could stay in the canyon. Many do. Some deny their deeds. "Fall? Me? Are you kidding? These aren't bruises. These aren't cuts. Me and Jesus? We are tight." Some distort their deeds. "I'm not to blame. Don't point the finger at me."

When we fall, we can dismiss it, deny it, distort it, or deal with it. Luke adds a chilling phrase to his account of Peter's denial of Christ. When the rooster crowed, "the Lord turned and looked straight at Peter" (22:61). The rooster reminds Peter of Jesus' warning. Peter lifts his eyes and looks across the courtyard, only to find Jesus looking at him. Jesus is being assailed by accusations, but he doesn't hear them. He hears only the denial of his friend.

If Peter ever thought he could keep his fall a secret, he now knows he can't. "Nothing in all creation is hidden from God's sight. Everything is uncovered and laid bare before the eyes of him to whom we must give account" (Hebrews 4:13).

There is an old story about the time Emperor Frederick the Great visited Potsdam Prison and spoke with the prisoners. Each man claimed to be innocent, a victim of the system. One man, however, sat silently in the corner. The ruler asked him, "And you, sir, who do you blame for your sentence?" His response was, "Your majesty, I am guilty and richly deserve my punishment." Surprised, the emperor shouted for the prison warden: "Come and get this man out of here before he corrupts all these innocent people!"[38]

The ruler can set us free once we admit we are wrong. We do ourselves no favors in justifying our deeds or glossing over our sins. Sometimes we come to Christ with our sin, but all we want is a covering. We want to skip the treatment. We want to hide our sin. And one wonders if God, even in his great mercy, will heal what we conceal. "If we say we have no sin, we are fooling ourselves, and the truth is not in us. But if we confess our sins, he will forgive our sins, because we can trust God to do what is right" (1 John 1:8–9 NCV).

How can God grant us pardon when we don't admit our guilt?

Ah, there's that word: *guilt*. Isn't that what we avoid? What we detest? But is guilt so bad? What does guilt imply if not that we know right from wrong, that we aspire to be better than we are, that we know there is a high country and we are in the low country? That's what guilt is: a healthy regret for telling God one thing and doing another.

Guilt is the nerve ending of the heart. It yanks us back when we are too near the fire. When Peter saw Jesus looking at him from across the courtyard, he was flooded with guilt. "Peter remembered what the Lord had said: 'Before the rooster crows this day, you will say three times that you don't know me.' Then Peter went outside and cried painfully" (Luke 22:61–62 NCV). Each tear a confession, each sob an admission.

Peter remembers the words of Jesus and weeps. But what if Peter hadn't dealt with his feelings of guilt? What if Peter had dismissed, denied, or distorted his sin? What if he had never exited the canyon? How many sermons would have gone unpreached? How many lives would have gone untouched or epistles gone unwritten? Had Peter not felt the guilt in the courtyard, he never would have proclaimed the grace on Pentecost.

Which leads us to wonder how many untold stories walk the canyon floor today. How many lives are being neutralized by guilt? How many Peters are in the shadows, wanting to come out, if only they knew the way?

Peter shows the way to a repentant heart. Mingle the tears of the sinner with the cross of the Savior and the result is a joyful escort out of the canyon of guilt.

THE HEART OF THE MATTER

- When you fall, you can dismiss it, deny it, distort it, or deal with it.
- You do yourself no favor in justifying your deeds or glossing over your sins.
- Guilt is healthy regret for telling God you will do one thing and then doing another.
- Jesus can forgive you, restore you, and lead you out of the canyon of guilt.

MEMORY VERSE

Your memory verse for this unit is James 5:16. Take a few moments to review this verse, and then write it out from memory in the space below.

After God's Own Heart

The sinking feeling after we've gossiped about a coworker. The flood of heat to our cheeks after we tell what we know is a lie. The rock in our gut after getting away with cheating at a game with friends. While the feeling of guilt isn't pleasant, it's necessary.

If we never felt guilt, there is a good chance we would continue gossiping, lying, and cheating. Guilt keeps us in check. Guilt says, "I did something wrong." It is unlike shame in this respect, which tells us we are something wrong. Healthy guilt helps us to move forward and repent of our sin. Unhealthy guilt traps us in the canyon.

Where are you? Are you stuck on the canyon's floor, believing you didn't just do something bad but that you are something bad? Will you let God pull you out? Yes, what you did was bad, but according to him, it's not who you are. You are his beloved child.

WEEKLY BIBLE STUDY

READ: LUKE 22:31–34, 54–62 AND 2 CORINTHIANS 7:8–13

1. What did Jesus understand that his disciples would be facing after his arrest? What was his specific prayer for the disciple Peter (see Luke 22:31–32)?

2. Peter promised to accompany Jesus to prison and even death (see Luke 22:33). However, what is he doing immediately after Jesus' arrest (see verses 54–55)?

3. Peter had heard Jesus say that he would deny him three times (see verse 34). What do you think caused Peter to lose his courage at this moment (see verses 56–60)?

4. Jesus turned and looked at Peter after his third denial. What was Peter's response when this caused him to remember what Jesus had said (see verses 61–62)?

5. What does Paul write about godly sorrow—the type of sorrow that Peter experienced after denying Christ—in 2 Corinthians 7:8–10?

6. What does Paul say godly sorrow had produced in the lives of the Corinthian believers? What caused Paul to be encouraged about them (see verses 11–13)?

7. Perhaps you find yourself today in the canyon of guilt. What do you learn from the passages you've studied this week about the way out of that canyon?

Week 42: HOPE FOR HEAVY HEARTS

The hill of regret. Heavy-hearted, the figure walked it alone. The trail was rock-strewn with his shame and hurt. The landscape was as barren as his soul. Thorns of remorse tore at his ankles and calves. The lips that had kissed a king were cracked with grief. On his shoulders he bore a burden that bowed his back—his own failure.

Why Judas betrayed his master is really not important. Whether motivated by anger or greed, the end result was the same: regret.

Several years ago I visited the Supreme Court. As I sat in the visitors' chambers, I observed the splendor of the scene. The chief justice was flanked by his colleagues. Robed in honor, they were the apex of justice. They represented the efforts of countless minds through thousands of decades. Here was humanity's best effort to deal with its failures.

How pointless it would be, I said to myself, *if I approached the bench and requested forgiveness for my mistakes*. Forgiveness for talking back to my fifth-grade teacher. Forgiveness for being disloyal to my friends. Forgiveness for pledging "I won't" on Sunday and saying "I will" on Monday. Forgiveness for the countless hours I have spent wandering in society's gutters.

It would be pointless because the judge could do nothing. Maybe a few days in jail to appease my guilt, but forgiveness? It wasn't his to give. Maybe that's why so many of us spend so many hours on the hill of regret. We haven't found a way to forgive ourselves.

So up the hill we trudge. Weary, wounded hearts wrestling with unresolved mistakes. Sighs of anxiety. Tears of frustration. Words of rationalization. Moans of doubt. For some the pain is on the surface. For others the hurt is submerged, buried in a rarely touched substrata of bad memories. Parents, lovers, professionals. Some trying to forget, others trying to remember, all trying to cope. We walk silently in single file with leg irons of guilt.

Paul was the one who posed the question that is on all our lips: "Who will rescue me from this body that is subject to death?" (Romans 7:24).

At the end of the trail are two trees. One is weathered and leafless. It is dead but still sturdy. Its bark is gone, leaving smooth wood bleached white by the years. Twigs and buds no longer sprout from it. Only bare branches fork from the trunk. On the strongest of these branches is tied a hangman's noose. It was here that Judas dealt with his failure.

> When Judas, who had betrayed him, saw that Jesus was condemned, he was seized with remorse and returned the thirty pieces of silver to the chief priests and the elders. "I have sinned," he said, "for I have betrayed innocent blood." . . . Then he went away and hanged himself (Matthew 27:3–5).

If only Judas had looked at the adjacent tree. It is also dead; its wood is also smooth. But there is no noose tied to its crossbeam. No more death on this tree. Once was enough. "By one sacrifice [Jesus] has made perfect forever those who are being made holy" (Hebrews 10:14).

Those of us who have also betrayed Jesus know better than to be too hard on Judas for choosing the tree he did. To think that Jesus would really unburden our shoulders and unshackle our legs after all we've done to him is not easy to believe. In fact, it takes just as much faith to believe that Jesus can look past our betrayals as it does to believe that he rose from the dead. Both are just as miraculous.

Perhaps this is why the Bible leaves no doubt about God's grace. His "perfect love expels all fear" (1 John 4:18 NLT). If God loved with an imperfect love, we would have high cause to worry. Imperfect love keeps a list of sins and consults it often. But God keeps no list of our wrongs. His love casts out fear because he casts out our sin!

We can tether our hearts to this promise: "If our heart condemns us, God is greater than our heart, and knows all things" (1 John 3:20 NKJV). When we feel unforgiven, we need only look to the tree on which Jesus was crucified—and then evict the feelings. Emotions don't get a vote. What God says in his Word holds rank over self-criticism and self-doubt.

As Paul told Titus, "God's readiness to give and forgive is now public. Salvation's available for everyone! . . . Tell them all this. Build up their *courage*" (Titus 2:11,15 MSG, emphasis added). Do you know God's grace? Then you can love boldly, live robustly. You can swing from trapeze to trapeze. His safety net will break your fall.

Nothing fosters courage like a clear grasp of grace.

And nothing fosters fear like an ignorance of mercy. May I speak candidly? If you haven't accepted God's forgiveness, you are doomed to live in fear. Nothing can deliver you from the gnawing realization that you have disregarded your Maker and disobeyed his instruction. No pill, pep talk, psychiatrist, or possession can set the sinner's heart at ease. You may deaden the fear, but you can't remove it. Only God's grace can. "If we confess our sins, He is faithful and just to forgive us our sins and to cleanse us from all unrighteousness" (1 John 1:9 NKJV).

What a pair, these two trees. Only a few feet from the tree of despair stands the tree of hope for heavy hearts. Life so paradoxically close to death. Goodness within arm's reach of darkness. A hangman's noose and a life preserver swinging in the same shadow.

But here they stand.

One can't help but be a bit stunned by the inconceivability of it all. Why does Jesus stand on life's most barren hill and await us with outstretched, nail-pierced hands? A "crazy, holy grace" it has been called.[39] A type of grace that doesn't hold up to logic. But then, grace doesn't have to be logical. If it did, it wouldn't be grace.

THE HEART OF THE MATTER

- We haven't found a way to forgive ourselves—so up the hill of regret we trudge.
- Some of us, like Judas, deal with our heavy hearts by choosing the tree of despair.
- But Jesus offers a different choice through his sacrifice: the tree of hope.
- God's act of mercy toward us is nothing less than "crazy, holy grace."

MEMORY VERSE

Your memory verse for this unit is James 5:16. Take a few moments to review this verse, and then write it out from memory in the space below.

After God's Own Heart

The hill of regret. The weight of remorse, guilt, and shame slows your steps, bends your back, and causes your head to tilt downward as you trudge up the trail. You don't see the sky or the sun. You don't make eye contact with friends or loved ones. All you can see is the magnitude of your failures as you place one weary foot in front of the other.

It's a destination in the opposite direction of grace. Even though your burdens keep your eyes downcast, you hear footsteps behind you, then beside you, traveling with you. Curious, you glance up and see his face—the face of a Jewish carpenter with kind eyes. He understands your heavy heart and, better yet, has the remedy: Repent and be healed. He takes you by the hand and turns you around on the path—toward his full, heart-healing grace.

WEEKLY BIBLE STUDY

READ: MATTHEW 27:1–10, ACTS 1:15–19, AND 1 JOHN 1:5–10

1. What did Judas do after he learned that the Jewish chief priests and elders had made plans to execute Jesus? What "seized" him in that moment (see Matthew 27:1–4)?

2. What similarities do you see between the responses of Judas and Peter when they each recognized they had denied Christ? What is the primary difference (see verse 5)?

3. What did the chief priests acknowledge about the money that Judas returned? Why does Matthew record this particular episode (see verses 6–10)?

4. What does Peter say about Judas's role in God's story of redemption in Acts 1:15–17? What details does Luke add about Judas (see verses 18–19)?

5. The apostle John declared that in Jesus "there is no darkness at all" (1 John 1:5). What does he say is likewise true of those who have fellowship with Christ (see verses 6–7)?

6. However, what does John say about those who claim to be without sin (see verse 8)? What is the promise for those who choose to confess their sins (see verse 9)?

7. Maybe you're standing at the top of the hill of regret today. How do the passages you have studied this week help you to know what to do next?

Week 43: THEY CAME BACK

"On the evening of that first day of the week, when the disciples were together, with the doors locked for fear of the Jewish leaders, Jesus came and stood among them and said, 'Peace be with you!'" (John 20:19). There is something striking in the simple fact the disciples got together again. I mean, they had to have been embarrassed. As they sat gawking at each other that Sunday, they must have felt a bit foolish.

Only two nights earlier the kitchen had gotten hot and they had taken off. It was as if someone had thrown a pan of scalding water on a bunch of cats. *Bam!* Off they scampered. They didn't stop until they had ducked into every available hole in Jerusalem.

Have you ever wondered what the disciples did that weekend? I have. I've wondered if any walked the streets or thought of going home. I've wondered what they said when people asked them what happened. "Uh . . . well . . . you see . . ." I've wondered if they stayed in pairs or small groups or alone. I've wondered what they thought, what they felt.

"We had to run! They would have killed us all!"

"I don't understand what happened."

"I let him down."

"He should have warned us!"

I have wondered where they were when the sky turned black. I've wondered if they were near the temple when the curtain ripped or near the cemetery when the graves opened. I've wondered if any of them even dared to sneak back up to the hillside and stand at the edge of the crowd and stare at the three silhouettes on the hill.

No one knows. Those hours are left to speculation. Any guilt, any fear, any doubts are all unrecorded.

But we do know one thing. They came back. Slowly. One by one. They came back. Matthew, Nathaniel, Andrew. They came out of hiding. Out of the shadows. James, Peter, Thaddeus. Perhaps some were already on their way home, back to Galilee, but they turned around and came back. Perhaps others had given up in disgust, but they changed their minds. Maybe others were flooded with shame, but still they returned.

One by one, they appeared at that same upper room. From all sections of the city, they appeared. Too convicted to go home, yet too confused to go on. Each with a desperate hope that it had all been a nightmare or a cruel joke. Each hoping to find some kind of solace in numbers. They came back. Something in their nature refused to let them give up. Something in those words spoken by the Master pulled them back together.

It certainly was an awkward position in which to be. Caught on that uneven ground between failure and forgiveness. Suspended somewhere between "I can't believe I did it" and "I'll never do it again." Too ashamed to ask for forgiveness, yet too loyal to give up. Too guilty to be counted in, but too faithful to be counted out.

I guess we've all been there. I daresay all of us have witnessed our sandcastle promises swept away by the pounding waves of panic and insecurity. I imagine that all of us have seen our words of promise and obedience ripped into ribbons by the chainsaw of fear and fright. And I haven't met a person yet who hasn't done the very thing he swore he would never do. We've all walked the streets of Jerusalem.

Why did the disciples come back? Rumors of the resurrection? That had to be part of it. Those who walked next to Jesus had learned to expect him to do the unusual. But it had to be more than just rumors of an empty tomb. There was something in their hearts that wouldn't let them live with their betrayal. For as responsible as their excuses were, they weren't good enough to erase the bottom line of the story: They had betrayed their Master. When Jesus needed them, they scampered. And now they were having to deal with the shame.

So, seeking forgiveness, but not knowing where to look for it, they came back. They gravitated to that same upper room that contained the sweet memories of broken bread and symbolic wine. The simple fact that they returned says something about their leader. It says something about Jesus that those who knew him best could not stand to be in his disfavor. For the original twelve, there were only two options—surrender or suicide. Yet it also says something about Jesus that those who knew him best knew that though they had done exactly what they had promised they wouldn't, they could still find forgiveness.

So they came back. Each with a scrapbook full of memories and a thread of hope. Each knowing it was all over but in their hearts hoping the impossible would happen once more. "If I had just one more chance." There they sat. What little conversation there was focused on the rumors of an empty tomb. Someone sighed. Someone locked the door. Someone shuffled his feet. And just when the gloom got good and thick, a familiar face walked through the wall.

My, what an ending. Or, better said, what a beginning! Don't miss the promise unveiled in this story. For those of us who, like the disciples, have turned and run when we should have stood and fought, this passage is pregnant with hope. A repentant heart is all he demands.

Come out of the shadows! Be done with your hiding! A heart of repentance is enough to summon the Son of God to walk through your walls of guilt and shame. He who forgave his followers stands ready to forgive you. All you have to do is trust, obey, and come back.

No wonder they call him the Savior.

THE HEART OF THE MATTER

- It is significant that the disciples got together again after Jesus' crucifixion.
- Something in their hearts wouldn't let them live with their betrayal.
- A repentant heart is all that Jesus requires to break through guilt and shame.
- Failure isn't the *end* but the opportunity for a new *beginning.*

MEMORY VERSE

Your memory verse for this unit is James 5:16. Take a few moments to review this verse, and then write it out from memory in the space below.

After God's Own Heart

"Then everyone deserted him and fled" (Mark 14:50). Peter gets a lot of attention for vowing to stay with Jesus unto death and then denying he even knew Jesus three times. But the reality is that all the disciples abandoned Christ and fled. They hid in the shadows in the streets of Jerusalem, too convicted to go home and yet too confused to continue on.

What is significant is that they all came back, one by one, to that upper room. Perhaps they did so to share their stories of their shame . . . and try to figure out what to do next. It was there that Jesus met them and restored them. He gave them a new story to share with the world—how the Savior came to save people from their sins—and a new path to follow.

The story of God's children is one of repentance. We've all walked the streets of Jerusalem. We've all been guilty of doing the thing we swore we would never do. But we can be sure that when we go back to our upper room, we will find Jesus waiting there.

WEEKLY BIBLE STUDY

READ: LUKE 15:11–32 AND JOHN 20:19–23

1. Jesus told the parable in Luke 15:11–32 to illustrate how God welcomes a repentant heart. What caused the younger son to rebel against his father (see verses 11–16)?

2. The younger son, at a certain point, "came to his senses" (verse 17). What plan did he devise to get himself back into his father's good graces (see verses 17–19)?

3. What was the father's response when he saw the younger son returning home (see verses 20–24)? What does this say about how God treats all who repent?

4. What was the older brother's response to his father's act of mercy (see verses 25–32)? What warning do you think Jesus was giving in these verses?

5. According to John 20:19, what was the disciples' state of mind when they returned together? How do you think Jesus' initial words comforted them?

6. What commission did Jesus give the disciples at this point? What did he say to them about forgiving as they had been forgiven (see verses 21–23)?

7. How has Jesus met you in your repentance? How did this encounter encourage you to return to him whenever you fall into sin?

Week 44: COMING CLEAN

"If we say we have no sin, we are fooling ourselves, and the truth is not in us. But if we confess our sins, he will forgive our sins, because we can trust God to do what is right. He will cleanse us from all the wrongs we have done" (1 John 1:8–9 NCV).

Confession. The word conjures up many images, not all of which are positive. Backroom interrogations. Admitting dalliances to a priest who sits on the other side of a black curtain. Walking down the church aisle and filling out a card. Is this what John had in mind?

Confession is not telling God what he doesn't know. (Impossible.) Confession is not complaining. (Reciting our problems and rehashing our woes is just whining.) Confession is a radical reliance on grace. A proclamation of our trust in God's goodness. "What I did was bad," we acknowledge, "but God's grace is greater than my sin, so I confess it." If our understanding of grace is small, our confession will be small: reluctant, hesitant, hedged with excuses and qualifications, full of fear of punishment. But great grace creates an honest confession.

The best-known prayer of confession comes from King David, even though he took an interminably long time to offer it. Our Old Testament hero dedicated a season of his life to making godless decisions. David, the man after God's own heart, allowed his own to calcify.

He suppressed his wrongdoing and paid a steep price for doing so. He later described it this way: "When I refused to confess my sin, my body wasted away, and I groaned all day long. Day and night your hand of discipline was heavy on me. My strength evaporated like water in the summer heat" (Psalm 32:3–4 NLT).

Bury misbehavior and expect pain, period. Unconfessed sin is a knife blade lodged in the soul. You cannot escape the misery it creates. Just ask Li Fuyan. This Chinese man tried every treatment imaginable to ease his throbbing headaches. Nothing helped. An X-ray finally revealed the culprit. A rusty four-inch knife blade had been lodged in his skull for four years. In an attack by a robber, Fuyan had suffered lacerations on the right side of his jaw. He didn't know the blade had broken off inside his head. No wonder he suffered such stabbing pain.[40]

We can't live with foreign objects buried in our bodies. Or our souls. What would an X-ray of your interior reveal? Shame about the marriage that didn't work, the habit you couldn't quit, the temptation you didn't resist, the courage you couldn't find? Guilt lies hidden beneath the surface, festering, irritating. Sometimes so deeply embedded you don't know the cause.

You become moody, cranky. You're prone to overreact. You're angry, irritable. Understandable, since you have a shank of shame lodged in your soul. Interested in an extraction? Request a spiritual MRI. "Search me, O God, and know my heart; try me, and know my anxieties; and see if there is any wicked way in me" (Psalm 139:23–24 NKJV). As God brings misbehavior to mind, agree with him and apologize. Let him apply grace to the wounds.

Don't make this inward journey without coming clean with God. You need a prayer of grace-based confession, like David's. After a year of denial, he finally prayed, "God, be merciful to me because you are loving. Because you are always ready to be merciful, wipe out all my wrongs. Wash away all my guilt and make me clean again. I know about my wrongs, and I can't forget my sin. You are the only one I have sinned against; I have done what you say is wrong. You are right when you speak and fair when you judge" (Psalm 51:1–4 NCV).

David came clean with God. And you? Your moment might look something like this.

Bedtime. The pillow beckons. But so does your guilty conscience. An encounter with a coworker turned nasty earlier in the day. Words were exchanged. Accusations made. Names called. Tacky, tacky, tacky behavior. You bear some, if not most, of the blame.

The old version of you would have suppressed the argument. But you aren't the old version of you. Grace is happening, rising like a morning sun over a wintry meadow, scattering shadows, melting frost. Now you know better. You are indwelled by Christ. You can risk honesty with God. So you tell the pillow to wait and step into the presence of Jesus. "Can we talk about today's argument? I'm sorry I reacted in the way I did. I was harsh and impatient. You have given me so much grace. I gave so little. Please forgive me."

The prayer will likely prompt an apology, and the apology will quite possibly preserve a friendship. You might even hang a sign on your office wall: "Grace happens here."

Or maybe your prayer needs to probe deeper. Beneath the epidermis of today's deeds are the unresolved actions of years past. Like King David, you tried cover-ups instead of repentance. You looked when you should have turned, seduced when you should have abstained, hurt when you should have helped, denied when you should have confessed.

Talk to God about these buried blades. Go to him as you would go to a trusted physician. Explain the pain and revisit the transgression together. Welcome his healing touch. And, this is important, trust his ability to receive your confession more than your ability to make it. The power of confession lies not with the one who makes it but with the God who hears it.

God may send you to talk to the church. "Confess your sins *to one another*, and pray for one another so that you may be healed" (James 5:16 NASB, emphasis added). James calls us not only to confess *up* to God but also to confess *out* to each other. Followers of Christ have been given authority to hear confession and proclaim grace. "If you forgive anyone's sins, their sins are forgiven; if you do not forgive them, they are not forgiven" (John 20:23).

Confessors find a freedom that deniers don't. "If we confess our sins, he will forgive our sins, because we can trust God to do what is right. He will cleanse us from all the wrongs we have done" (1 John 1:9 NCV).

Oh, the sweet certainty of these words. He *will* cleanse you. Not he *might*, *could*, *would*, or *has been known to*. He *will* cleanse you. Tell God what you did. Again, it's not that he doesn't already know, but the two of you need to agree. Spend as much time as you need. Share all the details you can. Then let the pure water of grace flow over your mistakes.

THE HEART OF THE MATTER

- Confession is a radical proclamation of your trust in God's goodness.
- Unconfessed sin is like a knife blade lodged deep into the soul.
- Trust in God's ability to receive your confession more than your ability to make it.
- God calls you to confess not only *up* to him but also *out* to others.

MEMORY VERSE

Your memory verse for this unit is James 5:16. Take a few moments to review this verse, and then write it out from memory in the space below.

After God's Own Heart

It's hard enough to confess our sins to God, much less a friend, family member, or elder in our congregation. We cave to the pressure to appear perfect, put together, polished, sinless. "People who have it all together don't confess their sin because they don't have sin to confess." What a brilliant lie Satan convinces us to believe. If we all think we have to look perfect, we'll never confess our sins and, therefore, never receive the healing we need.

What if we called the lie what it is? What if we chose to confess up to God but also out to others? What if we created a culture of confession in our churches where it was safe to share our sins because we knew we would be met with empathy and forgiveness rather than judgment or shame? Our faith communities are meant to be havens, not prisons. We free ourselves, and those around us, when we confess and trust that God's grace will catch us.

WEEKLY BIBLE STUDY

READ: PSALM 32:1–11 AND JAMES 5:13–20

1. What does David write about the power of confession in Psalm 32:1–2? What does this reveal that he had learned about repentance?

2. How does David describe the inner turmoil he experienced when he kept silent about his sins? How did God lead him to confession (see verses 3–5)?

3. What imagery does David use in verse 9 to describe those who do not follow God's guidance—including his instruction to repent?

4. What do you read in James 5:13–15 about the power of praying with your fellow brothers and sisters in Christ? What is the result of a prayer offered in faith?

5. Why do you think James advises you to confess your sins to other believers and to pray for each other (see verse 16)? What is the promise contained in this verse?

6. What does James add about a believer in Christ who has wandered from the truth (see verses 19–20)? What does this say about your role in the church?

7. What are some of the ways that God has made you aware of the sin in your life? What have you learned about the power of confession and repentance? How has it changed you?

Week 45: THE LIST OF YOUR FAULTS

Dare we think of the list God could compile if he were to tally up the faults in our hearts? After all, he has taken up residence there.

The door hinges to the prayer room have grown rusty from underuse. The stove called jealousy is overheating. The attic floor is weighted with too many regrets. The cellar is cluttered with too many secrets. And won't someone raise the shutter and chase out the pessimism?

The list of our weaknesses. Would you like anyone to see yours? Would you like them made public? How would you feel if they were posted high so that everyone, including Christ himself, could see? May I take you to the moment when they were?

Oh yes, there is a list of your failures. Christ has chronicled your shortcomings. And, yes, that list has been made public. But you've never seen it. Neither have I.

Come with me to the hill of Calvary and I'll tell you why. Watch as the soldiers shove the Carpenter to the ground and stretch his arms against the beams. One presses a knee against a forearm and a spike against a hand. Jesus turns his face toward the nail just as the soldier lifts the hammer to strike it.

Couldn't Jesus have stopped him? With a flex of the biceps, with a clench of the fist, he could have resisted. Is this not the same hand that stilled the sea? Cleansed the temple? Summoned the dead?

But the fist doesn't clench . . . and the moment isn't aborted. The mallet rings and the skin rips and the blood begins to drip, then rush. Then the questions follow. Why? Why didn't Jesus resist? "Because he loved us," we reply. That is true, wonderfully true, but—forgive me—only partially true. There is more to his reason. He saw something that made him stay.

As the soldier pressed his arm, Jesus rolled his head to the side, and with his cheek resting on the wood he saw:

A mallet? Yes.

A nail? Yes.

The soldier's hand? Yes.

But he saw something else. He saw the hand of God. It appeared to be the hand of a man. Long fingers of a woodworker. Calloused palms of a carpenter. It appeared common. It was, however, anything but.

These fingers formed Adam out of clay and furrowed truth into tablets. With a wave, this hand toppled Babel's tower and split the Red Sea. From this hand flew the locusts that plagued Egypt and the ravens that fed Elijah. Is it any wonder the psalmist celebrated liberation by declaring, "You drove out the nations with Your hand. . . . It was Your right hand, Your arm, and the light of Your countenance" (Psalm 44:2–3 NKJV)?

The hand of God is a mighty hand.

Oh, the hands of Jesus. Hands of incarnation at his birth. Hands of liberation as he healed. Hands of inspiration as he taught. Hands of dedication as he served.

And hands of salvation as he died.

The crowd at the cross concluded that the purpose of the pounding was to skewer the hands of Christ to a beam. But they were only half-right. We can't fault them for missing the other half. They couldn't see it. But Jesus could. And heaven could. And we can.

Through the eyes of Scripture, we see what others missed but what Jesus saw. "He canceled the record of the charges against us and took it away by nailing it to the cross" (Colossians 2:14 NLT).

Between his hand and the wood, there was a list. A long list. A list of our mistakes: our lusts and lies and greedy moments and prodigal years. A list of our sins. Dangling from the cross is an itemized catalog of *your* sins. The bad decisions from last year. The bad attitudes from last week. There, in broad daylight for all of heaven to see, is a list of your mistakes.

God has penned a list of our faults. The list God has made, however, cannot be read. The words can't be deciphered. The mistakes are covered. The sins are hidden. Those at the top are hidden by his hand; those down the list are covered by his blood. "He has forgiven you all your sins: Christ has utterly wiped out the damning evidence of broken laws and commandments which always hung over our heads, and has completely annulled it by nailing it over his own head on the cross" (Colossians 2:14 PHILLIPS).

This is why he refused to close his fist. He saw the list! What kept him from resisting? This warrant, this tabulation of your failures. He knew the price of those sins was death. He knew the source of those sins was you, and since he couldn't bear the thought of eternity without you, he chose the nails.

The hand squeezing the handle was not a Roman infantryman. The force behind the hammer was not an angry mob. The verdict behind the death was not decided by jealous Jews. Jesus himself chose the nails.

So the hands of Jesus opened up. Had the soldier hesitated, Jesus himself would have swung the mallet. He knew how; he was no stranger to the driving of nails. As a carpenter he knew what it took. And as a Savior he knew what it meant. He knew that the purpose of the nail was to place your sins where they could be hidden by his sacrifice and covered by his blood.

So Jesus himself swung the hammer. The same hand that stilled the seas stills your guilt. The same hand that cleansed the temple cleanses your heart. The hand is the hand of God.

The nail is the nail of God.

And as the hands of Jesus opened for the nail, the doors of heaven opened for you.

THE HEART OF THE MATTER

- The list of your sins has been made public—but no one has ever seen it.
- Jesus could have escaped the cross, but he saw something that made him stay.
- He couldn't bear the thought of eternity without you, so he chose the nails.
- Your sins have been hidden by his sacrifice and covered by his blood.

MEMORY VERSE

Your memory verse for this unit is James 5:16. Take a few moments to review this verse, and then write it out from memory in the space below.

After God's Own Heart

The sin you've confessed but that still replays in your head? Nailed to the cross. The sin from years ago that you question is forgiven? Nailed to the cross. The sin you committed against your own loved one who still isn't speaking to you? Nailed to the cross.

Dangling from the cross is an itemized catalog of your sins. But the words can't be deciphered, for the sins have been covered by the blood of Christ. Those who repent have the assurance that Jesus "purifies us from all sin" (1 John 1:7).

Do you believe this—that your confessed sins have a permanent place not on your conscience but on Jesus' cross? This trust in God's forgiveness will transform you. Confession will become not a monthly event but a way of life. Though we are quick to sin, we can be quick to confess because we are confident that our confession will be met with total forgiveness.

WEEKLY BIBLE STUDY

READ: ROMANS 6:15–23 AND COLOSSIANS 2:9–15

1. It is important to understand that sinning against God comes at a cost. What does Paul write in Romans 6:15–16 about choosing to be an obedient slave to sin?

2. What is Paul saying about the power that sin can have over us? What enables a person to instead become a slave to righteousness (see verse 17–18)?

3. What does Paul say about those who are slaves to sin? What does he say about those who choose the path of righteousness (see verses 19–23)?

4. Something powerful occurs when a person repents of sin and finds salvation in Christ. What does Paul say about this in Colossians 2:9–12?

5. When Jesus willingly chose to go to the cross for our sake, what transaction occurred?

6. Who does Paul say Jesus disarmed when all of this took place at the cross? Why is this important for every believer in Christ to recognize?

7. What is your prayer of thanksgiving to Jesus when you consider the list of your sins that were nailed to the cross? Take a few moments to write this out today.

Week 46: AMAZING GRACE

"So Jacob was left alone, and a man wrestled with him till daybreak. When the man saw that he could not overpower him, he touched the socket of Jacob's hip so that his hip was wrenched as he wrestled with the man" (Genesis 32:24–25).

I can identify with Jacob. I, too, have a limp.

I find great inspiration in the stories of other Bible heroes. Joseph and Daniel are wunderkinds and overachievers. The apostle John and Mary are the stuff of sages and mystics. Paul is the patron saint of the theologian and philosopher. But Jacob? His story exists for the times that the Jacob within us wonders, "Can God use a person like me?"

The answer—the reassuring and resounding answer—is *yes*. Pure grace.

Grace is God's greatest idea. That he would treat us according to his heart and not ours. That he would see us and see his Son. That he would relentlessly attach himself to us in a love that no sin can sever. That he would swing the doors of heaven open to anyone who would not *impress* him but *trust* him. Amazing grace!

God does not stand on a ladder and tell us to climb it and find him. He lowers a ladder in the wilderness of our lives and finds us. He does not offer to use us if we behave. He pledges to use us, knowing all the while we will misbehave. Grace is not a gift for those who avoid the shadows of Shechem. Grace exists because none of us succeed in doing so.

God loving. God stooping. God offering. God caring and God carrying.

Do you know this grace?

Grace does for us what I did for my grandson. Denalyn and I were enjoying an afternoon chat when, from outside our back door, I heard these words: "Help! It's an emergency!"

I knew the voice because I know the girl. Rosie, our granddaughter. She was one month shy of six years, redheaded, blue-eyed, and in that moment sounded very urgent.

Rosie and her three-year-old brother, Max Wesley, were engaged in their favorite pastime, rock collecting. No need to spend money on toys for this duo. Just turn them loose in the open field behind our house so they can search for glittering, sparkly stones.

As we hurried out the back door, Jenna asked Rosie, "What happened?"

"Max can't stand up!"

I assumed the worst. Rattlesnake bite. A tumble into the ravine.

"Why can't he stand up?"

"He loaded rocks in his pockets. His pants fell down to his ankles. He's stuck and can't stand up."

We stopped, looked at each other, and smiled.

"Looks like a sermon illustration in the making," Denalyn told me.

She was right. It was an illustration deluxe. Little Max could not stand up. He was plopped on the path. His knees were drawn to his chest. His jeans were down to his ankles. The only thing separating his rear from the asphalt was his Spiderman underwear.

Each pocket was laden with rocks. Side pockets, rear pockets, all four pockets made heavy with stones.

"Do you need help?" I asked.

He said, "Yes." He let me help him remove the unnecessary loads one by one, rock by rock, weight by weight. Next thing you know he hitched up his jeans and began to play again.

What keeps you from rising up? What entangles your feet?

What prevents you from moving forward? What load pilfers your peace?

Would you follow Max's example?

Max trusted us.

Won't you trust the grace of God?

Like Jacob, you struggle. Yet like Jacob, you are never disqualified by your struggles. "But we have this treasure in earthen vessels, that the excellence of the power may be of God and not of us" (2 Corinthians 4:7 NKJV).

Your treasure? A birthright. A spiritual heritage and destiny. Yet these earthen vessels don't match our treasure. We have minds that wander. Bodies that age. Hearts that doubt. Eyes that lust. Convictions that crumble. We crack under pressure. Our porcelain has fissures. Who wants to use a broken vessel? God does. God does great things through brokenness. Broken soil gives crops. Broken eggs give life. Broken skies give rain. Broken crayons still color. Broken cocoons give flight. Broken alabaster jars give fragrance. The broken bread of the Eucharist gives hope. The broken body of Christ on the cross is the light of the world.

Which is precisely the point. God does great things through the greatly broken. It's not the strength of the vessel that matters; it's the strength of the One who can use it.

You are not the sum of your sins. You are the sum of Jesus' death, burial, and resurrection. "God made him who had no sin to be sin for us, so that in him we might become the righteousness of God" (2 Corinthians 5:21). You "give off a sweet scent rising to God, which is recognized by those on the way of salvation—an aroma redolent with life" (2:15 MSG).

You don't have to be strong to be saved. You don't have to be perfect to be redeemed. You don't have to score straight A's. You simply need to trust in the God of Jacob—a God who sticks with the unworthy and the underachievers until they are safely home. He is the God of second chances and new beginnings. The God of grace.

And he never gives up on you.

THE HEART OF THE MATTER

- Jacob's story exists for the times you ask, "Can God use a person like me?"
- God lowers a ladder in the wilderness of your life and finds you.
- You, like Jacob, struggle, but you are never *disqualified* by your struggles.
- God's relentless grace offers second chances and new beginnings to the unworthy.

MEMORY VERSE

Your memory verse for this unit is James 5:16. Take a few moments to review this verse, and then write it out from memory in the space below.

After God's Own Heart

It has been said to "never trust a leader without a limp." After Jacob wrestled with God, he was left with a limp—a constant reminder that God can, and will, humble those who trust in their own strength, cunning, and skill. It's not a stretch to say this was a turning point in Jacob's life. Encounters with God's grace always have a way of changing our hearts.

Jacob's limp didn't disqualify him for God's service. It didn't nullify the covenant he made with Jacob at Bethel. It didn't remove him from the list of patriarchs. On the contrary, Jacob's limp became a part of his enduring testimony of what the Lord had done for him. It was a reminder that God can, and will, work through imperfect vessels.

We all carry limps. We bear the marks of our struggles, failures, and brokenness. Those marks represent where God's mercy and love have shone the brightest in our lives. If we allow God to use them, our testimony will serve as a powerful message of his grace to others.

WEEKLY BIBLE STUDY

READ: GENESIS 32:9–32 AND 2 CORINTHIANS 4:1–12

1. What did Jacob acknowledge about himself in his prayer to the Lord (see Genesis 32:9–10)? What was the cause of his immediate distress (see verses 11–12)?

2. What happened after Jacob sent his family and all of his possessions across the River Jabbok? How did Jacob end up with a limp (see verses 22–25)?

3. Jacob's name literally meant "he grasps the heel," a Hebrew idiom for "he deceives." What new name did God give to him—and what did it mean (see verses 26–28)?

4. In 2 Corinthians 4:1–2, what does Paul say that followers of Jesus have renounced and no longer do? What "new name" have you been given in Christ?

5. You, like Jacob, are never disqualified because of your struggles. What does Paul say you have within you? What are you in God's sight (see verses 5–7)?

6. You will be hard-pressed at times in your life. In spite of this, what promise does Paul say you can carry with you throughout your days (see verses 8–12)?

7. What does the story of Jacob reveal about the types of people that God will use for his service? How does this specifically give you encouragement today?

Week 47: A GRACE-SHAPED HEART

Some years ago I underwent a heart procedure. My heartbeat had the regularity of a telegraph operator sending Morse code. Fast, fast, fast. Sloooow.

After several failed attempts to restore healthy rhythm with medication, my doctor decided I should have a catheter ablation. The plan went like this: A cardiologist would insert two cables into my heart via a blood vessel. One was a camera; the other was an ablation tool. To ablate is to burn. Yes, burn, cauterize, singe, brand. If all went well, the doctor, to use his coinage, would destroy the "misbehaving" parts of my heart.

As I was being wheeled into surgery, he asked if I had any final questions. (Not the best choice of words.) I tried to be witty.

"You're burning the interior of my heart, right?"

"Correct."

"You intend to kill the misbehaving cells, yes?"

"That is my plan."

"As long as you are in there, could you take your little blowtorch to some of my greed, selfishness, superiority, and guilt?"

He smiled and answered, "Sorry, that's out of my pay grade."

Indeed it was, but it's not out of God's. He is in the business of changing hearts.

We would be wrong to think this change happens overnight. But we would be equally wrong to assume change never happens at all. It may come in fits and spurts—an "aha" here, a breakthrough there. But it comes. "The grace of God that brings salvation has appeared" (Titus 2:11 NKJV). The floodgates are open, and you just never know when grace will seep in.

Grace. We talk as though we understand the term. The bank gives us a *grace* period. The seedy politician falls from *grace*. Musicians speak of a *grace* note. We describe an actress as *gracious*, a dancer as *graceful*. We use the word for hospitals, baby girls, kings, and premeal prayers. We talk as though we know what *grace* means.

Especially at church. *Grace* graces the songs we sing and the Bible verses we read. *Grace* shares the church parsonage with its cousins: *forgiveness*, *faith*, and *fellowship*. Preachers explain it. Hymns proclaim it. Seminaries teach it.

But do we really understand it?

Here's my hunch: We've settled for wimpy grace. It politely occupies a phrase in a hymn, fits nicely on a church sign. Never causes trouble or demands a response. When asked, "Do you believe in grace?" who could say no?

The deeper question is whether you have been *changed* by grace—shaped by it, emboldened by it, softened by it. Have you been snatched by the nape of your neck and shaken to your senses by grace? God's grace has a drenching about it. A wildness about it. A white-water, riptide, turn-you-upside-downness about it. Grace comes after you. It rewires you.

When grace happens, you receive not a nice compliment from God but a new heart. Give your heart to Christ, and he returns the favor. "I will give you a new heart and put a new spirit within you" (Ezekiel 36:26 NKJV). You might call it a spiritual heart transplant.

Tara Storch understands this miracle as much as anyone can. A skiing accident took the life of her thirteen-year-old daughter, Taylor. What followed for Tara and her husband, Todd, was every parent's worst nightmare: a funeral, a burial, a flood of questions and tears. They decided to donate their daughter's organs to needy patients.

Few people needed a heart more than Patricia Winters. Her heart had begun to fail five years earlier, leaving her too weak to do much more than sleep. Taylor's heart gave Patricia a fresh start on life. Tara had only one request: She wanted to hear the heart of her daughter. She and Todd flew from Dallas to Phoenix and went to Patricia's home to listen to Taylor's heart.

The two mothers embraced for a long time. Then Patricia offered Tara and Todd a stethoscope.[41] When they listened to the healthy rhythm, did they not hear the still-beating heart of their daughter? It indwelt a different body, but the heart was the heart of their child. And when God hears your heart, does he not hear the still-beating heart of his Son?

As Paul said, "It is no longer I who live, but Christ lives in me" (Galatians 2:20 NKJV). The apostle sensed within himself not just the philosophy, ideals, or influence of Christ but the person of Jesus. Christ had moved in. He still does. When grace happens, Christ enters. "Christ in you, the hope of glory" (Colossians 1:27 NKJV).

Grace is God as heart surgeon cracking open your chest, removing your heart—poisoned as it is with pride and pain—and replacing it with his own. His dream isn't just to get you into heaven but to get heaven into you. What a difference this makes! Can't forgive your enemy? Can't forgive your past? Christ can, and he is on the move, budging you from graceless to grace-shaped living. Forgiven people forgiving people. Stumbles aplenty but despair seldom.

Grace lives because Jesus does, works because he works, and matters because he matters. He placed a term limit on sin and danced a victory jig in a graveyard. To be saved by grace is to be saved by him—not by an idea, doctrine, creed, or church membership—but by Jesus himself, who will sweep into heaven anyone who so much as gives him the nod.

If you fear you've written too many checks on God's kindness account, drag regrets around like a broken bumper, huff and puff more than you delight and rest, and wonder whether God can do something with the mess of your life, then grace is what you need.

Let's make certain it happens to you.

THE HEART OF THE MATTER

- For as much as we use the word *grace*, we often misunderstand its meaning.
- We settle for wimpy grace—one that never causes trouble or demands a response.
- Grace is God removing your heart and replacing it with his own.
- Jesus is on the move, budging you from graceless to grace-shaped living.

MEMORY VERSE

Your memory verse for this unit is James 5:16. Take a few moments to review this verse, and then write it out from memory in the space below.

After God's Own Heart

Checking your bag at the airport requires trust. You hand your suitcase over to the airline attendant and believe it will be waiting for you when you arrive at your destination. Is this trust well-founded? The research suggests yes. Only a fraction of luggage—less than one percent—are deemed permanently lost or stolen each year.

In the same way that checking a bag requires trust, so does repentance. When you hand your baggage (your sins) over to God, you believe that he will wipe them from your record and create in you a new heart. You trust that God's grace is enough. You don't repent and then work to try and make up for your sins. No, you recognize that grace is enough.

Is this trust in God's goodness well-founded? Well, the Bible reveals that his record is flawless. He has never once failed to deliver on his promise of forgiving sins that are entrusted to him through confession. For this reason, we trust God when he says, "We have been made holy through the sacrifice of the body of Jesus Christ once for all" (Hebrews 10:10).

WEEKLY BIBLE STUDY

READ: EZEKIEL 36:24–32 AND GALATIANS 2:15–21

1. Ezekiel 36:24–32 contains a promise from God about the restoration of his people. What type of cleansing does he say he will do (see verses 25–26)?

2. What does the Lord say about the new heart and spirit that he will put in his people? What will this "spiritual surgery" allow them to do (see verses 27–28)?

3. What will the new heart and spirit that God puts into his people allow them to remember about their former practices (see verses 31–32)?

4. The word justified means to be made righteous in the sight of God. According to the apostle Paul, what makes a person justified (see Galatians 2:15–16)?

5. What kind of death does Paul say he experienced as a result of receiving a new heart in Christ? What does it mean to be crucified with Christ (see verses 19–20)?

6. Paul concludes, "I no longer live, but Christ lives in me" (verse 20). How should this reality shape how you see both yourself and how you see others?

7. As you look back on your life, what evidence do you see of God giving you a grace-shaped heart? How are you actively showing God's mercy to others?

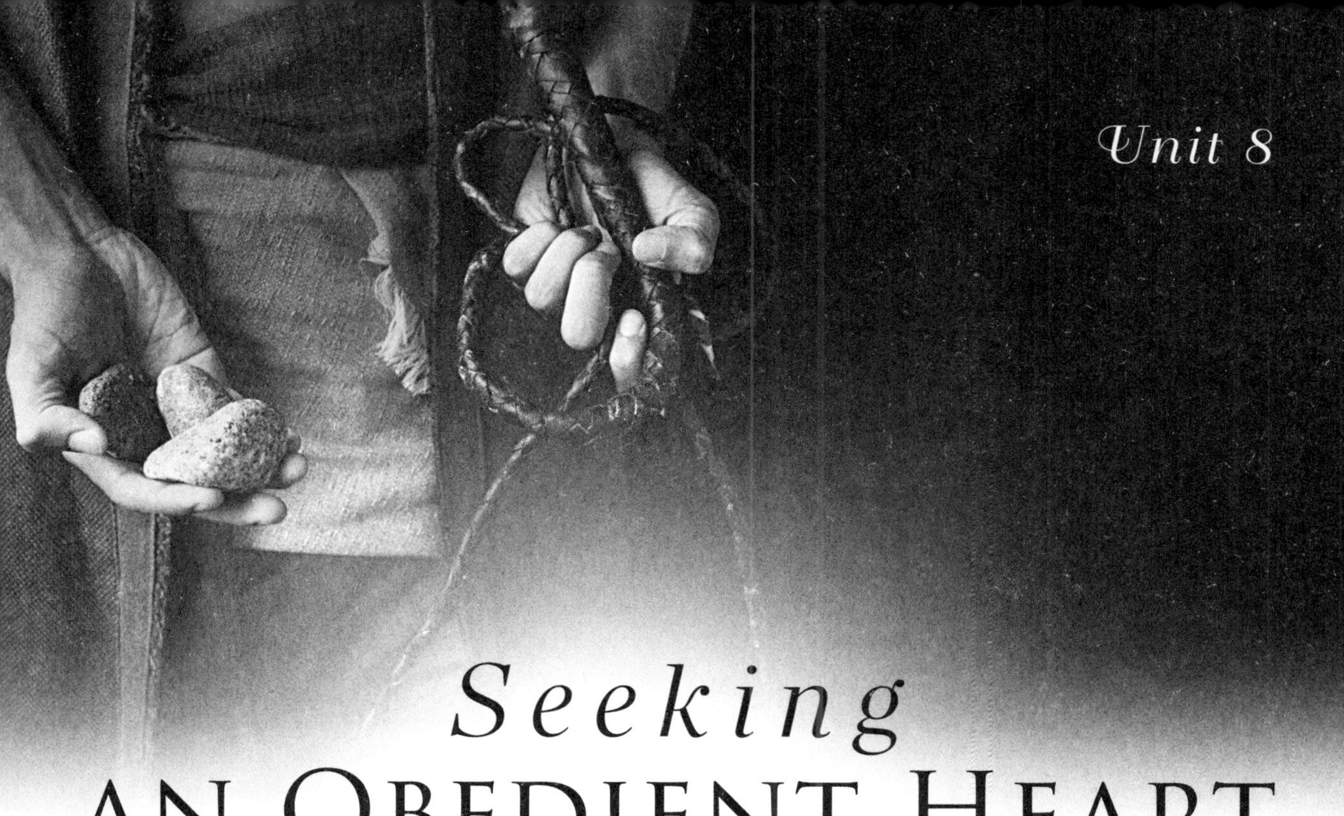

Unit 8

Seeking AN OBEDIENT HEART

WEEK 48: A CONJUNCTION IN LIFE
WEEK 49: THE VOICE YOU HEED
WEEK 50: EARS TO HEAR
WEEK 51: GOD'S WAITING ROOM
WEEK 52: IT BEGAN IN BETHLEHEM

Back when Moses was preparing the Israelites to enter into the promised land, he said to them, "These commandments that I give you today are to be on your hearts. Impress them on your children. Talk about them when you sit at home and when you walk along the road, when you lie down and when you get up" (Deuteronomy 6:6–7).

David knew the commands of the Lord. He had impressed them on his heart, even declaring, "The law of the LORD is perfect, refreshing the soul" (Psalm 19:7). But we have to wonder how much effort he took in impressing God's commands on his *children*.

Thirteen years have passed since Nathan told him, "The sword will never depart from your house" (2 Samuel 12:10). The prophecy has proven painfully true. One of David's sons, Amnon, fell in lust with his half-sister Tamar, one of David's daughters by another marriage. Amnon pined, plotted, and raped her. After the rape, he discarded Tamar like a worn doll.

Tamar, understandably, came undone. "[She] remained desolate in her brother Absalom's house" (13:20 NKJV). The next verse tells us David's response: "When King David heard of all these things, he was very angry" (verse 21 NKJV).

That's it? That's all? Nothing? No lecture, no penalty, no imprisonment, no dressing down, no chewing out? No . . . David did *nothing* to Amnon. And, even worse, he did nothing for Tamar. She needed a dad. What she got was silence. So Absalom, her brother, filled the void. He sheltered his sister, plotted to get Amnon drunk, and had him killed.

Again it was time for David to step up. His family needed to see the best of him. But they saw none of David. He didn't intervene or respond. He wept in solitude. David did so much so well. But when it came to his family, he blew it.

The seeds of bitterness in Absalom spread deep roots. He resolved to overthrow his father. He recruited from David's army and staged a coup. His takeover set the stage for David's sad walk out of Jerusalem—up the Mount of Olives and into the wilderness. No crown. No city. Just a heavy-hearted, lonely, old man.

Loyalists eventually chased Absalom down. When he tried to escape on horseback, his long hair got tangled in a tree, and soldiers speared him. David heard the news and fell to pieces: "O my son Absalom—my son, my son Absalom—if only I had died in your place!" (18:33 NKJV). Tardy tears. David succeeded everywhere except at home.

David would be restored as the king of Israel. He would later say to Solomon, his son and heir, "Observe what the LORD your God requires: Walk in obedience to him, and keep his decrees and commands, his laws and regulations, as written in the Law of Moses" (1 Kings 2:3). Sound advice . . . that his other children would have benefitted from hearing.

Don't make the same mistake. Impress God's commands on your heart. Obey his commands. But don't forget to impress those commands on those who follow after—with your words, your time, and your example. In the words of Paul, "Do not exasperate your children; instead, bring them up in the training and instruction of the Lord" (Ephesians 6:4).

— PRAYER —

Father, your ways are higher than mine. You have called me to follow you, but some days I choose my own way. Give me a heart of obedience. May I desire to do your will because of the grace I've received rather than as an attempt to earn it. May I remember that your way is best. And let my life be an example of obedience to those who follow after me. Amen.

— MEMORY VERSE —

Blessed are all who fear the LORD, who walk in obedience to him.

PSALM 128:1

Week 48: A CONJUNCTION IN LIFE

"*I had intended . . .*" The David who speaks the words is old. The hands that swung the sling hang limp. The feet that danced before the ark now shuffle. Though his eyes are still sharp, his hair is gray, and skin sags beneath his beard.

"*I had intended to . . .*" A large throng listens. Courtiers, counselors, chamberlains, and caretakers. They've assembled at David's command. The king is tired. The time for his departure is near. They listen closely as he speaks.

"*I had intended to build . . .*" Odd way to start a farewell speech. David mentions not what he did but what he wanted to do yet couldn't.

"I had intended to build a permanent home for the ark of the covenant of the LORD and for the footstool of our God" (1 Chronicles 28:2 NASB).

A temple. David had wanted to build a temple. What he had done for Israel, he wanted to do for the ark—protect it. What he had done with Jerusalem, he wanted to do with the temple—establish it. And who better than he to do so? Hadn't he, literally, written the book on worship? Didn't he rescue the ark of the covenant? The temple would have been his swan song, his signature deed. David had expected to dedicate his final years to building a shrine to God.

At least, that had been his intention.

"So I had made preparations to build it" (verse 2 NASB).

Preparations. Architects chosen. Builders selected. Blueprints and plans, drawings and numbers. Temple columns sketched. Steps designed.

Intentions. Preparations. But no temple. Why? Did David grow discouraged? No. He stood willing. Were the people resistant? Hardly. They gave generously. Were the resources scarce? Far from it. David "supplied more bronze than could be weighed, and . . . more cedar logs than could be counted" (22:3–4 NCV). Then what happened?

A conjunction happened.

Conjunctions operate as the signal lights of sentences. Some, such as *and*, are green. Others, such as *however*, are yellow. A few are red. Sledgehammer red. They stop you. David got a red light. "I had made preparations to build it. *But* God said to me, 'You shall not build a house for My name because you are a man of war and have shed blood. . . . Your son Solomon is the one who shall build My house and My courtyards" (28:2–3, 6 NASB, emphasis added).

David's bloodthirsty temperament cost him the temple privilege. All he could do was say, "I had intended . . . I had made preparations . . . *But* God . . ."

Willem was a man who uttered similar words. By the age of twenty-five, he knew he was made for the ministry. He sold art, taught language, and traded in books. He made a living, but it wasn't a life. His life was in the church. His passion was with the people.

So his passion took him to the coalfields of southern Belgium. There, in the spring of 1879, this Dutchman began to minister to the hardworking miners of Borinage. Within weeks his passion was tested. A mining disaster injured scores of villagers. Willem nursed the wounded and fed the hungry, even scraping the slag heaps to give his people fuel.

After the rubble was cleared and the dead were buried, the young preacher had earned a place in their hearts. The tiny church overflowed with people hungry for his simple messages of love. Young Willem was doing what he'd always dreamed of doing.

But . . . one day his superior came to visit. Willem's lifestyle shocked him. The young preacher wore an old soldier's coat. His trousers were cut from sacking, and he lived in a simple hut. "You look more pitiful than the people you came to teach," the church official said. Willem asked if Jesus wouldn't have done the same. The older man would have none of it. This was not the proper appearance for a minister. He dismissed Willem from the ministry.

The young man was devastated. He only wanted to build a church. He only wanted to honor God. Why wouldn't God let him do this work?

"I had intended . . . I had made preparations . . . *But* God . . ."

What do you do with the "but God" moments in life? When God interrupts your good plans, how do you respond? When God changed David's plans, how did he reply?

"Yet, the Lord, the God of Israel, chose me from all the household of my father to be king over Israel forever" (1 Chronicles 28:4 NASB). David followed the "but God" with a "yet God."

Reduce this to a phrase and it reads, "Who am I to complain?" David had gone from runt to royalty, from herding sheep to leading armies, from sleeping in the pasture to living in the palace. When you are given an ice cream sundae, you don't complain over a missing cherry. David faced the behemoth of disappointment with "yet God." He trusted and obeyed.

So did Willem. Initially, he was hurt and angry. He lingered in the small village, not knowing where to turn. But one afternoon he noticed an old miner bending beneath an enormous weight of coal. Caught by the poignancy of the moment, Willem began to sketch the weary figure. His first attempt was crude, but then he tried again. He didn't know it, but at that very moment, Willem discovered his true calling.

Not the robe of clergy, but the frock of an artist. Not the pulpit of a pastor, but the palette of a painter. Not the ministry of words, but of images. The young man the leader would not accept became an artist the world could not resist: Vincent Willem van Gogh.[42] In obedience, he found his true calling. His "but God" became a "yet God."

Who's to say yours won't become the same?

THE HEART OF THE MATTER

- Conjunctions are the signal lights of sentences. Some are red . . . they stop you.
- You have a choice in how to react when you encounter "but God" moments.
- When you respond in obedience, God leads you where he wants you to go.
- Respond to setbacks with "yet God" and trust his wisdom in all things.

MEMORY VERSE

Your memory verse for this unit is Psalm 128:1. Take a few moments to review this verse, and then write it out from memory in the space below.

After God's Own Heart

Put yourself in David's sandals for a moment. You've worked hard to get where you are. You've overcome people's doubts in you and envy of you. At each fork, you've asked God where to go and credited each success to him. You've been an obedient shepherd of God's people.

But there's one thing you haven't accomplished. A dream you made decades before in your reign that hasn't been fulfilled. You wanted to build a temple for the Lord. Not for *you*. Not a memorial to *your* success. A memorial for God! And what did God say? *No.*

David could have questioned, doubted, and ignored God's response. He could have just proceed with his plan. Who would know it wasn't divinely sanctioned? Yet a lifetime of faithful service had taught him that wasn't the way. He and God had a history. So, as hard as it was, he did what his grace-shaped heart told him that he must. He chose to obey.

WEEKLY BIBLE STUDY

READ: 1 CHRONICLES 28:1–10 AND EPHESIANS 2:8–10

1. What did King David announce to all the officials of Israel regarding the plans he had made to build the temple (see 1 Chronicles 28:1–2)?

2. What had God said to David when he made those plans (see verses 3, 5–7)? What charge was David now giving to Solomon "in the sight of all Israel" (verse 8)?

3. What did David choose to remember about God in spite of this disappointment (see verse 4)? How did David prove that his heart was obedient to the Lord?

4. What was Solomon's role in taking up this task of building the temple? What would be the consequences if he was not obedient toward God (see verses 9–10)?

5. What does the apostle Paul say that believers in Christ should remember when it comes to considering the blessings they have received (see Ephesians 2:8–9)?

6. What does Paul say about the reason as to why you were created (see verse 10)? How can this help you to submit your plans to the Lord?

7. What are some of the plans you have made that God has altered or told you not to pursue? Looking back, why do you think God directed you in the way he did?

Week 49: THE VOICE YOU HEED

I had a dog, named Andy, who ran away one time. A neighbor had tipped me off to a great place for dogs to romp and run. So I told Andy about it.

"Andy, I know of a dog's dream come true. It's a creek bed with a wide meadow. No cars. No fences. No leashes. Just stuff to sniff and trees to wet and crevices to explore."

"Oh, Master Max," he barked, "you put the wow in *bowwow.* That sounds like the doggy version of the promised land."

"Indeed it is. A canine promised land. But let me warn you. You must stay close to me. This pasture is several miles from our home. Deer will entice. Rabbits will lure. There may even be a seductive poodle on the path. You must stay alert. Heed my voice. Stay with me."

"I will," he yelped.

But did he? No. The moment I let him out of the car and unleashed him, he ran. He dashed through a grove of trees and scampered up a twenty-foot-tall bluff.

"Andy!" I shouted. He stopped and looked down at me. He had a moral dilemma. On one side he heard the luring voices of the pasture. The wild life beckoned, "Come on, Andy. Let's have fun." On the other side he heard the voice of his wise, seasoned, and very handsome master: "Come here, Andy."

He looked my way. Then away. My way, then away. And then in a flash he was gone.

My first thought was, *Denalyn is going to kill me.*

I ran after him, but he ran faster. "My next dog is going to be a basset hound," I resolved. My voice grew hoarse from yelling and my legs grew weak from climbing. It took me forty-five minutes to find him. Finally, there he was. Lying beneath a tree. Exhausted, thirsty, and, can I say, repentant. "Go ahead," he offered. "Use me in your book. I entered the promised land, but I failed to heed my master's voice."

When the Israelites were preparing to enter the promised land, God was also concerned they would fail to heed his voice. Canaan was full of new, strange, alluring voices. Hence, the pre-promised land caution: "Be careful to obey all the law my servant Moses gave you; do not turn from it to the right or to the left, that you may be successful wherever you go. Keep this Book of the Law always on your lips; meditate on it day and night, so that you may be careful to do everything written in it" (Joshua 1:7–8).

God was calling Joshua to lead two million ex-slaves into Canaan to inherit their inheritance. He was equipping their general for the mission of a lifetime. And what command did God give Joshua? Read the Word of God.

Like you and me, Joshua had a Bible. His Bible had five books—Genesis, Exodus, Leviticus, Numbers, and at least portions of Deuteronomy—which were carried alongside the ark of the covenant. But it wasn't enough for Joshua to possess the Scriptures; God wanted the Scriptures to possess Joshua. "Keep this Book of the Law always on your lips" (verse 8).

This was God's command to the commander of Israel. Though he was the unquestioned five-star general of the army, Joshua was subject to God's law. God did not tell him to create law or invent statutes but to be regulated by what was "written."

Notice that the Lord also told Joshua, "Meditate on it day and night" (verse 8). Literally, "you shall . . . mutter over this torah document."[43] The image is one of a person reciting, rehearsing, reconsidering God's Word over and over again. Canaan is loud with enemy voices. The devil megaphones doubt and death into our ears. Take heed to the voice you heed.

"Let the word of Christ dwell in you richly in all wisdom, teaching and admonishing one another" (Colossians 3:16 NKJV). Chew it. Swallow it. Speak it.

Great rewards come to those who do. God promised Joshua, "You will make your way prosperous, and then you will have good success" (Joshua 1:8 NKJV). This is the only place in the Old Testament where the words *prosperous* and *success* are found together. This is an emphasized promise. Align yourself with God's Word and expect prosperity and success.

Don't cringe. Joshua 1:8 isn't a guarantee of early retirement. In the United States we often associate prosperity and success with money. The Bible is not so narrow. Its promise of prosperity *occasionally* includes money, but it far more often refers to a wealthy spirit, mind, and body. God prospers the leader with new skills, the worker with good sleep, the teacher with added patience, the mother with deeper affection, the elderly with greater hope. Scriptural fluency leads to spiritual affluence.

God's command was enough for Joshua. He responded with direct obedience. He told his men, "Prepare provisions for yourselves, for within three days you will cross over this Jordan, to go in to possess the land which the LORD your God is giving you to possess" (Joshua 1:11 NKJV). No hesitation. No reservation.

Do likewise. Learn a lesson from Joshua. And learn a lesson from my dog, Andy. Knowing that I would be writing about him, he spoke to me today.

"Master Max . . ." (I love it when he calls me by that title.)

"Yes, Andy."

"Can you tell your readers something for me?"

"Of course."

"Tell them that I learned my lesson. Whenever I wander too far from my master's voice, my life is ruff, ruff, ruff."

THE HEART OF THE MATTER

- You have a choice when it comes to whose voice you will heed.
- God wants his Word—the Bible—to take hold of your life.
- Meditate on God's Word daily and let it shape your decisions.
- Obey God's Word without hesitation and without reservation.

MEMORY VERSE

Your memory verse for this unit is Psalm 128:1. Take a few moments to review this verse, and then write it out from memory in the space below.

After God's Own Heart

Ancient myths told of deadly creatures called sirens who dwelt on rocky shoals and used their voices to lure sailors to their deaths. Over time, the English word *siren* came to represent a warning. Today, when you hear a siren, you know that an imminent danger is near.

God's Word serves as a warning about all the voices in this world that want to lure you to their rocky shoals. Obedience to what the Lord says thus isn't about restriction but about protection. He is sounding the call to the imminent dangers that are near.

Obedience to this "siren" requires trust. It means believing that God's way is better—as difficult as it may be—when the world promises an easy way ahead. And it involves tuning your heart to God's voice so that you can hear him in the midst of all the other voices.

WEEKLY BIBLE STUDY

READ: JOSHUA 1:1–11 AND JOHN 17:6–19

1. After the death of Moses, God commanded Joshua to lead the people into the promised land. What promise did God make to him at this time (see Joshua 1:1–5)?

2. What did God say that Joshua was to be careful to do (see verses 7–8)? Why did God need to stress this to the Israelites before they entered into Canaan?

3. Joshua not only had to *hear* God's words but also *act* on God's words. How did Joshua demonstrate he was willing to obey the Lord (see verses 10–11)?

4. God had called out the Israelites from the rest of the world. How is this similar to the way that he had called out the disciples from the world (see John 17:6–9)?

5. Jesus understood that his disciples would need to be strong and courageous after his departure. What was his prayer for them (see verses 11–12)?

6. Why did the world hate the disciples (see verses 13–14)? What does this say about the treatment you can expect from the world when you obey Christ?

7. What voices from the world are preventing you from clearly hearing God's voice? What do you need to do this week to stifle those competing voices?

Week 50: EARS TO HEAR

"Let he who has ears to hear, use them." More than once Jesus said these words. Eight times in the Gospels and eight times in the book of Revelation we are reminded that it's not enough just to have ears. It's necessary to use them.[44]

Jesus told a parable in Mark 4:1–20 in which he compared our ears to soil. He told about a farmer who scattered seed (symbolic of the Word) in four different types of ground (symbolic of our ears). Some people's ears are like a hard path—unreceptive to the seed. "As soon as they hear it, Satan comes and takes away the word that was sown in them" (verse 15).

Others have ears like rocky soil. "[They] hear the word and at once receive it with joy. But since they have no root, they last only a short time. When trouble or persecution comes because of the word, they quickly fall away" (verses 16–17).

Still others have ears akin to a weed patch—too overgrown, too thorny, with too much competition for the seed to have a chance. "Still others, like seed sown among thorns, hear the word; but the worries of this life, the deceitfulness of wealth and the desires for other things come in and choke the word, making it unfruitful" (verses 18–19).

And then there are some who have ears that hear: well-tilled, discriminate, and ready to hear God's voice. "Others, like seed sown on good soil, hear the word, accept it, and produce a crop—some thirty, some sixty, some a hundred times what was sown" (verse 20).

In all four cases the seed is the same seed. The sower is the same sower. What's different is not the message or the messenger—it's the listener. And if the ratio in the story is significant, three-fourths of the world isn't listening to God's voice. Whether the cause is hard hearts, shallow lives, or anxious minds, seventy-five percent of us are missing the message.

It's not that we don't have ears; it's that we don't use them.

Scripture has always placed a premium on hearing God's voice. Indeed, the great command from God through Moses began with the words, "Hear, O Israel: The LORD our God, the LORD is one! You shall love the LORD your God with all your heart, with all your soul, and with all your strength" (Deuteronomy 6:4–5 NKJV). Nehemiah and the people gathered in Jerusalem were commended because they were "attentive to the Book of the Law" (Nehemiah 8:3 NKJV). "Happy are those who listen to me" is the promise of Proverbs 8:34 (NCV).

Jesus urges us to learn to listen like sheep. "The shepherd walks right up to the gate. The gatekeeper opens the gate to him and the sheep recognize his voice. He calls his own sheep by name and leads them out. When he gets them all out, he leads them and they follow because they are familiar with his voice. They won't follow a stranger's voice but will scatter because they aren't used to the sound of it" (John 10:3–5 MSG).

Our ears, unlike our eyes, do not have lids. They are to remain open, but how easily they close.

Denalyn and I were shopping for luggage some time back. We found what we wanted in one store but wanted to go to another store to compare prices.

The salesclerk asked me if I wanted to take his business card. I told him, "No, your name is easy to remember, Bob."

To which he replied, "My name is Joe."

I had heard the man, but I hadn't listened.

Pilate didn't listen either. He had the classic case of ears that didn't hear. Not only did his wife warn him, "Don't do anything to that man, because he is innocent" (Matthew 27:19 NCV), but the very Word of Life stood before Pilate in his chamber and proclaimed, "Everyone who belongs to the truth listens to me" (John 18:37 NCV). But Pilate had selective hearing. He allowed the voices of the people to dominate the voices of conscience and the carpenter.

"They were urgent, demanding with loud cries that he should be crucified. And their voices prevailed" (Luke 23:23 RSV). In the end Pilate inclined his ear to the crowd and away from the Christ and ignored the message of the Messiah. "Faith comes from hearing the message" (Romans 10:17), and since Pilate didn't hear, he never found faith.

"Let he who has ears to hear, use them." How long has it been since you had your hearing checked? When God throws seed your way, what is the result?

God seems to send messages as he did his manna: one day's portion at a time. On the morning I wrote this, for example, my quiet time found me in Matthew 18. I was only four verses into the chapter when I read, "Whoever takes the lowly position of this child is the greatest in the kingdom of heaven." I needed to go no further. I copied the words in my journal and pondered them on and off during the day.

Several times I asked God, "How can I be more childlike?" By the end of the day, I was reminded of my tendency to hurry and my proclivity to worry.

Will I learn what God intends? If I listen, I will.

Don't be discouraged if your reading reaps a small harvest. Some days a lesser portion is all we need. A little girl returned from her first day at school. Her mom asked, "Did you learn anything in your classes today?" "I guess not," the girl responded. "I have to go back tomorrow and the next day and the next day . . ."

Such is the case with learning how to have a listening and obedient heart. And such is the case with Bible study. Understanding comes a little at a time over a lifetime.

THE HEART OF THE MATTER

- Hearing God's voice requires the "soil" of open, attentive, and receptive hearts.
- Jesus urges you to learn to listen to him like sheep learn to listen to the shepherd.
- God sends his messages as he did his manna: one day's portion at a time.
- Understanding God's voice comes a little at a time and over a lifetime.

MEMORY VERSE

Your memory verse for this unit is Psalm 128:1. Take a few moments to review this verse, and then write it out from memory in the space below.

After God's Own Heart

Imagine that you are standing in a quiet forest. Nearby, you hear a bird erupt in song. A cricket chirps. A frog croaks. But you're not listening for those sounds. You close your eyes. Ah, there it is . . . a gentle rustle among the leaves. The wind doesn't shout; it "whispers" like this. If you want to hear it, you have to be still, patient, and—most of all—attentive.

Jesus would often end his parables with the statement, "Whoever has ears to hear, let them hear" (Mark 4:9). Having ears to hear means not allowing the noises of life to drown out God's whispers. Worries, ambitions, busyness . . . these all cry out for our attention. But when we pause and listen for God's "gentle whisper" (1 Kings 19:12), we allow the seed of his Word to fall upon the good soil of our hearts. As a result, God's voice transforms us.

Today, quiet your heart. Listen for God's whisper. And obey what he says.

WEEKLY BIBLE STUDY

READ: MARK 4:1–20 AND JOHN 10:1–6

1. Jesus told the parable of the sower to the crowds in Mark 4:1–8. What invitation did he then give to go deeper into the meaning of the parable (see verse 9)?

2. Who took Jesus up on the offer (see verse 10)? What did Jesus say had been given to this group that the crowds had not received (see verses 11–12)?

3. What did Jesus say the seed represented in his parable? What did Jesus reveal about what the different kinds of soils represented (see verses 14–19)?

4. What did Jesus ultimately reveal about the kind of heart that accepts his word? What did Jesus say that kind of heart produces (see verse 20)?

5. What did Jesus, the "good shepherd," say in John 10:1–3 about those who have accepted his words? What do these "sheep" do to reveal that they belong to him?

6. How do these sheep of Jesus respond when they hear the voice of a stranger (see verse 5)? What does this say about the importance of hearing God's voice?

7. In what ways are you showing Jesus that you have "ears to hear" his voice? What small step can you take this week to further open up your heart to him?

Week 51: GOD'S WAITING ROOM

Here I sit in the waiting room. The receptionist took my name, recorded my insurance data, and gestured to a chair. "Please have a seat. We will call you when the doctor is ready." I look around. A mother holds a sleeping baby. A fellow dressed in a suit thumbs through a magazine. A woman looks at her watch, sighs, and continues the task of the hour: waiting.

The waiting room. Not the examination room. That's down the hall. Not the consultation room. That's on the other side of the wall. Not the treatment room. Exams, consultations, and treatments all come later.

We in the waiting room understand our assignment: to wait. We don't treat each other. I don't ask the nurse for a stethoscope or blood pressure cuff. I don't pull up a chair next to the woman with the newspaper and say, "Tell me what prescriptions you are taking." That's the job of the nurse. My job is to wait. So I do.

Can't say that I like it. Time moves like an Alaskan glacier. Someone pressed the pause button. Life in slow-mo. We don't like to wait. We are the giddy-up generation. We weave through traffic, looking for the faster lane. We frown at the person who takes eleven items into the ten-item express checkout. We drum our fingers while the song downloads or the microwave heats our coffee. "Come on, come on." We want six-pack abs in ten minutes and minute rice in thirty seconds. We don't like to wait. Not on the doctor, the traffic, or the pizza.

Not on God?

Take a moment and look around you. Do you realize where we sit? This planet is God's waiting room. The young couple in the corner? Waiting to get pregnant. The fellow with the briefcase? He has résumés all over the country, waiting on work. The elderly woman with the cane? A widow. Been waiting a year for one tearless day. Waiting on God to give, help, heal. We indwell the land betwixt prayer offered and prayer answered. The land of waiting.

Paul wrote, "God is always at work for the good of everyone who loves him" (Romans 8:28 CEV). To wait, biblically speaking, is not to assume the worst, worry, fret, make demands, or take control. Nor is waiting inactivity. Waiting is a sustained effort to stay focused on God through prayer and belief. It requires action . . . and obedience.

Nehemiah provides us with an example of how to do this. His book is a memoir of his efforts to reconstruct the walls of Jerusalem. His story starts with a date. "It happened in the month of Chislev, in the twentieth year, as I was in Susa the citadel, that Hanani . . . came with certain men from Judah" (Nehemiah 1:1–2 ESV). They brought bad news. Hostile forces had flattened the walls that had once guarded the city. Even the gates had been burned. The few remaining Jews were in "great trouble and shame" (verse 3 ESV).

Nehemiah responded with prayer. "O LORD, let your ear be attentive to the prayer of your servant . . . and give success to your servant today, and grant him mercy in the sight of this man" (verse 11 ESV). This "man" was King Artaxerxes, the monarch of Persia. Nehemiah was his personal cupbearer, on call twenty-four hours a day, seven days a week. Nehemiah could not leave his post and go to Jerusalem. Even if he could, he had no resources with which to rebuild the walls. So he resolved to wait on the Lord in prayer.

The first verse of the second chapter reveals the length of his wait. "In the month of Nisan" Nehemiah was appointed to a spot on the king's Jerusalem Commission. How far apart were the dates? Four months. Nehemiah's request, remember, was immediate: "Give your servant success today." God answered the request four months (!) after Nehemiah made it.

And what of this command? "Three times a year all your men are to appear before the Sovereign LORD, the God of Israel. I will drive out nations before you and enlarge your territory, and no one will covet your land when you go up three times each year to appear before the LORD your God" (Exodus 34:23–24). God instructed the promised land settlers to stop their work three times a year and gather for worship. All commerce, education, government, and industry came to a halt while the people assembled. Can you imagine this happening today?

Yet God promised to protect the territory. No one would encroach upon the Israelites. What's more, they wouldn't even desire to do so. "No one will covet your land." God used the pilgrimage to teach this principle: If you will wait in worship, I will work for you.

Daniel did this. In one of the most dramatic examples of waiting in the Bible, this Old Testament prophet kept his mind on God for an extended period. His people had been oppressed for almost seventy years. Daniel entered into a time of prayer on their behalf. For twenty-one days he abstained from pleasant food, meat, and wine. He labored in prayer. He persisted, pleaded, and agonized. No response.

Then on the twenty-second day, a breakthrough. An angel of God appeared. He revealed that Daniel's prayer was heard on the first day it was offered. The angel was dispatched with a response. "But for twenty-one days the mighty Evil Spirit who overrules the kingdom of Persia blocked my way. Then Michael, one of the top officers of the heavenly army, came to help me, so that I was able to break through these spirit rulers of Persia" (Daniel 10:13 TLB).

From an earthly perspective nothing was happening. But from a heavenly perspective a battle was raging in the heavens. While Daniel was waiting, God was working.

So, for heaven's sake, don't give up, lose faith, or walk away, for all of heaven is warring on your behalf. Have a heart of obedience . . . and wait on him to move.

THE HEART OF THE MATTER

- Waiting on God is active trust that requires prayer, belief, and obedience.
- While you wait, God is always working behind the scenes for your good.
- Worship during waiting invites God to work on your behalf and protect you.
- Don't lose faith! Heaven is fighting for you, even when you can't see it.

MEMORY VERSE

Your memory verse for this unit is Psalm 128:1. Take a few moments to review this verse, and then write it out from memory in the space below.

After God's Own Heart

When Jesus taught about how people receive the word of God, he used the parable of a farmer sowing seed. If you've ever planted a seed, you know the process involves digging a hole in the soil, placing the seed, watering it, and then . . . a lot of waiting. Days pass, and nothing happens. But beneath the surface, unseen to you, the seed is preparing to break through.

Waiting on God's timing can feel much the same. You pray, you hope, you trust, and yet, the answers seem delayed. Like Nehemiah, who waited four months for God to move, or Daniel, who prayed for twenty-one days before seeing a breakthrough, the waiting can feel endless. But just as the seed grows unseen, so God is working in ways you cannot see.

Waiting is active. It's believing in God even when you don't understand what he is doing beneath the surface. It's watering your faith with prayer and trusting in the Gardener, knowing that—in his perfect timing—he will cause the seed to burst forth into life.

WEEKLY BIBLE STUDY

READ: ISAIAH 40:27–31 AND JOHN 15:5–10

1. The prophecy in Isaiah 40:27–31 was written to God's people during their exile in Babylon. What was their complaint against God (see verse 27)?

2. God's people had grown weary of waiting for him to restore them to their homeland. But what reminder did Isaiah give them about the Lord (see verse 29)?

3. How did Isaiah encourage those who were waiting in exile to persevere (see verses 28–31)? How do these promises encourage you today?

4. What reminder did Jesus give to his followers in John 15:5? What does this say about your natural tendency (as a human being) to want to do things on your own?

5. What is the warning for those who do not abide in Jesus (see verse 6)? Ultimately, what is God's purpose for asking his followers to do this (see verse 8)?

6. How do followers of Jesus demonstrate they are devoted to him and abiding in his love? How are they actually modeling Christ when they do this (see verses 9–10)?

7. What do you find difficult when it comes to waiting on God's timing? What does it mean for you to just abide in Christ and obey his commands?

Week 52: IT BEGAN IN BETHLEHEM

His story started in a pasture. Woolly heads witnessed his early days. Quiet fields welcomed his childish eyes. Before people heeded his message, sheep turned at his cry. Queue up the billions of creatures that have heard his voice, and grass-grazers claim a place near the front.

His story began in a pasture.

A Bethlehem pasture. Such a small hamlet sleeping on the gentle slopes. The home of shepherds. The land of figs, olives, and vines. Not lush, but sufficient. Not known to the world but known to God, who, for his reasons, chose Bethlehem as the incubator of this chosen child.

Chosen, indeed. Chosen by God. Anointed from on high, set apart by heaven. The prophet declared the call. The family heard it. The lad of the sheep would be a shepherd of souls. Bethlehem's boy would be Israel's king.

List a dozen facts, and each describes twin traits of David and Jesus. The stories of both share many names: Bethlehem, Judea, Jerusalem, the Mount of Olives, the Dead Sea, En Gedi. But while their stories are similar, don't for a second think they are identical.

Jesus had no Bathsheba collapse, Uriah murder, or adultery cover-up. Jesus never pillaged a village, camped with the enemy, or neglected a child. No one accused the fairest son of Bethlehem of polygamy, brutality, or adultery.

In fact, no one successfully accused Jesus of anything. They tried. My, how they tried. But when accusers called him a son of Satan, Jesus asked for their proof. "Can any one of you convict me of a single misleading word, a single sinful act?" (John 8:46 MSG). No one could. Disciples traveled with him. Enemies scrutinized him. Admirers studied him.

But no one could convict him of sin.

No one spotted him in the wrong place, heard him say the wrong words, saw him respond the wrong way, or witnessed him disobey even one of God's commands. Peter, three years Jesus' companion, said, "He never did one thing wrong, not once said anything amiss" (1 Peter 2:22 MSG). Pilate was the head of the Roman version of the CIA, yet when he tried to find fault in Jesus, all he could say was, "I find no basis for a charge against him" (John 18:38). Even the demons called Jesus "the Holy One of God" (Luke 4:34).

Jesus never missed the mark.

Equally amazing, he never distances himself from those who do.

Just read the first verse of Matthew's Gospel.

Jesus knew David's ways. He witnessed the adultery, winced at the murders, and grieved at the dishonesty. But David's failures didn't change Jesus' relation to David. The initial verse of the first chapter of the first Gospel calls Christ "the son of David" (Matthew 1:1). The title contains no disclaimers, explanations, or asterisks. I'd have added a footnote: "This connection in no way offers tacit approval to David's behavior." No such words appear. David blew it. Jesus knew it. But he claimed David anyway.

He did for David what my father did for my brother and me. Back in our elementary school days, my brother received a BB gun for Christmas. We immediately set up a firing range in the backyard and spent the afternoon shooting at an archery target. Growing bored with the ease of hitting the circle, my brother sent me to fetch a hand mirror.

He placed the gun backward on his shoulder, spotted the archery bull's-eye in the mirror, and did his best Buffalo Bill imitation. But he missed the target. He also missed the storehouse behind the target and the fence behind the storehouse. We had no idea where the BB pellet flew. Our neighbor across the alley knew, however. He soon appeared at the back fence, asking who had shot the BB gun and who was going to pay for his sliding glass door.

At this point I disowned my brother. I changed my last name and claimed to be a holiday visitor from Canada. My father was more noble than I. Hearing the noise, he appeared in the backyard, freshly rousted from his Christmas Day nap, and talked with the neighbor.

Among his words were these:

"Yes, they are my children."

"Yes, I'll pay for their mistakes."

Christ says the same about you. He knows you won't always have an obedient heart. He knows you miss the target. He knows you can't pay for your mistakes. But he can. "God sent Jesus Christ to take the punishment for our sins" (Romans 3:25 TLB).

Since he was sinless, he could. Since he loves you, he did. "This is love: not that we loved God, but that he loved us and sent his Son as an atoning sacrifice for our sins" (1 John 4:10).

He became one of us to redeem all of us. "Jesus, who makes people holy, and those who are made holy are from the same family. So he is not ashamed to call them his brothers and sisters" (Hebrews 2:11 NCV). He wasn't ashamed of David. He isn't ashamed of you. He calls you brother; he calls you sister. The question is, do you call him Savior?

Take a moment to answer this question. Perhaps you never have. Perhaps you never knew how much Christ loves you. Now you do. Jesus didn't disown David. He won't disown you. He simply awaits your invitation. One word from you and God will do again what he did with David and millions like him: He'll claim you, save you, and use you.

Any words will do, but these seem appropriate: *Jesus, my Savior, I trust you with my heart and give you my life. I ask for mercy, strength, and eternal life. Amen.*

Pray such words with an obedient and honest heart and be assured of this: Your greatest Goliath has fallen. Your failures are flushed and death defanged. The power that made weaklings out of David's giants has done the same with yours.

THE HEART OF THE MATTER

- Jesus, the Holy One of God, never missed the mark.
- Equally amazing, he never distances himself from those who do.
- Jesus obediently became one of us to redeem all of us.
- One word from you and he will claim you, save you, and use you.

MEMORY VERSE

Your memory verse for this unit is Psalm 128:1. Take a few moments to review this verse, and then write it out from memory in the space below.

After God's Own Heart

David's life is a virtual tapestry of triumphs and failures. From the quiet pastures of Bethlehem to the throne of Israel, his story is marked by moments of faithful obedience and devastating missteps. Yet, through it all, David remained a man after God's own heart. As the apostle Paul would later say of him, "God testified concerning him: 'I have found David son of Jesse, a man after my own heart; he will do everything I want him to do'" (Acts 13:22).

David wasn't perfect. But he was a man who sought after God's own heart. Because of this, he had a courageous, trusting, prayerful, worshipful, honest, obedient, and—yes—a repentant heart. David's story reminds us that having a heart attuned to God isn't about *perfection* but *surrender*. It's trusting God enough to follow him even after we fall.

Jesus, the Son of David, never faltered in obedience to God. Yet he chose to redeem those who do. He doesn't disown us in our failures. He calls us his own. So today, like David, choose a heart of obedience. Trust God to use your life, flaws and all, for his glory.

WEEKLY BIBLE STUDY

READ: ROMANS 3:9–26 AND HEBREWS 2:10–18

1. Paul writes in Romans 3:9 that everyone is under the power of sin. What picture of the human condition does Paul go on to paint in verses 11–18?

2. What does Paul say is the purpose of God's law (the Mosaic law)? What does the law of God actually reveal to a person (see verses 19–20)?

3. The law cannot save anyone, "for all have sinned and fall short of the glory of God" (verse 23). Given this, how are you made righteous before God (see verses 25–26)?

4. According to Hebrews 2:11, what new standing are you given when you accept Jesus' sacrifice for your sin? What is Jesus "not ashamed" to call you?

5. What did Jesus accomplish by choosing to become flesh and blood and obediently offering up his life as a perfect sacrifice for sin (see verses 14–15)?

6. Jesus became fully human "in order that he might become a merciful and faithful high priest in service to God" (verse 17). What does this say about his love for you?

7. Jesus was fully obedient to God's plan of salvation. As you close this study, what is your prayer to have a heart of obedience like Christ?

About Max Lucado

Photography by Amanda Mae Steele

Since entering the ministry in 1978, Max Lucado has served churches in Miami, Florida; Rio de Janeiro, Brazil; and San Antonio, Texas. He currently serves as the teaching minister of Oak Hills Church in San Antonio. He is the recipient of the 2021 ECPA Pinnacle Award for his outstanding contribution to the publishing industry and society at large. He is America's bestselling inspirational author with more than 150 million products in print. Visit his website at MaxLucado.com.

Join the Max Lucado Community:
Facebook.com/MaxLucado
Instagram.com/MaxLucado
X.com/MaxLucado
YouTube.com/MaxLucadoOfficial

NOTES

1. The Hebrew terms translated as "heart" (*leb* and *lebab*) appear eight hundred and fifty-three times in the Old Testament. See Bruce Waltke, *An Old Testament Theology: An Exegetical, Canonical, and Thematic Approach* (Zondervan Academic, 2007), 225. The Greek term translated as heart (*kardia*) appears one hundred and fifty-six times in the New Testament. See Verlyn D. Verbrugge, *New International Dictionary of New Testament Theology* (Zondervan Academic, 200), 289.
2. Verbrugge, *New International Dictionary of New Testament Theology*, 288.
3. Adapted from Max Lucado, *A Gentle Thunder* (Thomas Nelson, 1995), 46.
4. Robinson Risner, *The Passing of the Night: My Seven Years as a Prisoner of the North Vietnamese* (1973; reprinted: World Wide Printing, 2001), and a conversation with the author, February 24, 2004.
5. Risner, *The Passing of the Night* and a personal conversation.
6. Shelley Wachsmann, *The Sea of Galilee Boat: An Extraordinary 2000 Year Old Discovery* (Plenum Press, 1995), 39, 121.
7. "Oh, the comfort—the inexpressible comfort of feeling safe with a person, having neither to weigh thoughts nor measure words—but pouring them all out, just as they are, chaff and grain together, certain that a faithful hand will take and sift them, keep what is worth keeping, and with the breath of kindness, blow the rest away." This quote, often attributed to George Eliot, was written by Dinah Maria Mulock Craik in her 1859 novel, *A Life for a Life*.
8. As recounted in an interview with Joy Veron on October 10, 2013, and used by permission.
9. Fall of Jericho: *Unearthing One of the Bible's Greatest Mysteries* (Gateway Films/Vision Video, 2008).
10. H. I. Hester, *The Heart of Hebrew History: A Study of the Old Testament* (Quality Press, 1962), 143–44.
11. "The work of salvation never started with the efforts of any man. God the Holy Spirit must begin it. Now, the reasons no man ever started the work of grace in his own heart are very apparent: first, because he cannot; second, because he won't. The best reason of all is because he cannot; he is dead. The dead may be made alive, but the dead cannot make themselves alive, for the dead can do nothing." Charles Spurgeon, *Spurgeon on the Holy Spirit* (Whitaker, 2000), 16.
12. George Arthur Butterick, ed., *The Interpreter's Dictionary of the Bible: An Illustrated Encyclopedia* (Abingdon, 1962), s.v. "Urim and Thummim," and Merrill C. Tenney, gen. ed., Pictorial Bible Dictionary (Nashville: Southwestern Company, 1975), s.v. "Urim and Thummim."
13. Martin Luther, *Luther's Small Catechism*, "The Lord's Prayer," fourth petition.
14. As quoted in Timothy Jones, *The Art of Prayer* (Ballantine Books, 1997), 133.
15. Jones, *The Art of Prayer*, 140.
16. Charles R. Swindoll, *The Finishing Touch* (Thomas Nelson, 1994), 292.
17. Some scholars suggest that "sons of Abinadab" in 2 Samuel 6:3 should be understood in the broader sense of "descendants of Abinadab." See Earl D. Radmacher, general editor, *Nelson's New Illustrated Bible Commentary* (Thomas Nelson, 1999). See also 1 Samuel 7:1, where Eleazar is called Abinadab's son.
18. Wayne Carson, Johnny Christopher, and Mark James, "Always on My Mind" (1972).
19. Harold Boulton, "All Through the Night" (1884).
20. "Bertie Felstead," The Economist, August 2, 2001, http://www.economist.com/node/718781.
21. Horatio G. Spafford, "It Is Well with My Soul" (1873).
22. Kent and Amber Brantly with David Thomas, *Called for Life: How Loving Our Neighbor Led Us into the Heart of the Ebola Epidemic* (WaterBrook, 2015), 97.
23. Brantly, *Called for Life*, 97.
24. Thomas Obediah Chisholm, "Great Is Thy Faithfulness" (1923).
25. Annie S. Hawks, "I Need Thee Every Hour" (1873).
26. Brantly, Called for Life, 115.
27. John Milton, *Paradise Lost*, book IV (Samuel Simmons, 1667).
28. Used by permission.
29. Daniel Webster, "Argument on the Murder of Captain Joseph White" (April 6, 1860), as reported in Edward Everett, editor, *The Works of Daniel Webster*, volume vi (Little Brown and Company, 1851).

30. Paul (Harvey) Aurandt, *Paul Harvey's The Rest of the Story*, edited and compiled by Lynne Harvey (Bantam Books, 1977), 123. See also Richmond Morcom, "They All Loved Lucy," American Heritage Magazine, volume 21, issue 6 (October 1970).
31. The fifth occasion is 1 John 2:1.
32. See Acts 8:29; 16:6–7 (led and commanded the disciples); Romans 8:26 (intercedes for the believer).
33. See Acts 20:28 (appoints elders); 1 Corinthians 2:10 (searches all things); 1 Corinthians 2:11 (knows the mind of God); 1 Corinthians 2:13 (teaches the content of the gospel).
34. See 1 Corinthians 3:16; Romans 8:11; 2 Timothy 1:14 (dwells among and within believers); 1 Corinthians 12:11 (distributes spiritual gifts); 2 Corinthians 3:6 (gives life to those who believe).
35. See Romans 8:26 (helps in our weaknesses); Romans 8:28 (works all things together for our ultimate good); Ephesians 3:16 (strengthens believers).
36. Lifeway Research, *2018 State of American Theology Study, Research Report*, http://lifewayresearch.com/wp-content/uploads/2018/10 /Ligonier-State-of-Theology-2018-White-Paper.pdf, p. 3.
37. Chris Weller, "There's a Place for Thieves with a Guilty Conscience to Return Money to the Government Anonymously," Business Insider, March 12, 2017, https://www.businessinsider.com/conscience-fund-us-treasury-2017-3.
38. James F. Colianni, *The Book of Pulpit Humor* (Voicings Publications, 1992), 128.
39. Frederick Buechner, *The Sacred Journey* (Harper and Row, 1982), 52.
40. "Doctors Remove Knife from Man's Head After Four Years," AOL News, February 18, 2011, www.aolnews.com/2011/02/18/doctors-remove-knife-from-li-fuyans-head-after-4-years.
41. Todd and Tara Storch, parents of Taylor and founders of Taylor's Gift Foundation (www.TaylorsGift.org), tell the ongoing story of their journey of regifting life, renewing health, and restoring families in their book (with Jennifer Schuchmann) *Taylor's Gift: A Courageous Story of Life, Loss, and Unexpected Blessings* (Revell, 2013).
42. Aurandt, *Paul Harvey's The Rest of the Story*, 107–109.
43. Dale Ralph Davis, *Joshua: No Falling Words* (Christian Focus Publications, 2000), 19.
44. See Matthew 11:15; 13:9; 13:43; Mark 4:9; 4:23; 8:18; Luke 8:8; 14:35; Revelation 2:7, 11, 17, 29; 3:6, 13, 22; 13:9.

ALSO AVAILABLE FROM

MAX LUCADO

The Life Lessons Bible Study Series

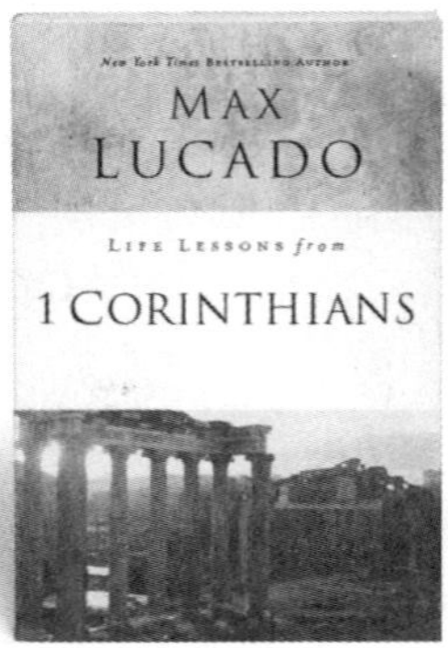

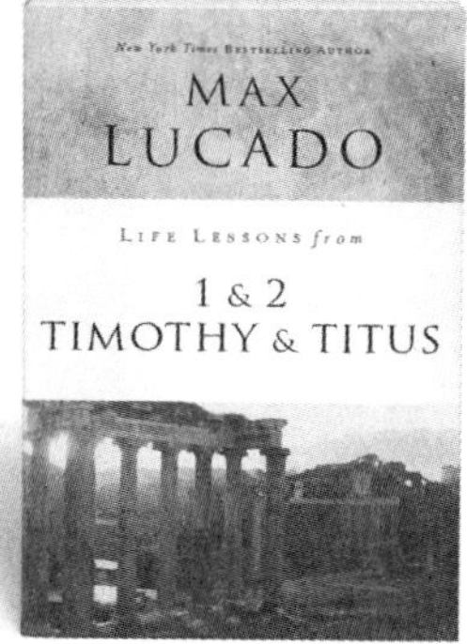

Bible Studies Include

Genesis
Psalms
1 & 2 Samuel
Psalms
Ezra & Nehemiah
Daniel & Esther
Matthew
Mark
Luke
John
Acts
Romans
1 Corinthians
2 Corinthians
Galatians
Ephesians
Philippians
Colossians & Philemon
1 & 2 Thessalonians
1 & 2 Timothy & Titus
Hebrews
James
1 & 2 Peter
1, 2, 3 John & Jude
Revelation

HARPERCHRISTIANRESOURCES.COM

From the Publisher

GREAT STUDIES

ARE EVEN BETTER WHEN THEY'RE SHARED!

Help others find this study:

- Post a review at your favorite online bookseller.
- Post a picture on a social media account and share why you enjoyed it.
- Send a note to a friend who would also love it—or, better yet, go through it with them!

Thanks for helping others grow their faith!